Grammar Dimensions

Book Two

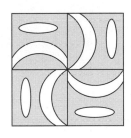

Grammar Dimensions

Book Two
Form, Meaning, and Use

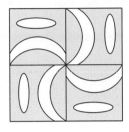

Heidi Riggenbach
University of Washington

Virginia Samuda
Sonoma State University

Heinle & Heinle Publishers
A Division of Wadsworth, Inc.
Boston, Massachusetts 02116 U.S.A

Photo Credits:

Photos on page 2 (photos 1–3) courtesy of H. Armstrong Roberts.

Photo on page 2 (photo 4) by J. Myers courtesy of H. Armstrong Roberts.

Photos on page 2 (photos 5, 6) courtesy of the University of Illinois.

Photo on page 2 (photo 7) courtesy of the *Illio,* University of Illinois yearbook.

Photo on page 38 of John Lennon courtesy of Kahana/Shooting Star.

Photo on page 177 of Diana Ross (recent) courtesy of Kahana/Shooting Star, page 178 (yearbook) courtesy of Seth Poppel Yearbook Archives.

Photo on page 177 of Tina Turner (recent) courtesy of McAfee/Shooting Star, page 178 (yearbook) courtesy of Seth Poppel Yearbook Archives.

Photo on page 177 of Madonna (recent) courtesy of Archer/Shooting Star, page 178 (yearbook) courtesy of Seth Poppel Yearbook Archives.

Photo on page 177 of Meryl Streep (recent) courtesy of Leonelli/Shooting Star, page 178 (yearbook) courtesy of Seth Poppel Yearbook Archives.

Photo on page 177 of Bruce Springsteen (recent) courtesy of Gallo/Shooting Star, page 178 (yearbook) courtesy of Seth Poppel Yearbook Archives.

Photo on page 177 of Warren Beatty (recent) courtesy of Fotex/Shooting Star, page 178 (yearbook) courtesy of Seth Poppel Yearbook Archives.

The publication of the Grammar Dimensions series
was directed by the members of the Heinle & Heinle
ESL Publishing Team:

David C. Lee, Editorial Director
Susan Mraz, Marketing Manager
Lisa McLaughlin, Production Editor
Nancy Mann, Developmental Editor

Also participating in the publication of this program were:

Publisher: Stanley J. Galek
Editorial Production Manager: Elizabeth Holthaus
Assistant Editor: Kenneth Mattsson
Manufacturing Coordinator: Mary Beth Lynch
Full Service Production/Design: Publication Services, Inc.
Cover Designer: Martucci Studio
Cover Artist: Susan Johnson

10   9   8   7   6   5   4   3   2   1

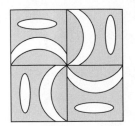

Table of Contents

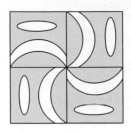

Preface to *Grammar Dimensions: Form, Meaning, and Use*

To the Teacher

ABOUT THE SERIES

With the recent emphasis on communication, the teaching of grammar has often been downplayed, or even overlooked entirely. Although one would not want to argue the goal of having students be able to communicate successfully, it is important to recognize that a major means to this end is to teach students to use grammatical structures. Some grammatical structures may be acquired naturally without instruction, but it is assumed by the creators of this series that explicit focus on the troublesome aspects of English will facilitate and accelerate their acquisition. The teaching needs to be done, however, in such a way that the interdependence of grammar and communication is appreciated.

In this regard, it is crucial to recognize that the use of grammatical structures involves more than having students achieve formal accuracy. Students must be able to use the structures meaningfully and appropriately as well. This series, therefore, takes into account all three dimensions of language: syntax/morphology (form), semantics (meaning), and pragmatics (use). The relevant facts about the **form, meaning,** and **use** of English grammatical structures were compiled into a comprehensive scope and sequence and distributed across a four-book series. Where the grammatical system is complex (e.g., the verb-tense system) or the structure complicated (e.g., the passive voice), it is revisited in each book in the series. Nevertheless, each book is free-standing and may be used independently of the others in the series if the student or program needs warrant.

Another way in which the interdependence of grammar and communication is stressed is that students first encounter every structure in a meaningful context where their attention is not immediately drawn to its formal properties. Each treatment of a grammatical structure concludes with students being given the opportunity to use the structure in communicative activities. The point of the series is not to teach grammar as static knowledge, but to have students use it in the dynamic process of communication. In this way grammar might better be thought of as a skill, rather than as an area of knowledge.

It is my hope that this book will provide teachers with the means to create, along with their students, learning opportunities that are tailored to learners' needs, are enjoyable, and will maximize everyone's learning.

ABOUT THE BOOK

This book deals with basic sentence and subsentence grammatical structures. It also introduces language forms that support certain social functions such as making requests and seeking permission.

Units that share certain features have been clustered together. No more than three or four units are clustered at one time, however, in order to provide for some variety of focus. As the units have been designed to stand independently, it is possible for a syllabus to be constructed that follows a different order of structures than the one presented in the book. It is also not expected that there will be sufficient time to deal with all the material that has been introduced here within a single course. Teachers are encouraged to see the book as a resource from which they can select units or parts of units which best meet student needs.

Unit Organization

TASKS

One way in which to identify student needs is to use the **Tasks**, which open each unit as a pre-test. Learner engagement in the Tasks may show that students have already learned what they need to know about a certain structure, in which case the unit can be skipped entirely. Or it may be possible, from examining students' performance, to pinpoint precisely where the students need to work. For any given structure, the learning challenge presented by the three dimensions of language is not equal. Some structures present more of a form-based challenge to learners; for others, the long-term challenge is to learn what the structures mean or when to use them. The type and degree of challenge varies according to the inherent complexity of the structure itself and the particular language background and level of English proficiency of the students.

FOCUS BOXES

Relevant facts about the form, meaning, and use of the structure are presented in **Focus Boxes** following the Task. Teachers can work their way systematically through a given unit or can pick and choose from among the Focus Boxes those points on which they feel students specifically need to concentrate.

EXERCISES

From a pedagogical perspective, it is helpful to think of grammar as a skill to be developed. Thus, in this book, **Exercises** have been provided to accompany each Focus Box. Certain of the Exercises may be done individually, others with students working in pairs or in small groups. Some of the Exercises can be done in class, others assigned as homework. Students' learning styles and the learning challenge they are working on will help teachers determine the most effective way to have students use the Exercises. (The Instructor's Manual should be consulted also for helpful hints in this regard.)

ACTIVITIES

At the end of each unit are a series of **Activities** that help students realize the communicative value of the grammar they are learning and that offer them further practice in using the grammar to convey meaning. Teachers or students may select the Activities from which they believe they would derive the most benefit and enjoyment. Student performance on these Activities can be used as a post-test as well. Teachers should not expect perfect performance at this point, however. Often there is a delayed effect in learning anything, and even some temporary backsliding in student performance as new material is introduced.

OTHER COMPONENTS

An **Instructor's Manual** is available for this book. The Manual contains answers to the Exercise questions and grammatical notes where pertinent. The Manual also further discusses the theory underlying the series and "walks a teacher through" a typical unit, suggesting ways in which the various components of the unit might be used and supplemented in the classroom.

A student **Workbook** also accompanies this book. It provides additional exercises to support the material presented in this text. Many of the workbook exercises are specially designed to help students prepare for the TOEFL (Test of English as a Foreign Language).

To the Student

All grammar structures have a form, a meaning, and a use. We can show this with a pie chart:

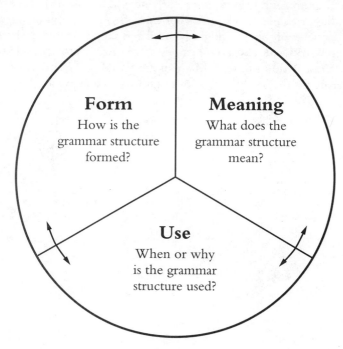

Often you will find that you know the answer to one or more of these questions, but not to all of them, for a particular grammar structure. This book has been written to help you learn answers to these questions for the major grammar structures of English. More importantly, it gives you practice with the answers so that you can develop your ability to use English grammar structures accurately, meaningfully, and appropriately.

At the beginning of each unit, you will be asked to work on a **Task.** The Task will introduce you to the grammar structures to be studied in the unit. However, it is not important at this point that you think about grammar. You should just do the Task as well as you can.

In the next section of the unit are **Focus Boxes** and **Exercises.** You will see that the boxes are labeled with **FORM, MEANING, USE,** or a combination of these, corresponding to the three parts of the pie chart. In each Focus Box is information that answers one or more of the questions in the pie. Along with the Focus Box are Exercises that should help you put into practice what you have studied.

The last section of each unit contains communicative **Activities.** Hopefully, you will enjoy doing these and at the same time receive further practice using the grammar structures in meaningful ways.

By working on the Task, studying the Focus Boxes, doing the Exercises, and engaging in the Activities, you will develop greater knowledge of English grammar and skill in using it. I also believe you will enjoy the learning experience along the way.

Diane Larsen-Freeman

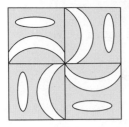

Acknowledgments

Series Director Acknowledgments

As with any project this ambitious, a number of people have made important contributions. I need to thank my students in the MAT Program at the School for International Training and audiences worldwide for listening to me talk about my ideas for reconciling the teaching of grammar with communicative language teaching. Their feedback and questions have been invaluable in the evolution of my thinking. One student, Anna Mussman, should be singled out for her helpful comments on the manuscript that she was able to provide based on her years of English teaching. A number of other anonymous teacher reviewers have also had a formative role in the development of the series. I hope they derive some satisfaction in seeing that their concerns were addressed wherever possible. In addition, Marianne Celce-Murcia not only helped with the original scope and sequence of the series, but also provided valuable guidance throughout its evolution.

I feel extremely grateful, as well, for the professionalism of the authors, who had to put into practice the ideas behind this series. Their commitment to the project, patience with its organic nature, and willingness to keep at it are all much appreciated. I insisted that the authors be practicing ESL teachers. I believe the series has benefited from this decision, but I am also cognizant of the demands it has put on the authors' lives these past few years.

Finally, I must acknowledge the support of the Heinle and Heinle "team." This project was "inherited" by Heinle and Heinle during its formative stage. To Dave Lee, Susan Mraz, Lisa McLaughlin, and especially Susan Maguire, who never stopped believing in this project, I am indeed thankful. And to Nancy Mann, who helped the belief become a reality, I am very grateful.

Author Acknowledgments

We would like to thank our families, friends, students, colleagues, cats—and each other—for hanging in there. We would also like to thank Diane Larsen-Freeman for her guidance during the process of writing this book, and the following reviewers for their valuable suggestions: Brian Hickey (Manhattanville College), Marilyn Santos (Valencia Community College), Marjore Walsleben (UCLA), Martha Low (University of Oregon), Jonathan Seeley (University of Arizona), and the field tester, Mary Monogue (University of Colorado, Boulder).

Simple Present
Facts, Habits, and Routines

Task

How Do You Learn Grammar?

Complete this questionnaire about the way you learn by circling the number beside each statement.

1 = never true for me	2 – rarely true for me	3 = sometimes true for me	4 = often true for me	5 = always true for me

1. I take every opportunity to practice the the English I know.   1 2 3 4 5
2. To learn grammar, I study grammar books and memorize the rules.   1 2 3 4 5
3. To learn grammar, I read newspapers, watch TV and movies, and listen to songs.   1 2 3 4 5
4. When I don't know how to say something exactly, I don't say anything at all.   1 2 3 4 5
5. To learn grammar, I observe native speakers in different situations and notice what they say and do.   1 2 3 4 5
6. I am not afraid of making mistakes because mistakes help me learn.   1 2 3 4 5
7. Working in groups with my classmates helps me learn.   1 2 3 4 5
8. I ask questions when I do not understand.   1 2 3 4 5
9. When I can't think of how to say something, I try to say it another way.   1 2 3 4 5
10. I try to think in English.   1 2 3 4 5
11. I think of grammar rules when I speak.   1 2 3 4 5

Now compare your answers with those of another student. In what ways are your learning habits similar and in what ways are they different? What other things do you do to learn grammar? Share and compare your findings with the rest of the class and with your teacher.

Focus 1

Simple Present Tense

USE

- The simple present talks about habits: things you do again and again.
  (a) I ask questions when I don't understand.
- The simple present also talks about everyday routines: things you do regularly.
  (b) My sister gets up at 6:00.

Focus 2

FORM
Simple Present Tense

Statement	Negative	Question	Short Answers
I You We They } work.	I You We They } do not/don't work.	Do { I you we they } work?	Yes, { I you we they } do.
He She It } works.	He She It } does not/doesn't work.	Does { he she it } work?	Yes, { he she it } does.
			No, { I you we they } don't.
			No, { he she it } doesn't.

Exercise 1

What are some of the *other* things you do (or do not do) to help you learn English grammar? Complete the following, using full sentences.

Some things I do:

1. I _____ .

2. I _____ .

3. I _____ .

Some things I don't do:

1. I _____ .

2. I _____ .

3. I _____ .

Now share your sentences with a partner. Then, without showing your books to each other, write about your partner here.

My partner, _____ (name), does several different things to learn English.

She or he _____.

_____.

_____.

Now get together with a *different* partner. Tell him or her what you and your first partner do (and do not do) to learn English grammar. Compare your findings with your new partner's findings. Together with your new partner, decide on the three most useful strategies that you and your partners use. Share your findings with the rest of the class.

Focus 3

FORM ● MEANING

Adverbs of Frequency

FORM
MEANING

- To show **how often** you do something, you can use an adverb of frequency:

**Most
Frequently**

I	always	
	usually	
	often	
	sometimes	ask questions.
	seldom	
	rarely	
	hardly ever	
	never	

**Least
Frequently**

Position of Adverbs of Frequency	
Before the main verb: **(a)** I **usually** get up at 6:00. **(b)** He **never** calls me.	After the verb *be:* **(c)** She is **always** late. **(d)** They are **rarely** happy.

- For more information on adverbs of frequency, see Unit 16, Focus 7.

Exercise 2

Complete the chart with information about the habits and routines of these people when they are in the classroom. The first one has been done for you as an example.

	Teachers in My Country	Students in This Country	Teachers in My Country	Students in This Country
Usually	give a lot of homework			
Sometimes				
Hardly ever				
Never				

Now get together with a student from another country, if possible, and ask eight questions about the information from his or her chart:

What do $\begin{Bmatrix} \text{teachers} \\ \text{students} \end{Bmatrix}$ in your country $\begin{Bmatrix} \text{often} \\ \text{sometimes} \\ \text{hardly ever} \\ \text{never} \end{Bmatrix}$ do?

EXAMPLE: *Tell me one thing students in your country sometimes do.*

Now make as many true sentences as you can, using the information from your chart (and from your partner's if possible).

EXAMPLE: *Students in this country never stand up when the teacher enters the classroom.*

Exercise 3

Read the job descriptions below and match them to the occupations in the list below.

1. He wears a uniform and usually travels many miles a day. He serves food and drink, but he hardly ever prepares them himself.
2. She works in an office, but she often takes work home with her. She generally earns a high salary, but often feels a lot of stress. She sometimes entertains clients in the evening.
3. He usually wears a uniform and always carries a gun. He leads a dangerous life, so his job rarely gets boring.
4. He often works at night and meets many different people. He serves drinks and gets tips when people like his work.

5. She wears a uniform and drives many miles a day. She never serves food or drinks.

6. He spends many hours in the classroom and asks questions. He always has a lot of work to do and sometimes writes on the blackboard.

7. She often wears a uniform and walks many miles a day. She works very hard and does not earn very much money, although she sometimes gets generous tips.

8. They spend a lot of time in the classroom and like to ask questions. They often write on the blackboard.

a student	a policeman	a businesswoman	secretaries
	a flight attendant	mechanics	teachers
a nurse	a bartender	an architect	a bus driver	a waitress

Now write similar descriptions for the jobs that are still left in the box.

9. _____

_____

10. _____

_____

11. _____

_____

12. _____

_____

Now think of two more jobs. Write a short job description for each one and get together with another student. Read your descriptions to each other and ask and answer questions until you guess the jobs your partner has described:

EXAMPLE: Does she or he . . . ?

Is she or he a . . . ?

13. _____

_____

14. _____

_____

Exercise 4

Sam is looking for a roommate to share his house, and Dave is looking for a place to live. They are trying to find out if they will be compatible as roommates. Complete their conversation, using verbs that will complete the meaning. Sometimes more than one answer is possible.

Sam: What do you usually do on weekends?

Dave: Well, I usually (1) _____ early, about 5:30, and then I (2) _____

by the river for an hour or so before breakfast.

Sam: Really? And what (3) _____ you _____ next?

Dave: After breakfast, I (4) _____ a cold shower, and then I usually

(5) _____ my bike or I sometimes (6) _____ tennis for a couple

of hours. What (7) _____ you _____ on Saturday mornings?

Sam: I like to relax on weekends; I (8) _____ home and (9) _____

the newspaper and (10) _____ TV.

Dave: All weekend?

Sam: No. On Sundays, I often get in my sports car and (11) _____ to the beach.

Dave: Great! I like swimming too. My brother (12) _____ in the ocean every day

of the year, even in the winter.

Sam: Well, I rarely (13) _____ in the ocean. I usually (14) _____ on

the beach and try to get a good sun tan. Then I (15) _____ some of my

friends and we go to a bar and (16) _____ beer.

Dave: Don't you ever exercise?

Sam: Well, I (17) _____ (not) to a health club or gym, but every Saturday night, I

go to a disco and I (18) _____ for hours. That's my idea of exercise.

Focus 4

Simple Present Tense

USE

- You can also use simple present to talk about statements of **fact**—things that are always true:

    The sun **rises** in the east and sets in the west.

- Thus, we use the simple present to talk about routines, habits, and facts.

Exercise 5

Match these facts by connecting the information in Column A with the appropriate information in Column B.

A	B
Horses	have twelve eyes.
Scorpions	live for about two years.
Spiders	sleep standing up.
Elephants	use their ears to "see."
Ducks	run at a speed of 70 miles per hour.
Antelopes	stay with the same mate all their lives.
Bats	sometimes go for four days without water.

Do you know any other unusual facts about animals or insects? Share them with the rest of the class.

Activities

Activity 1

The purpose of this activity is to *prove* or *disprove* the following statements about your classmates. Survey your classmates by asking questions to see if the following are true or false.

1. Most people in this class do not eat breakfast.

2. Women drink more coffee than men.

3. Three people come to school by bike.

4. The people in this room sleep an average of seven hours a night.

5. 50 percent of the people here watch TV every night.

6. At least half of the people in this room smoke.

7. At least three people wear contact lenses.

8. The people in this room have an average of three brothers and sisters.

9. Most people in this room do not like opera.

10. At least half of the people here read a newspaper in English every day.

Activity 2

The purpose of this activity is to find out what North Americans usually do on certain special days. Interview several different people (native speakers if possible) and find out what usually happens on these days. Share your findings with the class.

St. Patrick's Day:_____

_____

Valentine's Day:_____

_____

Thanksgiving Day:_____

_____

Halloween:_____

_____

Activity 3

Complete the following with information that is true about yourself. Write complete sentences.

SOMETHING I USUALLY DO IN SUMMER:_____

_____

SOMETHING I OFTEN DO ON WEEKENDS:_____

_____

SOMETHING I RARELY DO IN THIS COUNTRY:_____

_____

SOMETHING I SOMETIMES DO ON FRIDAYS:_____

_____

1. Memorize these four sentences about yourself.
2. Walk around the room. When your teacher tells you to stop, find the nearest person. Tell her or him your four sentences. When she or he tells you *her or his* sentences, memorize them.
3. Walk around the room. When your teacher tells you to stop, find a different person. Tell him or her about the habits of **the last person you spoke to**. Do not talk about your own. Memorize what he or she tells you.
4. Find someone different. Tell him or her **the information the last person told you**. Memorize what he or she tells you.
5. Now find someone new. Continue the process for as long as possible. Remember, you always pass along **the information the last person tells you**. Try to speak to as many different people as possible.
6. At the end, tell the rest of the class the information you heard from the last person. Is all the information true?

Activity 4

Write a letter to a friend or family member describing what usually happens in your English classes or what you usually do on weekends here.

Activity 5

Prepare a short talk for your classmates, describing a special day or holiday that people celebrate in your country, city, or region. Talk about what people usually do on this day and how they celebrate.

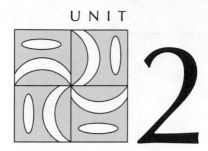
Present Progressive
Stative and Nonstative Verbs

Task

What do you think is probably happening in this picture? Draw the missing parts and be ready to describe your interpretation of the picture to the rest of the class. Decide who has the most interesting theory.

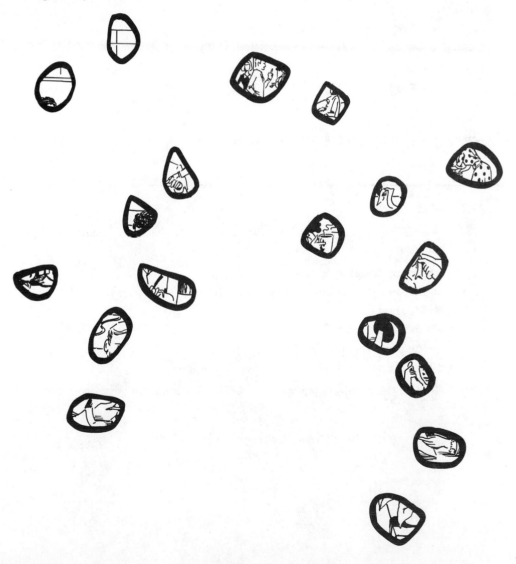

Focus 1

Present Progressive

USE

- Use verbs in the present progressive to talk about actions and situations that are **in progress** or in the middle of happening at the time of speaking:

    (a) Right now, I **am sitting** on the couch and my brothers **are cooking** dinner.

    (b) It **is raining** at the moment and Oscar **is waiting** for the bus.

- You may also use the present progressive to talk about actions and situations that are going on **around** the time of speaking, although they may not be in progress **exactly** at the time of speaking. These actions or situations are often temporary, and we expect them to end in the future:

    (c) This semester, I **am taking** three math classes.

- Some common time expressions associated with present progressive:

right now	this year
at the moment	this semester
today	this week
at present	these days

Exercise 1

Look at the following statements about the picture in the Task and decide which ones are *probably* true (T) and which ones are *probably* false (F).

1. Some coats are hanging on a rack.	T	F
2. A customer in a restaurant is checking the bill.	T	F
3. Somebody is typing.	T	F
4. Somebody is gardening.	T	F
5. Somebody is writing a letter.	T	F
6. Several people are waiting to see a doctor in a hospital.	T	F

Now look at the complete picture on page 22. How many of your guesses were correct?

Focus 2

Present Progressive

- To form the present progressive, use *be* + *present participle* (*-ing*) of the main verb:

Statement	Negative	Question	Short Answers
I am (I'm) working.	I am not (I'm not) working.	Am I working?	Yes, I am. No, I'm not.
You are (you're) work-ing.	You are not (aren't) working.	Are you working?	Yes, you are. No, you aren't. OR you're not.
She/He/It is (She's/He's/It's) working.	She/He/It is not (isn't) working.	Is she/he/it working?	Yes, she/he/it is. No, she/he/it isn't. OR She's/He's/It's not.
We are (We're) work-ing.	We are not (aren't) working.	Are we working?	Yes, we are. No we aren't. OR we're not.
They are (They're) working.	They are not (aren't) working.	Are they working?	Yes, they are. No, they aren't OR They're not.

Exercise 2

Study the complete picture in the Task for one minute. Turn the page and, from memory, write as many sentences as possible to describe what is going on in the picture. Compare your results with those of the rest of the class. Who can remember the most?

Focus 3

Simple Present versus
Present Progressive

USE

- Use the simple present tense to talk about events or actions that happen regularly and repeatedly (see Unit 1). Thus, the simple present refers to permanent or habitual situations.

  (a) Philippe **smokes** 20 cigarettes a day.

- Use the present progressive to talk about events or actions that are already going on **at** the time of speaking or **around** the time of speaking. Thus, the present progressive refers to temporary situations:

  (b) Philippe **is smoking** a cigarette right now.

  (c) Philippe **is smoking** more cigarettes than usual these days because he is nervous about his final exams.

Exercise 3

Complete the following using either simple present or present progressive. Use the words in parentheses. The first one has been done for you.

1. A: Ray! The phone *is ringing* (ring).

   B: I can't get it. I _____ (wash) my hair.

2. A: Look at Juan. He _____ (smoke).

   B: That's strange. He _____ (smoke + never)!

   A: Maybe he's nervous about something.

3. A: Hey, Pam! What a surprise! What _____ you _____

   (do) on campus?

   B: I _____ (take) an art class this semester. It's great!

   I _____ (learn) a lot.

4. A: Please be quiet, we _____ (study) for a test!

   B: What kind of test?

   A: Math. We _____ (have + always) a math test on Mondays.

5. (The phone rings.)

A: Hi, honey. How _____ you _____ (do)?

B: Mom! What a coincidence! I was about to write you a letter.

A: Really? You _____ (write + hardly ever) me letters. Is something wrong?

6. A: What's the matter?

B: It _____ (rain) and I _____ (have + not) an umbrella.

7. A: Why _____ Brian _____ (wear) a suit today?

B: It's Tuesday. He _____ (go + always) to lunch with his boss on Tuesdays.

8. A: I have to find a different roommate.

B: Why?

A: Because my current roommate and I have completely different life-styles. For example, she _____ (get up) early, but I _____ (sleep) late. We _____ (like + not) the same food; she _____ (eat + not) meat or fish or eggs. It's really hard sharing an apartment.

A: Why don't you two get together right now and talk the problem over? What _____ she _____ (do) at the moment?

B: She _____ (sleep). She _____ (go + always) to bed at 8:00.

Exercise 4

Can you translate the following into English? Write your answers below. After that, underline the verbs in each sentence and write each verb in the appropriate box. The first one has been done for you.

1. 👁 ♡ U. *I love you*

2. 👁 C U. _____

3. 👁 H ÷ 8 U. _____

4. 👁 H ÷ 🗣 U. _____

5. He 🐝 U. _____

6. RU 21 ? _____

7. 👁 C U R YY 4 me. _____

8. 👁 TH ÷ 🖋 UR GR ÷ 8. _____

You can find the answers to this puzzle on page 22.

Now underline all the verbs in your sentences and write them in the appropriate boxes below. The first one has been done for you.

Verbs that express emotions and feelings
love

Verbs that express senses and perceptions

Verbs that express cognition: knowledge, thoughts, and beliefs

Verbs that express ownership and possession

Which verb does not fit into these boxes? _____

All these verbs have something in common. Can you tell what it is?

Focus 4

MEANING
Stative Verbs

- Some verbs are not used in the progressive in English. These are called **stative** because they refer to states which we do not expect to change, not actions which may be temporary.

   (a) He **loves** me, but he **hates** my cats.
   NOT: He is loving me, but he is hating my cats.

   (b) I **know** your sister.
   NOT: I **am knowing** your sister.

- The most common stative verbs are in these categories:

Emotion		Perception	Cognition	Possession
love	prefer	see	think	have
like	want	hear	believe	own
hate	dislike	taste	know	belong
appreciate		smell	understand	

Other Common Stative Verbs		
be	need	owe
seem	weigh	cost
exist		

Exercise 5

Complete the following with simple present or present progressive, using the verbs in parentheses.

Today, more and more people (1) _____ (discover) the joys of riding a bicycle.

In fact, mountain biking (2) _____ (become) one of America's most popu-

lar recreational activities. The bicycle business (3) _____ (grow) fast, and every

year it (4) _____ (produce) hundreds of new-model bikes. In general, bike shops

(5) _____ (sell) not only bicycles but also a full range of accessories and equipment.

Paul Brownstein (6) _____ (manage) a popular bike shop in Boston. Many of his customers (7) _____ (be) avid cyclists, and several (8) _____ (own) more than one bicycle. These people usually (9) _____ (ride) several times a week for pleasure, although according to Paul, more and more people these days (10) _____ (ride) their bicycles to work too, because they (11) _____ (believe) that bicycles (12) _____ (provide) an alternative to the automobile. Paul(13) _____ (sell) all kinds of bikes, but these days he (14) _____ (sell) a lot of bicycle clothing as well. In fact, one of his customers regularly (15) _____ (come) into the shop and (16) _____ (buy) clothes, even though she (17) _____ (not + own) a bicycle. She (18) _____ (like) the clothes, but (19) _____ (hate) the sport! Unfortunately, this attitude (20) _____ (not + be) unusual these days, because as everybody (21) _____ (know), some people (22) _____ (think) style and appearance (23) _____ (be) more important than anything else in life.

Focus 5

MEANING

Stative versus Nonstative Meaning

MEANING

- Stative verbs usually express a regular state or quality, **not** an action:
  (a) I love you.
  (b) I hate my job.
- Some verbs look like stative verbs because they describe a state, but they also have nonstative meanings when they describe action:

State	Action
(c) I weigh 120 pounds.	I am weighing myself (to see if I have gained weight).
(d) Mmm—dinner smells great!	I'm smelling the milk (to see if it is spoiled).
(e) The soup tastes good.	He is tasting the soup (to see if it needs salt).

- Therefore, when these verbs express a nonstative meaning, they can take the progressive forms.
  - *Be* is generally considered a stative verb because it describes a regular state or quality:
    - **(f)** She is very polite.
  - *Have* is considered a stative verb when it describes possession:
    - **(g)** She has a dog and two cats.
- However, when you use *have* to describe an experience and not possession, you use the progressive forms:

Possession	Experience
(h) They have three cars.	**(i)** We are having fun.

- Some common expressions using *have* and expressing an experience:

have fun	*have a good time*	*have trouble with*
have problems	*have difficulty with*	

- When *have* describes a medical condition or physical discomfort, it does not usually take progressive forms:
  - **(j)** I can't talk to you right now because I **have** a really sore throat.
  - **(k)** Sandy **has** a headache and a high fever today; maybe she **has** the flu.

Exercise 6

Work with a partner or in a small group. You need a die and a small object (like a coin) to represent each person. First, take turns throwing the die. The person who throws the highest number starts. Put your coins (or objects) on the square marked *Start* on the following page. Throw the die and move your coin to the appropriate square. Complete the sentence in the square; if everyone agrees with your answer, you may write it in the square. If you are not sure, your teacher will be the referee. If you make a mistake or do not know the answer, you miss your next turn. The winner is the first person to reach the final square.

I _____ (love) grammar! 25	A: The chef _____ (taste) the food right now. B: Is it good? A: Yes! It _____ (taste) wonderful! 26	MISS A TURN 27	Did you cut your hand? It _____ (bleed). 28
She _____ (write) a letter now, but she rarely _____ (write) letters. 24	MISS A TURN 23	The students _____ (have) some trouble with verbs today. 22	She _____ (take) three classes this semester, but she usually _____ (take) more. 21
MISS A TURN 17	How many pairs of shoes _____ she _____ (own) now? 18	This suitcase _____ (weigh) too much. I can't carry it. 19	A: What's wrong? B: I _____ (have) problems with my boyfriend at the moment. 20
A: Look! There's the President B: Where? I _____ (not + see) him. 16	A: _____ you _____ (like) your job? B: No, I _____ (hate) it. 15	A: _____ you always _____ (take) the bus? B: No, I usually _____ (walk) to work. 14	A: Where's Tim? B: I _____ (think) he _____ (take) a nap. 13
A: How are the kids? B: They both _____ (have) sore throats today. 9	A: Shhh! We _____ (study) for a test. 10	A: _____ you _____ (like) Mexican food? B: Yes, I _____ (love) it! 11	A: How's Joe? B: Great. He _____ (have) fun because he _____ (have) a new car. 12
MISS A TURN 8	Mmm! Is that a new perfume? You _____ (smell) great. 7	What _____ you _____ (think) Henry _____ (think) about right now? 6	People _____ (spend) less money on entertainment these days. 5
START 1	Moya always _____ (sit) at the back of the class, but today she _____ (sit) at the front. 2	Rose _____ (not + know) that it is my birthday today. 3	MISS A TURN 4

Activities

Activity 1

Go to a crowded place where you can safely sit and watch what is happening around you. Look carefully at everything that is happening. Pretend you are a journalist or radio or television reporter. Describe in writing everything that you see. Do not forget to include everything you hear as well.

Activity 2

Work with a partner or a small group and develop a short story including a sequence of actions and emotions. Act out your story without using words. Your classmates must try to guess what is happening in your story by providing a commentary of everything your group does, as they watch it happen.

Activity 3

Do you know how to play tic-tac-toe? In this activity, you will be playing a version of this well-known game. Work with a partner or in teams. First copy each of the following onto separate cards or different pieces of paper. Place these cards facedown on the table in front of you.

she/speak	they/think about	he/believe
we/hear	she/dance (?)★	you/write (?)★
I/understand	we/sing	you/live
they/eat	they/work(?)★	I/see

(?)★ = make a question

The first player chooses a tic-tac-toe square and draws the first card. She or he makes a meaningful statement including the words in the tic-tac-toe square and the words on the card. Each statement must have *at least* four words in it (not including the words in the tic-tac-toe square). If everyone accepts your statement, you may mark the square with either *X* or *O*. The next player chooses a different square and draws the next card. The first person to draw a straight line through three squares is the winner. You may play this game repeatedly by erasing the *X*s and *O*s at the end of each round, or by writing them on small pieces of paper and covering the squares with these. Good luck!

every day	today	usually
this week	occasionally	right now
often	at the moment	sometimes

DUANE GILLOGLY

ANSWERS TO EXERCISE 4

1. I love you.
2. I see you.
3. I hate you.
4. I hear you.
5. He knows you.
6. Are you 21?
7. I see you are too wise for me!
8. I think you are great.

Be Going To and Will

Task

In North America, Chinese restaurants traditionally give customers a fortune cookie at the end of the meal. This cookie is small and hollow. Inside you find a piece of paper that predicts something about your future. Can you match the two parts of these fortunes?

1 You will help

2 Your boss is going to

3 You will be lucky

4 You are going to take

5 Your friends and family

6 You are going to get

7 You will

8 You are going

9 Your life

10 An interesting stranger is

A a trip around the world.

B an "A" in this class.

C to have a large and happy family.

D and win a lot of money.

E are going to throw a big party in your honor.

F give you a big raise.

G make an important contribution to the world.

H is going to change dramatically.

I a friend in need.

J going to enter your life.

Focus 1

Talking about the Future with *Will* and *Be Going To*

- To talk about the future, you can use *be going to* and *will*:
  (a) It **will** rain some time next week.
  (b) It **is going to** rain in a few minutes.

Focus 2

Will and *Be Going To*

- *Will* is a modal auxiliary and does not change form to agree with the subject:

Statement	Negative	Question
I You We They } **will** leave. **'ll**	I You We They } **will not/won't** leave.	**Will** { I you we they } leave?
He She It } **will** leave. **'ll**	He She It } **will not/won't** leave.	**Will** { he she it } leave?

- *Be going to* is a phrasal modal and changes form to agree with the subject:

Statement	Negative	Question
I { **am going to** leave. **'m**	I { **am not** **'m not going to** leave.	**Am** I **going to** leave?
He She It } **is going to** leave. **'s**	He She It } **is not** **isn't going to** leave. **'s not**	**Is** { he she it } **going to** leave?
You We They } **are going to** leave. **'re**	You We They } **are not** **aren't going to** leave. **'re not**	**Are** { I you we they } **going to** leave?

Exercise 1

Write the complete predictions about the future from the fortune cookies in the Task.

1. _____ .

2. _____ .

3. _____ .

4. _____ .

5. _____ .

6. _____ .

7. _____ .

8. _____ .

9. _____ .

10. _____ .

Focus 3

USE

Be Going To versus *Will*: Immediacy and Formality

USE

- Both *be going to* and *will* are used to make predictions. However, you use *be going to* for actions or events that you believe will occur very soon:
  - **(a)** We're going to leave. (very soon)
  - **(b)** We'll leave some time next week.
- *Will* is more formal than *be going to*; therefore, the choice of *be going to* over *will* also depends on the situation and the relationship between the speakers:
  - **(c)** Mother to child: Daddy is going to be angry about this.
  - **(d)** School principal to student: Your father will be angry about this.

Exercise 2

For each of the following, decide on the best form to use: *be going to* or *will*. In some sentences, it is possible to use both. The first one has been done for you.

1. Quick! Catch the baby! I think he *is going to* fall off the sofa.

2. Excuse me, Mr. President. Do you think unemployment _____ decrease in the foreseeable future?

3. Uh-oh. Look at those clouds. It _____ rain.

4. I predict that you _____ meet a tall, dark, and handsome stranger and you _____ fall in love and get married.

5. One day we _____ look back at all this and laugh.

6. I don't believe it. Look at Paula! I think she _____ ask that guy to dance with her.

7. A: What do you think about my son's chances of getting into Harvard, Dr. Heath?

   B: I don't think he _____ have any problems at all, Mrs. Lee.

8. Meteorologists predict that the drought _____ end sometime this fall.

Focus 4

USE

Be Going To versus *Will:* Plans and Intentions

 USE

- *Be going to* also talks about future plans and intentions:
  (a) We are going to spend the month of August in Italy. We bought the tickets last week, and we are going to leave on August 3.
- *Be going to* is preferred to *will* here because it refers to plans that have already been made.

Exercise 3

In this exercise, you need to get information from one of your classmates. Use *be going to* or *will* in your answers, as appropriate.

1. Get together with a partner and find out three things she or he intends to do after class:

   My partner _____

   _____ .

2. Now find out three things she or he does not intend to do after class:

   My partner _____

   _____ .

3. Now make three predictions about your partner's future:

   My partner _____

   _____ .

Finally, look back at what you have written in this exercise. Where did you choose *be going to* and where did you choose *will*? Why did you make these choices?

Exercise 4

Read the following carefully and decide if the use of *be going to* or *will* is appropriate or not. Check (√) the sentences you think are acceptable. Correct the sentences you think are unacceptable.

1. A: Do you have any plans for tonight?
   B: Yes. We will go to the baseball game. Do you want to come with us?
2. A: Your nephew is a very talented artist, isn't he?
   B: Yes. We believe he'll be very famous one of these days.
3. A: Who do you think will win the next World Cup?
   B: I think Brazil is going to win next time.
   A: Really?
4. A: Where's Freddie?
   B: He will spend the night at his friend's house.
5. A: Have you heard the news? Heidi's going to get married.
   B: That's great!

Focus 5

Be Going To versus Will: Promises and Willingness

USE

- *Will* is also used to show willingness to do something, often at the moment that the speaker decides to do it:

  (a) A: I think there's someone at the front door.

  B: I'll go and check.

  Will is preferred to *be going to* here because it shows that the speaker has just decided to do something or is willing to do something right away. The contracted *'ll* form is usually used in this case.

- *Will* is also used to make promises:

  (b) I will always love you.

  (c) I'll give you my homework tomorrow, I promise!

Exercise 5

Complete the following, using *be going to, 'll*, or *will* as appropriate.

1. A: What are your plans for the weekend?

   B: We _____ take the boat and go fishing.

   A: Sounds great. Can I join you?

2. A: Excuse me, but I can't reach those books on the top shelf.

   B: Move over. I _____ get them down for you.

3. A: You've bought a lot of groceries today.

   B: Yes. I _____ cook dinner for the people who work in my office.

4. A: Here's $20.

   B: Thank you. I promise I _____ pay you back next week.

5. A: Can we have some volunteers to help paint the new homeless shelter?

   B: Harry and I _____ do it. We really want to help.

6. A: Oops! I've just spilled my drink all over everything.

   B: Don't panic. I _____ get a cloth.

7. A: What _____ (you) wear to Aki's party?

   B: Kuniko and I _____ wear jeans. What about you?

8. A: Now, kids, I want you to be very good this afternoon because I'm not feeling well.

   B: It's O.K., Mrs. Swanson. We promise we _____ behave.

9. A: What's up?

   B: I'm late for work and my car won't start.

   A: Don't worry. I _____ give you a ride.

10. A: What _____ (you) do with your brother when he comes to visit next

    weekend?

    B: First, Jody and I _____ take him out to brunch down by the beach, and

    after that Kate _____ show him the sights.

Activities

Activity 1

The purpose of this activity is to collect as much information as possible about the future plans and intentions of your classmates.

Look at the chart below. Your task is to complete as many squares as you can by finding the required information. Write the name or names of the people who gave you the information in the square. "Maybe" and "I don't know" are not acceptable answers! The first person to get a line of three squares—vertically, horizontally or diagonally—is the winner. Good luck!

Find someone who is going to take the TOEFL soon. When is she or he going to take it?	Find three people who are going to cook dinner tonight. What are they going to cook?	Find two people who are going to smoke after this class.
Find two people who are going to play the same sport this week. What sport are they going to play?	Find someone who is going to move to another city within a year. What city is she or he going to move to?	Find someone who is going to go to the movies today. What movie is she or he going to see?
Find someone who is going to get his or her hair cut in the next two weeks.	Find two people who are not going to watch TV this week.	Find two people who are going to celebrate their birthdays next month.

Activity 2

Write fortune cookie "fortunes" for your teachers and five of your classmates. Write each fortune on a small slip of paper, the same size as in real fortune cookies, and give each one to the appropriate person.

Activity 3

What are your predictions for the next ten years? What do you think will happen in the world? What do you think will happen in your country? Write a brief report on your predictions. Your report should include a short introduction to your topic. When you finish writing, read your report carefully and check your use of *will* and *be going to*. Remember, it is often possible to use either one. Remember also that it is not necessary to use *will* and *be going to* in every sentence you write!

We have written the beginning of a report to give you some ideas, but you probably have better ideas of your own.

LIFE IN THE FUTURE

Nobody knows exactly what will happen in the future, but in my opinion, we will see many important changes in the world in the next ten years. Some of them will be good and some of them will be bad. In this short report, I will talk about some of my predictions for the future of the world, as well as the future of my country.

First, let me tell you about my predictions for the world. . . .

Activity 4

In this activity, you will be interviewing young North Americans about their goals and future plans. If possible, try to interview young people at different stages of their lives: college students, high school students, and children. Find out what they are going to do when they leave school. Report your findings to the class.

If possible, tape your interviews. Later listen to your tape and take note of the different ways these native speakers talk about the future. Make a list of the most interesting plans and share them with the rest of the class.

Activity 5

In this activity, you will be creating a chain story about your teacher's next vacation. Your teacher will start by telling you where he or she is going for his or her next vacation and one thing he or she is going to do:

Teacher: I'm going to Hawaii for my vacation, and I am going to climb a mountain.

Student 1:   (Teacher's name) is going to Hawaii; he or she is going to climb a mountain and he or she is going to swim in the ocean too.

The next person repeats the first part and adds another statement about the teacher's vacation until everyone in the room has added to the description.

UNIT

4

Past Progressive and Simple Past with Time Clauses
When, While, and *As Soon As*

Task*

Last night Lewis Meyer died at his home in Miami. Phil Fork, a police detective, was the first person to arrive at the house after Mr. Meyer died. This is what he found:

Mr. Meyer's wife, Margo, told Fork: "It was an accident. My husband took a shower at about 10:00 P.M. After his shower, he slipped on a piece of soap and fell down."

*Based on the situation in "Tragedy in the Bathroom" in *Crime and Puzzlement* by Lawrence Treat, 1935, published by David R. Godine

32

DO YOU BELIEVE HER?

Look at the picture and work with a partner to decide what happened. Be ready to share your answers with your classmates and to say why you think each statement is true (T) or false (F).

1. Mr. Meyer died after Phil Fork arrived.	T F
2. Mr. Meyer died when Phil Fork arrived.	T F
3. Mr. Meyer died before Phil Fork arrived.	T F
4. Mr. Meyer brushed his teeth before he died.	T F
5. Mr. Meyer was brushing his teeth when he died.	T F
6. Mr. Meyer was taking a shower when he died.	T F
7. Mr. Meyer took a shower before he died.	T F
8. Mr. Meyer died when he slipped on a piece of soap.	T F
9. Somebody hit Mr. Meyer over the head while he was brushing his teeth.	T F
10. The murder weapon is still in the bathroom.	T F

YOU ARE THE DETECTIVE ... WHAT REALLY HAPPENED?
(You can find the solution to this problem at the end of this unit.)

Focus 1

USE

Past Progressive versus Simple Past

USE

- When we talk about actions or events that **started and finished** in the past, we usually use the simple past:

(a) Ramon left the party at 9:00 last night.

- When we talk about an action that **was in progress** at a specific time in the past, we use the past progressive:

(b) Ramon was leaving the party at 9:00 last night.

33

- We often use the past progressive with the simple past to describe two actions in the past:

(c) Ramon was leaving the party when I arrived.

Past   9:00 p.m.   Now

LAST NIGHT

- The past progressive refers to an action that was in progress when something else happened. It started before this time and possibly continued after it.

Focus 2

FORM

Form of the Past Progressive

FORM

- *was/were* + verb + *-ing*

Statement	Negative	Question
I She He It } **was sleeping.**	I She He It } **was not sleeping.** **(wasn't)**	**Was** { I she he it } **sleeping?**
We You They } **were sleeping.**	We You They } **were not sleeping.** **(weren't)**	**Were** { we you they } **sleeping?**

Exercise 1

Complete this newspaper report of Mr. Meyer's murder without turning back to the Task.

DAILY NEWS

BATHROOM MURDER

"I am innocent!" says Mrs. Meyer.

Last night police arrested Margo Meyer for the murder of her husband, Lewis. On her way to the police station, Mrs. Meyer told reporters: "I am innocent. I loved my husband very much. I didn't kill him."

According to Mrs Meyer, on the night of his

death, her husband _____

_____

when _____

_____ .

However, Detective Phil Fork believes _____

_____

while _____

_____ .

Focus 3

When, While, and As Soon As

MEANING

- *While, when,* and *as soon as* are time adverbials. *While* is associated with an action in progress. It means "during that time":

  (a) While I was reading the newspaper, Donald called.

- *When* is associated with a completed action. It means "at that time":

  (b) When Donald called, I was reading the newspaper.

  However, *when* and *while* are often used in the same way. *When* is more common, and we often use it in place of *while*, especially in informal situations.

- *As soon as* is also associated with a completed action. It means "immediately after":

  (c) As soon as we heard the good news, we started to celebrate.

Exercise 2

Make meaningful statements about Mr. Meyer's murder by matching information from A with information from B. The first one has been done for you.

A

1. Mrs. Meyer called the police
2. While she was waiting for the police to arrive
3. As soon as Phil Fork heard about the murder
4. Mrs. Meyer took him to the scene of the crime
5. While Phil Fork was searching the bathroom for clues
6. He saw that Mr. Meyer died
7. When Phil Fork charged Mrs. Meyer with murder
8. A crowd of news reporters tried to interview Mrs. Meyer

B

she insisted she was innocent.

as soon as he arrived.

when her husband died.

while the police were taking her to jail.

while he was brushing his teeth.

she placed a bar of soap on the bathroom floor.

he rushed to the Meyer's house.

he became suspicious of Mrs. Meyer's story.

Exercise 3

Look again at the sentences you created in Exercise 2. For each one, underline the part of the sentence that gives information about time. This is the part of the sentence that answers the question "When?" For example: He saw that Mr. Meyer <u>died while he was brushing his teeth.</u>

Focus 4

FORM

Time Clauses with *When, While,* and *As Soon As*

- Time clauses answer the question "When?" by giving information about the time an action or event happened. They contain a subject and a verb and are introduced by time terms like *when, while,* and *as soon as*:

   (a) **While Renata was crossing the street,** she ran into her ex-boyfriend.
   (b) We left **as soon as we got your phone call.**
   (c) **When Phyllis arrived home,** everyone rushed out to greet her.

- A time clause is a dependent clause; this means that it is not complete by itself. For example, in order to fully understand, *When Phyllis arrived home*, we need more information. A time clause therefore depends on the rest of the sentence (the independent or main clause) to complete its meaning:

    Dependent Time Clause   **Main (Independent) Clause**
    (d) When Phyllis arrived home, everybody rushed out to greet her.

- A time clause can come at the beginning of a sentence:

    (e) While my father was cooking the dinner, our guests arrived.

- A time clause can also come at the end:

    (f) Our guests arrived **while my father was cooking the dinner**.

- If the time clause comes at the beginning of the sentence, use a comma between the time clause and the main clause:

When _____ , _____ .
(time clause)   (comma)   (main clause)

While _____ , _____ .
(time clause)   (comma)   (main clause)

As soon as _____ , _____ .
(time clause)   (comma)   (main clause)

- If the main clause comes at the beginning of the sentence and the time clause comes last, do not use a comma between the two clauses:

_____ when _____ .
(main clause)   (time clause)

_____ while _____ .
(main clause)   (time clause)

_____ as soon as _____ .
(main clause)   (time clause)

Exercise 4

Turn back to the sentences you created in Exercise 2. Write them below and add punctuation, as necessary.

1. _____

2. _____

3. _____

4. _____

5. _____

6. _____

7. _____

8. _____

Exercise 5

Work with a partner and write down five things you know about John Lennon.

1. _____ .

2. _____ .

3. _____ .

4. _____ .

5. _____ .

Here is some more information about John Lennon's life. The wavy line (〰) indicates an action in progress. X indicates a completed action.

1. attend high school 〰〰〰〰〰 ___ X his mother dies	2. attend high school 〰〰〰〰〰 ___ X meet Paul McCartney
3. study at art school 〰〰〰〰〰 ___ X form The Beatles	4. perform in clubs 〰〰〰〰 in Liverpool 〰〰〰 ___ X sign his first recording contract
5. live in London 〰〰〰〰 ___ X fall in love with Yoko Ono	6. work for peace and 〰〰〰〰〰 write new songs 〰〰〰〰 ___ X die
7. leave his apartment 〰〰〰〰〰 ___ X one of his fans shoots him	

Use this information to finish the short biography below. Fill in the blanks, using simple past or past progressive. The first one has been done for you as an example.

John Lennon was one of the most famous singer/songwriters of his time. He was born in Liverpool, England, in 1940, but his childhood was not very happy.

(1) *His mother died* while *he was attending high school.* Life was difficult for John after his mother's death, but after a time things got better. (2) _____ while _____ . Soon Paul introduced him to George Harrison, and they began to play in a band together. After that, John left high school and became an art student. (3) While _____ . Soon after John formed the Beatles, he married his first wife, Cynthia, and they had a son, Julian. (4) _____ when _____ . John and the Beatles moved to London and became very famous throughout the world. (5) _____ while _____ . A couple of years later, the Beatles split up. John and Yoko got married and they moved to the United States, where their son Sean was born. John (6) _____ when _____ . On December 8, 1980, (7) _____ while _____ . John Lennon died many years ago, but he still has many fans all over the world.

Exercise 6

Complete the sentences in the story below using the word in parentheses. Decide whether you should use simple past or past progressive.

NOTE: *After* and *before* also introduce time clauses, but we use them with the simple past tense only, in contrast to *while* and *when*.

1. Yesterday morning at 10:00, Marie _____ (go) to see the dentist.

2. While she _____ (wait) for her appointment, her old friend

   Lin _____ (come) into the dentist's waiting room.

3. Before Marie _____ (get) her new job at the software company, she and Lin _____ (work) together at the bank.

4. When Marie and Lin _____ (see) each other in the waiting room, they _____ (be) surprised and delighted.

5. They _____ (realize) that they had not seen each other for several months.

6. While they _____ (wait) for their appointments, they _____ (talk and laugh) about old times.

7. When it _____ (be) finally time for Marie to see the dentist, they _____ (not + want) to stop talking.

8. Just before Marie _____ (leave) the waiting room, they _____ (make) a date to to see each other again.

9. While Marie _____ (leave) the waiting room, Lin _____ (say), "I hope you don't have any cavities!"

Exercise 7

Combine the two sentences below into one sentence. Use the time word on the left to make a time clause and put the verb into simple past or past progressive.

1. (as soon as) Event #1: I (finish) shopping for groceries.
               Event #2: I (drive) home.

    EXAMPLE: *As soon as I finished shopping for groceries, I drove home.*

           OR

           I drove home as soon as I finished shopping for groceries.

2. (when)   Event #1: I (get) home
               Event #2: I (put) the groceries away.

3. (as soon as) Event #1: I (finish) my homework.
               Event #2: I (make) dinner.

4. (while)   Event #1: I (make) dinner.
               Event #2: My roommate (come) home.

5. (when)   Event #1: I (ask) my roommate if he was hungry.
               Event #2: He got upset.

6.(while)   Event #1:   My roommate (explain) why he was upset.

6.(while)   Event #1:   My roommate (explain) why he was upset.
                Event #2:   I (load) his plate with food.
7.(when)   Event #1:   He (look) down at the food on his plate.
                Event #2:   He (calm) down.
8.(as soon as) Event #1:   He (start) to eat.
                Event #2:   He (apologize) to me.

Activities

Activity 1

Nan Silviera has just written her first book:

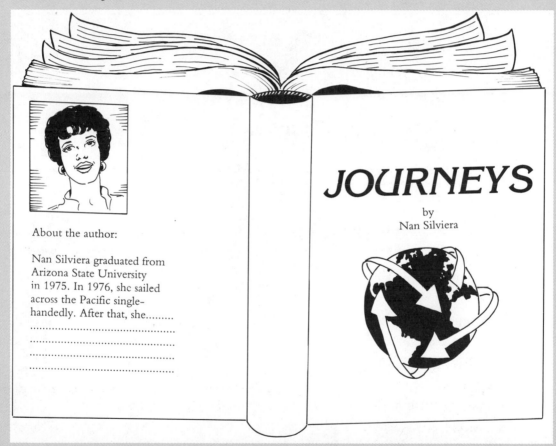

About the author:

Nan Silviera graduated from
Arizona State University
in 1975. In 1976, she sailed
across the Pacific single-
handedly. After that, she.........
....
....
....
....

JOURNEYS

by
Nan Silviera

As you can see, the author's life story on the back of the book is not complete. Work with a partner to finish writing it.

Student A is to turn to page 43 and Student B is to turn to page 45. You both have information about Nan's life, but some of the information is missing. Do not show your books to each other, but ask each other questions to get information about the parts marked "?". Write down the information your partner gives you so that when you finish, you will have the complete story.

Finally, use the information from your chart to write about Nan's life. You can use the biography on the back of her book to begin your story. When you finish writing, check your work to see if you have used time adverbials and the past progressive and past simple tenses appropriately.

Activity 2

In this activity, you will be finding information about your classmates' lives by asking about what they were doing at the times below. In the last box, add a time of your own choice.

Do not write information about yourself; go around the room and get as much information from as many different people as possible. Write the information in the boxes on the right. Be ready to share the most interesting or surprising information you find with the rest of the class.

TIME	
at 8:30 P.M. last Saturday	
in May 1989	
five hours ago	
ten years ago today	

Activity 3

Take a large sheet of paper and make a time line for your own life like the one in Activity 1. Bring your time line to class and describe the story of your life to your classmates.

Activity 4

The death of President Kennedy in 1963 was an enormous shock to Americans and to people all over the world. Most Americans who were alive at that time can remember exactly what they were doing when they heard the news of Kennedy's assassination. Interview at least three people who were alive at that time (you will probably have to find people over 35!) and find out what they were doing when they heard the news of Kennedy's death. Share your findings with the rest of the class. If possible, tape-record your interviews. Listen carefully to your recording and note if the speakers use any of the structures discussed in this unit.

A

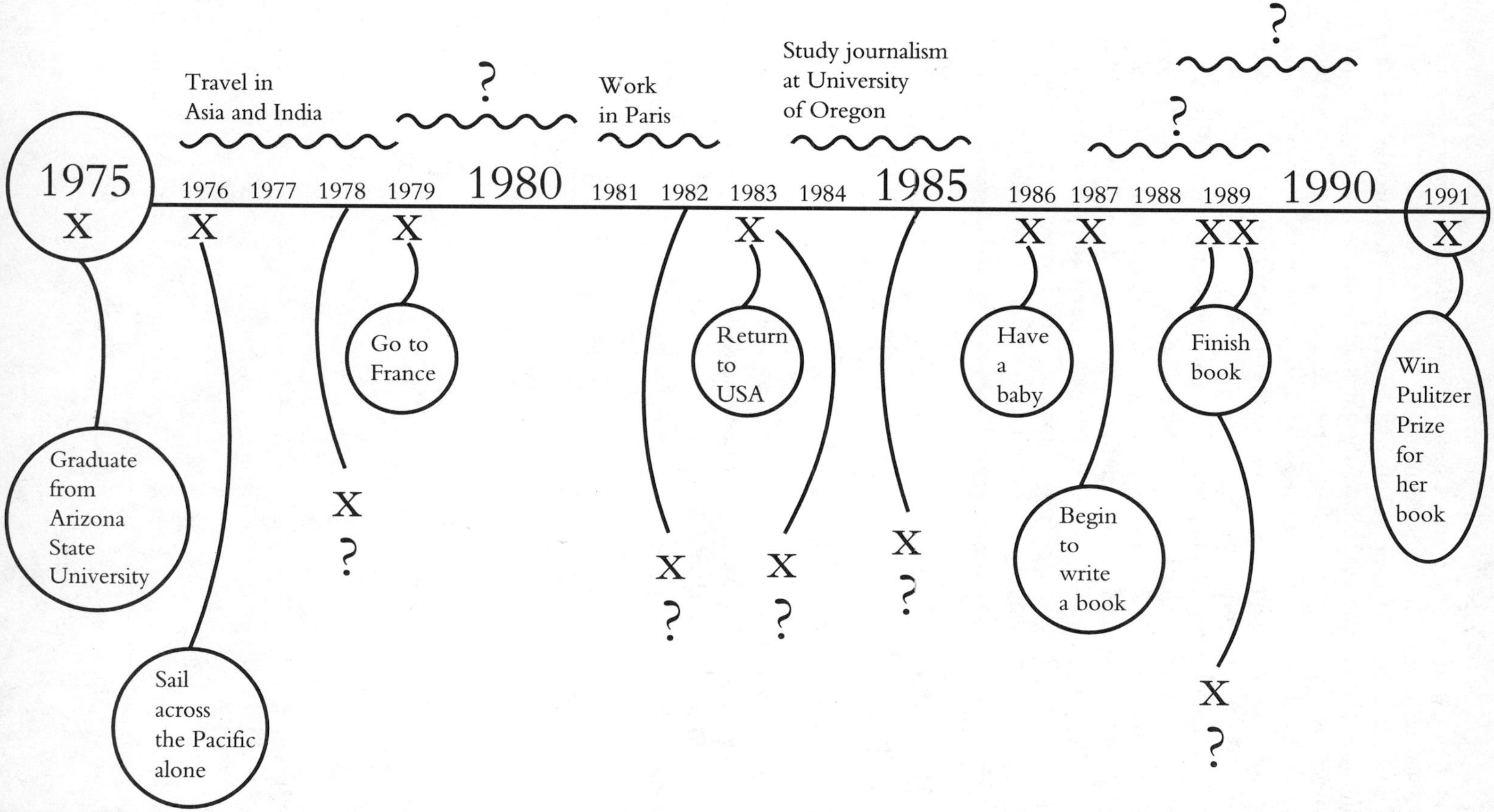

1975 X

Graduate from Arizona State University

Sail across the Pacific alone

Travel in Asia and India

1976 1977 1978 1979 1980 1981 1982 1983 1984 1985 1986 1987 1988 1989 1990 1991

X ~.

X

Go to France

?

Work in Paris

X ~.

X ~.

X

Return to USA

Study journalism at University of Oregon

X ~.

X ~.

X

Have a baby

X

Begin to write a book

?

?

X X

Finish book

X ~.

X

Win Pulitzer Prize for her book

Activity 5

Alibi

An alibi is a story that proves a person did not commit a crime because she or he was at a different place at the time of the crime.

A crime was committed around 10:00 P.M. last night. The purpose of this team game is to create an alibi for your team and to "break" the alibis of the other teams in the game.

Divide into teams of three or four people. You have five minutes to get together with your team to create an alibi for what you were all doing together between 9:00 P.M. and midnight last night. Try to agree on as many details as possible. For example, what were you doing? Where were you doing it? What were you wearing?

When everyone is ready, the first team goes out of the room. The rest of the class are now police detectives, and your job is to question the team one by one to see if they can keep to the same alibi. Call one person back into the room and ask questions about what she or he was doing. Keep notes of the answers. Next, call the second person into the room and ask *the same questions*. If she or he gives a different answer to any of the questions, his or her team must drop out of the game. (The rest of the team can now come back into the room and become police detectives.) The winning team is the team that keeps to the same story. Good luck.

Solution to the Task

Mrs. Meyer killed her husband. She entered the bathroom while he was brushing his teeth, and she hit him over the head with the bathroom scale. Then she turned on the shower and put the soap on the floor.

How Do We Know This?

From the toothbrush: He was brushing his teeth, not walking from the shower.

From the footprints: We can see his wife went into the shower.

From the soap: It was not possible to slip in this position.

From the bathroom scale: The scale does not indicate zero.

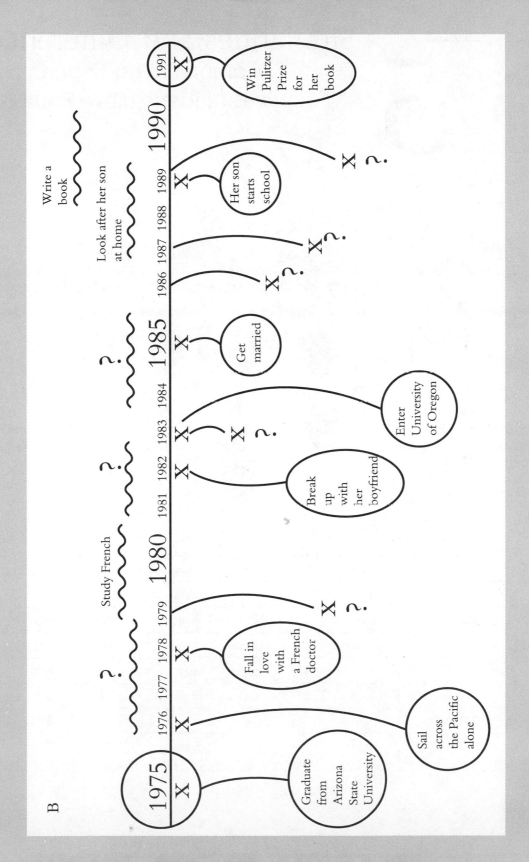

5 Similarities and Differences
Comparatives, Superlatives, Equatives, and Negative Equatives

Task

The silhouettes in this picture are from a photograph of a group of friends. Use the information from the chart and the list of clues to identify each person. Write their names in the correct position on the picture.

THE LEFT   THE RIGHT

Name	Likes	Age	Hair	Occupation	Eyes	Height
LINDA	football	75	red	doctor	green	5'9 1/2"
BOB	beer	19	brown	student	blue	5'9 1/2"
SUSAN	music	25	blonde	student	green	5'1"
FRANK	cats	43	gray	artist	brown	6'4"
CARLA	food	28	black	singer	blue	5'5"
GEORGE	movies	44	bald	writer	brown	5'10"
DIANA	opera	58	brown	engineer	gray	5'10"

CLUES

1. The oldest person is behind the youngest woman.
2. The tallest woman is behind someone who is thirty years younger than her.
3. The shortest person is in front of someone with green eyes.
4. The tallest man is next to the tallest woman.
5. The person who likes beer is not quite as tall as the person next to him on the right.
6. The man who is on the right of the youngest person is behind the tallest person.
7. The youngest person is as tall as the person next to him on the left.
8. The 28-year-old singer is not next to anybody.

When you finish, check your answers with the rest of the class to see if you all agree. You can find the solution to the Task at the end of the unit.

Focus 1

Expressing Difference: Comparatives and Superlatives

FORM
MEANING

- One of the most common ways of expressing difference is through the use of comparatives and superlatives.
  - Superlatives express **extremes** of difference among people or things:

    (a) Susan **is the shortest,** and Frank **is the tallest.**

- Comparatives show relative differences among people or things, but they do not show the extremes of difference:

(b) George **is taller than** Linda.
(c) Carla **is shorter than** George.

- Comparatives and superlatives can be used with all parts of speech:

		Comparative	Superlative
Adjectives			
One Syllable	young	young**er than**	**the** young**est**
One Syllable + -*y*	easy	eas**ier than**	**the** eas**iest**
Two or More Syllables	difficult	**more** difficult **than** **less** difficult **than**	**the most** difficult **the least** difficult
Adverbs	carefully	**more** carefully **than** **less** carefully **than**	**the most** carefully **the least** carefully
Verbs	weigh	weigh **more than** weigh **less than**	weigh **the most** weigh **the least**
Nouns	money	**more** money **than** **less** money **than**	**the most** money **the least** money

Exercise 1

First fill in the blanks or complete the words and then use the information from the task to decide if the statements are true (T) or false (F).

1. The oldest woman is taller __ __ __ __ the oldest man.   T F

2. George is tall __ __ than the person beside him.   T F

3. Diana is young __ __   __ __ __ __ the man beside her on the right.   T F

4. George is tall __ __   __ __ __ __ Frank.   T F

5. The singer is several years older __ __ __ __ the person behind her.   T F

6. The doctor is __ __ __ old __ __ __ .   T F

7. Bob is old __ __   __ __ __ __ the person in front of him.   T F

8. The young __ __ __ woman is in front of __ __ __ __ old __ __ __ woman.   T F

9. Frank is __ __ __ tall __ __ __ man, but he isn't __ __ __ old __ __ __ .   T F

10. __ __ __ old __ __ __ man is short __ __   __ __ __ __ __ __ __

   young __ __ __ woman.   T F

Focus 2

Degrees of Similarity and Difference

FORM
MEANING

- Expressing similarity:
  - To express similarity between people or things, you can use an **equative** (*as . . . as*):

(a) Linda is 5'9 1/2".   Linda is **as tall as** Bob.
(b) Bob is 5'9 1/2".   OR Bob is **as tall as** Linda.

- To emphasize the amount of similarity, you can add: *exactly, almost, nearly, not quite, just about,* or *practically:*

(c) George is 5'10".   George is **exactly as tall as** Diana.
(d) Diana is 5'10".   OR Diana is **exactly as tall as** George.

(e) George is 5'10".   Bob is $\begin{cases} \textbf{nearly} \\ \textbf{almost} \\ \textbf{not quite} \\ \textbf{practically} \end{cases}$ **as tall as** George.
(f) Bob is 5'9 1/2".

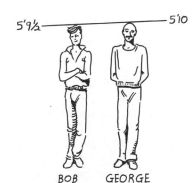

- Expressing difference:
  - Another way to express difference is by using a negative **equative** *(not as . . . as)*:
    (g) George is 5′10″.   Bob is **not as tall as** George.
    (h) Bob is 5′9 1/2″.
  - You can emphasize the amount of difference by adding *not nearly, nowhere near, not anywhere near:*

    (i) Susan is 5′1″.
    (j) Diana is 5′10″.

    Susan is $\begin{cases} \textbf{not nearly} \\ \textbf{nowhere near} \\ \textbf{not anywhere near} \end{cases}$ **as tall as** Diana.

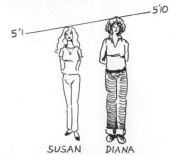

  - *Nowhere near as* and *not anywhere near as* are colloquial and are only used in conversation and informal speech.

Exercise 2

Use the information in the Task to complete the following, using the appropriate equatives, comparatives, or superlatives. Show the amount of difference or similarity as necessary.

1. Linda/Bob/height

Linda is as tall as Bob .

2. Susan/Frank/height

_____ .

3. Linda/Diana/height

_____ .

4. Linda/Carla/height

_____ .

5. George/Susan/height and age

_____ .

6. Bob/George/height

_____ .

50

7. Frank/George/age

_____

8. Diana/Linda/age

_____

9. Frank/height

_____

10. Linda/age

_____

11. George/Diana/height

_____

How many more meaningful comparisons can you make using the chart in the Task?

Focus 3

FORM

How to Use Equatives and Negative Equatives

FORM

- Like comparatives and superlatives, equatives and negative equatives can be used with all parts of speech:

Adjectives	(a) Susan is not as **tall** as Carla.
Adverbs	(b) Frank does not work as **quickly** as George.
Nouns	(c) Linda does not have as much **money** as Diana. (d) Diana does not have as many **friends** as Carla.
Verbs	(e) George **works** as much as Linda.

- *As* can be followed by:

Clauses	(f) Susan works as hard as **Carla works.** (g) Carla is not as tall as **Linda is.**
Reduced Clauses	(h) Susan works as hard as Carla **does.**
Noun Phrases	(i) Susan works as hard as **Carla.** (j) Carla is not as tall as **Linda.**
Subject Pronouns	(k) Susan works as hard as **I/you/he/she/we/they.**

- This is rarely used, except in very formal situations. Reduced clauses are generally preferred to subject pronouns by themselves:

  (l) Susan works as hard as **I do.**

  - Object Pronouns:

    (m) Susan works as hard as **me/you/her/him/us/them.**

- This is very common in conversation and informal writing.

  - Possessive Pronouns:

    (n) Susan's hair is not as short as **mine.**

  - Notice the change in meaning:

(o) Susan's hair is as long as me:

SUSAN'S HAIR   ME

(p) Susan's hair is as long as mine:

SUSAN'S HAIR   MY HAIR

Exercise 3

Correct the mistakes in the following sentences.

1. All her life, Hester has been lucky than her sister, Miriam.
2. Hester is not intelligent as Miriam but she was always more successful than Miriam in school.
3. For example, Hester's grades were always better than Miriam.
4. Both sisters are pretty, but many people believe that Miriam is prettier that her sister.
5. However, Miriam does not have as much boyfriends as her sister does.
6. They both have excellent jobs, but Miriam thinks her job isn't as interesting as her sister.
7. They both travel as part of their work, but Hester goes to more exciting places than Miriam is.
8. In spite of these differences, Miriam thinks that she is happier that her sister is.
9. However, Hester knows that she is lucky and she thinks that good luck is as important than good looks and intelligence.

Exercise 4

Work in a group to create a problem like the one in the Task. First use the picture and blank chart to record your information and then write the clues. Each clue must contain at least one of the following: a comparative; a superlative; an equative; a negative equative. Finally, exchange your problem with another group and see if you can solve each other's problems.

Name	Age	Height	Occupation	Likes

CLUES

_____

_____

_____

_____

Focus 4

FORM ● MEANING

Making Tactful Comparisons

FORM
MEANING

- Many of the adjectives that we use in comparisons express opposite meanings. These are called *polarity* or *opposite* adjectives:

tall	large		short	small
old	fast		young	slow
("MORE")			("LESS")	

- In general, the adjectives that express "more" are considered neutral because they do not give any special emphasis to the meaning of the adjective. For example, we usually ask:

  How **old** are you?
  NOT: How **young** are you?

  We only ask, "How young are you?" when we want to give special emphasis to *young*.

- To make comparisons using *as . . . as* and *not as . . . as,* we also usually choose the neutral adjective. For example:

  (a) Linda is **as tall as** Bob.

  (b) Linda is **as short as** Bob.

  (a) is neutral; we think only about Bob's and Linda's height. However, (b) draws attention to *short*, and we understand that both Bob and Linda are especially short.

  (c) Patricia is **as old as** Virginia. (Neutral)

  (d) Patricia is **as young as** Virginia. (Emphasis is on *young*.)

- The following statements express the same meaning:

  (e) Bob is **shorter than** Frank.

  (f) Bob is **not as tall as** Frank.

  (g) Frank is **not as short as** Bob.

BOB   FRANK

However, (f) is more polite than (e) and (g) because it is more positive about Bob's height. (e) and (g) both emphasize the difference between Frank and Bob and suggest that Bob is especially short. If Bob is sensitive about his height, it is more tactful to choose the neutral adjective.

- Therefore, when you know someone may be sensitive about the comparison you wish to make, you can use **not as . . . as + a neutral opposite adjective.** You can also use **not quite as** to soften the comparison and minimize the difference even more:

  (h) Otis is **not quite as bright as** Rocky.

  (i) His latest book is **not quite as good as** his earlier ones.

Exercise 5

Your boss has asked you to act as interpreter at an important business meeting with some foreign clients. He would like to do business with these clients, but there are some problems to be discussed because the two companies are very different. Unfortunately, your boss is very direct, and you believe that some of his statements will probably offend the clients.

Change his statements so that they will be less direct and more tactful. Use the adjectives in parentheses with *not as . . . as*. Add *not quite* if you want to be even more tactful. The first one has been done for you:

1. Your company is smaller than ours. (large)

   Your *company is not as large as ours*   .

2. Your factories are more old-fashioned than ours. (modern)

   Your _____.

3. Your workers are lazier than ours. (energetic)

   Your _____.

4. Your products are less popular than ours. (well known)

   Your _____.

5. Our advertising is more successful than yours. (effective)

   Your _____.

6. Your designs are more conservative than ours. (up to date)

   Your _____.

7. Your production is slower than ours. (fast)

   Your _____.

8. The quality of your product line is lower than ours. (high)

   The _____.

9. Your factories are dirtier than ours. (clean)

   Your _____.

10. Your factories are more dangerous than ours. (safe)

    Your _____.

Exercise 6

Omar is president of the international students' association at an American college located in a small town in the midwest. The chamber of commerce has asked him to give a speech to local businessmen on foreign students' reactions to life in America. He has made a survey of the foreign students on campus, and he is using the results of the survey for his speech. Some of the comments are not very complimentary, but he feels the local community should know what foreign students really think. He therefore decides to edit some of the more direct comments so that they will be informative but not offensive. He is having problems with the following. Can you help?

1. In America, people are less sincere.

   _____.

2. People in my country are much friendlier and are more hospitable.

   _____.

3. Americans are often very rude; people in my country are never rude.

   _____.

4. The cities here are dirtier and more dangerous than at home.

   _____.

5. Americans are lazy compared to people in my country.

   _____.

6. American food is tasteless compared to the food in my country.

   _____.

7. The nightlife in this town is really boring compared to the nightlife at home.

   _____.

8. People here watch too much television. We watch much less TV at home.

   _____.

Do you agree or disagree with these comments?

Do you have any comments of your own that Omar could include in his speech? Add them here:

Activities

Activity 1

Write a brief guide for American families who want to become host families for students from your country. What should American host families know about the differences between your culture and customs and those of the United States? Be tactful where necessary!

Activity 2

There are many common idioms in English that use the construction *as . . . as.*

Here are some common ones:

as stubborn as a mule

as happy as a clam

as strong as an ox

Interview several native speakers and ask them to tell you as many of these idioms as they can remember. Find out what they mean and share your findings with the rest of the class.

Idiom	Meaning
as _____ as _____	

Activity 3

Get together with another student. Observe him or her quietly for one minute and then write down all the similarities and all the differences between you that you can think of. Compare your lists. How many of your differences and similarities were the same? Together, can you think of any more? Share your findings with the rest of the class.

Activity 4

Go through as many newspapers and magazines as possible and clip all the examples of different types of comparisons that you can find (in headlines, advertisements, and so on). Bring these to class and get together with a group of three or four other students. Make a "Comparison Poster," using the examples you found. Share your posters with the rest of the class.

Solution to the Task

LINDA	BOB	GEORGE
SUSAN	DIANA	FRANK
	CARLA	

UNIT

6

Degree Complements

Too, Enough, Very

Task

Mary is looking for a place to rent. She is looking for a two-bedroom house or apartment with lots of light and plenty of closet space. She cannot pay more than $800 a month. She read the classified ads in the newspaper and went to see the following places. She also made notes on each place she saw. Can you match her notes to the appropriate classified ad? Which one do you think she probably chose?

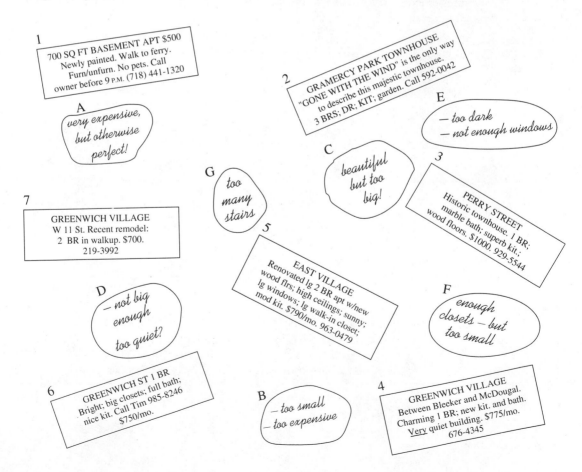

1
700 SQ FT BASEMENT APT $500
Newly painted. Walk to ferry.
Furn/unfurn. No pets. Call
owner before 9 P.M. (718) 441-1320

A
*very expensive,
but otherwise
perfect!*

2
GRAMERCY PARK TOWNHOUSE
"GONE WITH THE WIND" is the only way
to describe this majestic townhouse.
3 BRS; DR; KIT; garden. Call 592-0042

E
*— too dark
— not enough windows*

C
*beautiful
but too
big!*

G
*too
many
stairs*

3
PERRY STREET
Historic townhouse. 1 BR;
marble bath; superb kit.;
wood floors. $1000. 929-5544

7
GREENWICH VILLAGE
W 11 St. Recent remodel:
2 BR in walkup. $700.
219-3992

5
EAST VILLAGE
Renovated lg 2 BR apt w/new
wood flrs; high ceilings; sunny;
lg windows; lg walk-in closet;
mod kit. $790/mo. 963-0479

D
*— not big
enough
too quiet?*

F
*enough
closets — but
too small*

6
GREENWICH ST 1 BR
Bright; big closets; full bath;
nice kit. Call Tim 985-8246
$750/mo.

B
*— too small
— too expensive*

4
GREENWICH VILLAGE
Between Bleeker and McDougal.
Charming 1 BR; new kit. and bath.
Very quiet building. $775/mo.
676-4345

Focus 1

Expressing Sufficiency, Insufficiency, and Excess

MEANING

- *Enough* expresses sufficiency; it shows you have as much as you need and that you do not need any more:

    (a) There are **enough** closets.

    (b) The apartment is big **enough** for both of us.

- *Enough* suggests a positive feeling about the situation.

- *Not enough* expresses insufficiency; it shows you do not have all that is necessary or desirable for doing something:

    (c) There are **not enough** windows in this apartment. (I want more windows.)

    (d) The bedroom is **not** big **enough.** (I want a bigger bedroom.)

- *Not enough* suggests a negative feeling about the situation.

- *Too* expresses excess (more than you want or need) or insufficiency (less than you want or need), depending on the meaning of the word that follows:

    (e) The rent is **too** high. (EXCESS: The rent is **more** than I want to pay.)

    (f) The kitchen is **too** small. (INSUFFICIENCY: It is less than I want; I want something bigger.)

- In both contexts, *too* suggests a negative feeling about the situation:

    (g) This coffee is **too** hot. (I can't drink it.)

    (h) He speaks **too** quickly. (I can't understand him.)

    (i) She is **too** young to drink. (She can't drink alcohol here.)

Exercise 1

Can you find an appropriate cause for the following problems?

PROBLEM	CAUSE
1. My feet really hurt.	You don't go to the dentist often enough.
2. I'm broke!	Maybe you shouted too much at the ball game.
3. I failed my math test.	You didn't add enough salt.
4. I've gained a lot of weight recently.	Perhaps your shoes aren't big enough.
5. I never feel hungry at mealtimes.	You spend too much money.
6. I can't sleep at night.	Your stereo is too loud.
7. I have a sore throat.	You don't get enough exercise.
8. This soup is tasteless.	You eat too many snacks.
9. My neighbors are always angry with me.	You drink too much coffee.
10. My teeth hurt.	You didn't study enough.

Focus 2

FORM

How to Use *Enough, Not Enough,* and *Too*

FORM

- Enough
  - *Enough* follows adjectives, adverbs, and verbs:
    - **(a)** This house is **big enough.**   This house is **not big enough.**
    - **(b)** He speaks **clearly enough.**   He does **not** speak **clearly enough.**
    - **(c)** We **have seen enough.**   We **have not seen enough.**
    - **(d)** She **ate enough.**   She **did not eat enough.**
  - *Enough* precedes nouns:
    - **(e)** We have **enough money.**   We do not have **enough money.**
    - **(f)** There are **enough people** here.   There are not **enough people** here.

- *Enough* can be used with an adjective, adverb, verb, or noun followed by an infinitive.
  - **Adjective + infinitive:**
    - **(g)** She is **old enough to vote.**
    She is **not old enough to vote.**
  - **Adverb + infinitive:**
    - **(h)** They studied **hard enough to pass** the test.
    They didn't study **hard enough to pass** the test.
  - **Verb + infinitive:**
    - **(i)** We **earned enough to buy** a new car.
    We **didn't earn enough to buy** a new car.
  - **Noun + infinitive:**
    - **(j)** I have **enough chocolate to** make a cake.
    I don't have **enough chocolate to make** a cake.
- Too
  - *Too* precedes adjectives and adverbs:
    - **(k)** She is **too young.**
    - **(l)** They work **too slowly.**
  - *Too* + adjective is often followed by an infinitive:
    - **(m)** This tea is **too hot to drink.**
    - **(n)** We were **too tired to stay** at the party.
  - *Too* + adjective is often followed by *for* + noun / pronoun + infinitive:
    - **(o)** The book was **too difficult for him to understand.**
    - **(p)** He walked **too fast for the children to keep up.**

Exercise 2

Complete the following appropriately, using *too, enough,* or *not enough* as necessary. There are many different ways to make meaningful responses in this exercise. Compare your answers with a partner and see how many different responses you can make.

1. A: Why are you wearing so many sweaters?

   B: Because this room *is too cold / isn't warm enough*.

2. A: Does your brother have a car?

   B: No, he's only 14! He's _____.

3. A: Why did they move?

   B: They're expecting a baby, and their old house_____.

4. A: Would you like some more pie?

   B: No, thanks. It's delicious, but I _____.

5. A: Can we count on your support in next month's election?

   B: I'm sorry, but I _____ . I won't be 18 until next year.

6. A: What's wrong?

   B: My jeans _____ . I can't get them on.

   A: Why don't you buy a new pair?

   B: I don't get paid until next week, so I _____ .

7. A: Waiter!

   B: Yes, sir?

   A: We can't eat this. It _____ .

8. A: Let me help you carry that.

   B: Thanks. This suitcase _____ .

Focus 3

FORM ● MEANING

Too Much and *Too Many;*
Too Little and *Too Few*

FORM
MEANING

- *Too + much* is used with non-count nouns:
  (a) Jack has **too much money**.
- *Too + many* is used with count nouns:
  (b) There are **too many students** in this class.
- *Too much* and *too many* express excess, and suggest a negative feeling about the situation.
- *Too + little* is used with non-count nouns:
  (c) There is **too little time** to finish this.
- *Too + few* is used with count nouns:
  (d) The class was canceled because **too few students** enrolled.
- *Too few* and *too little* express insufficiency, and therefore suggest a negative feeling about the situation.

Exercise 3

Read the following and underline all the expressions or phrases that express the idea of insufficiency. Where possible, replace these with *too little* or *too few* as appropriate and change the verbs as necessary.

My sister's wedding was a disaster. First of all, she decided to get married very suddenly, so there
was too little time
<u>wasn't enough time</u> to plan it properly. Nevertheless, about 50 of her friends came to the reception in her

studio. Unfortunately, there wasn't enough room for everyone, so it was rather uncomfortable. She only

had a few chairs, and our 96-year-old grandmother had to sit on the floor. My father had ordered lots of

champagne, but there weren't enough glasses, so some people didn't get very much to drink. In addition,

we had several problems with the caterers. There wasn't enough cake for everyone, but there was too much

soup! We also had problems with the entertainment. My sister loves Latin music, so she hired a salsa band;

however, it was hard to move in such a small space, and my sister got upset when not enough people wanted

to dance. I got into trouble too. I was the official photographer, but I didn't bring enough film with me, so

now my sister is mad because she only has about ten wedding photographs—and all of them are pictures of

people trying to find a place to sit down!

Focus 4

MEANING
Too versus *Very*

MEANING

(a)	*We often see him.*	This writing is small.
(b)	*She usually doesn't call us.*	This writing is very small.
(c)	*They will arrive tomorrow around midnight.*	This writing is too small.

- *Very* adds emphasis, but *too* shows that something is excessive or more than enough. In (b) the writing is small, but I can read it; however, in (c) I cannot read the writing. Therefore, *too* suggests that you are unable to do something, but *very* does not.

Exercise 4

Complete the following with *too, too + to,* or *very* as appropriate.

1. A: Are you really going to buy that motorcycle?

    B: Yes. It's <u>very</u> expensive, but I think I've got enough money in the bank.

2. A: Why aren't you drinking your tea?

    B: I can't. It's _____ hot _____ drink.

3. A: Can I borrow your truck when I move to my new apartment?

    B: Sure.

    A: Thanks! My car is _____ small _____ carry all my stuff.

4. A: Can you turn your stereo down?

    B: Why?

    A: It's _____ loud! We've been trying to get to sleep for about an hour.

5. A: Do you need some help?

    B: No, thanks. This is _____ heavy, but I think I can manage by myself.

6. A: What do you think of Pat's new boyfriend?

    B: He's _____ quiet, but I like him.

7. A: We haven't heard from you for ages.

    B: I'm sorry. I've been _____ busy _____ call.

8. A: Did you like the movie?

    B: No, it was _____ long.

9. A: Do you want to go home now?

    B: No, not yet. I'm _____ tired, but I think I'll stay a little longer.

10. A: How's the water in the pool?

    B: It's _____ cold! I'm getting out right now.

11. A: Did Brian have fun at the party?

    B: Yes. He seemed to enjoy it _____ much.

12. A: Did Mary decide to rent that apartment?

    B: No, it was _____ small.

Exercise 5

Complete the following with *very, too, too + to, enough, not enough,* or *too much/many/little/few* as appropriate.

Dear Tom and Wendy,

I'm writing to answer your questions about life in in New York. In fact, this is quite hard to do because my opinions keep changing!

My apartment is nice, but the rent is (1) *very* high. Luckily, I earn a good salary and I can afford it. The main problem is that the apartment just is (2) _____ big _____ . I had to sell about half my furniture because I didn't have (3) _____ room for everything. I can't invite people for dinner because the kitchen is (4) _____ small _____ eat in! Luckily, the apartment has lots of windows, so all my plants are getting (5) _____ light. I live (6) _____ close to a subway station; it only takes me a couple of minutes to walk there. However, I never take the subway to work because it's (7) _____ crowded. You wouldn't believe it! There are just (8) _____ people crammed in like sardines, and you can't breathe because there is (9) _____ air. I haven't had the courage to ride my bike yet because there's just (10) _____ traffic. Mostly I walk everywhere, so the good news is that I am getting (11) _____ exercise!

Despite all this, there are lots of wonderful things about living here. There are (12) _____ museums and art galleries to keep me happy for years! However, at the moment, I have (13) _____ time to enjoy them because my job is driving me crazy! It's impossible to get all the work done because there are (14) _____ projects and (15) _____ good people to work on them. As a result, I am (16) _____ busy to make new friends or meet people. I don't sleep (17) _____ , and so I am always tired. Worst of all, I don't even have (18) _____ time to stay in touch with dear old friends like you! Nevertheless, I'm certain things will get better soon. Why don't you come and visit? That would really cheer me up!

Love,

Mary

Activities

Activity 1

Work with a partner or in teams to play this version of tic-tac-toe.

1. Decide who will be "X" and who will be "O" and toss a coin to see who will start the game.
2. For each round of the game, select a different topic from the list below.
3. Choose the square you want to start with. With your team, agree on a meaningful sentence expressing the idea written in the square and relating to the topic of the round. For example: TOPIC: This classroom. "This classroom is very small," "There aren't enough chairs in this classroom," "There are too few windows in this classroom," and so on.
4. The first team to get a line is the winner.

TOPICS

1. This campus
2. Television
3. The United States
4. This town or city

very	*enough*	*too*
too few	*not enough*	*too much*
not enough	*too many*	*too little*

Activity 2

First, look at the chart below. If you were responsible for making the laws in your community, at what ages would you permit the following activities? Write these in the column marked *ideal*. Now go around the room and collect information from your classmates about the ages at which these activities are permitted in the countries that they know about. Do not forget to include information about this country as well.

Activity	Ideal Age	Real Age/Countries					
drive a car							
drink alcohol							
vote							
join the military							
get married							
own a gun							
buy cigarettes							

When you have collected the information, prepare a report (oral or written) on the differences and similarities you found across different communities. Include your own opinions about the ideal ages for these activities and give reasons to support them. Remember to announce the purpose of the report in your introduction and to end with a concluding statement. You can use these headings to organize your information:

Introduction: Purpose of this report:

Most interesting similarities among countries:

Most interesting differences among countries:

Your opinions on ideal ages, with reasons to support them:

Brief concluding statement:

If you make a written report, remember to read it through carefully after you finish writing. Check to see if you were able to include any of the language discussed in this unit.

If you make an oral report, try to record your presentation and listen to it later. See if you were able to include any of the language discussed in this unit.

Activity 3

The purpose of this activity is to share opinions on different social issues. Work with a partner and look at the issues listed below. Relate the issues to this country and to other countries you know about. For each issue, think about sufficiency (enough–?), insufficiency (not enough—?), and excess (too —?), Try to be as specific as possible. Use the chart to record your ideas. We have offered some ideas to get you started, but you probably have better ideas of your own. Be ready to share your ideas with the rest of the class.

Issue	This Country	Other Countries
Public Transportation	—too expensive —not enough mass transit	Switzerland: very efficient
Health Care		
Housing		
Law and Order		
Employment		
Education		
Care of the Elderly		
Building and Public Transport Access For Disabled People		

Activity 4

Choose *one* of the social issues you discussed in Activity 3. Review the information you collected on different countries. In your opinion, which country has the best solution? Which country, in your opinion, is the least successful in dealing with this issue? Write a short report, describing the best and worst solutions. Give reasons to support your opinions. Remember to introduce your topic; we have suggested one possibility below, but you can probably think of a better way. When you finish writing, read your report carefully and check to see if you were able to include any of the language discussed in this unit.

In the modern world, many countries are trying to find solutions to the same social issues, and

it is interesting to see that different countries and cultures deal with these issues in different ways.

In my opinion, some countries have better solutions than others. To illustrate this point, I will talk

about _____ (social issue) _____ and show how _____

(country) _____ and _____ (country) _____ both deal

with it.

Activity 5

What is your ideal house or apartment like? Draw a plan of the house or apartment you would really like to live in. Next, write a short description of the house or apartment in which you are living at the moment, showing how it differs from your ideal house or apartment.

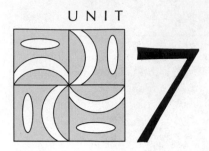

Giving Opinions and Advice
Should, Ought To, Had Better, Could, and Must

Task
Men's Work, Women's Work?

Look at the occupations below. Who *usually* does these jobs, men (♂), women (♀), or both (♂♀)? In your opinion, who is best suited to doing these jobs, men, women, or both? Write ♂, ♀, or ♂♀ in the appropriate column on the chart. Share your opinions with a partner.

Job	Who Usually Does It?		Who Should Do It?	
	in the U.S.	in your country	in the U.S.	in your country
elementary school teacher				
fire fighter				
airline pilot				
secretary				
cleric				
plumber				
nurse				
baby-sitter				
electrician				
fighter pilot				
cab driver				
college professor				

Focus 1

MEANING

Expressing Opinions and Beliefs

MEANING

- To show you think something is a good idea or that it is right for people to do, you can use *should* or *ought to:*

  (a) In my opinion, more men $\begin{Bmatrix} \textbf{should} \\ \textbf{ought to} \end{Bmatrix}$ teach in elementary schools.

- To show something is a bad idea or that it is not right for people to do, you can use *should not (shouldn't):*

  (b) In Alonso's opinion, women **should not** be cab drivers.

Focus 2

FORM

Should and *Ought To*

FORM

- *Should* and *ought to* are modal auxiliaries. They do not take *s* in the third person singular:
  (a) She **should** be a doctor.
  (b) He **ought to** work with children.
- Questions and negatives are made without *do:*
  (c) **Should** we go? No, you **shouldn't.**
- *Ought to* is rarely used in questions and negatives.
- It is important to remember that *should* does not take *to.*

Exercise 1

Get together with another student. Choose four of the occupations from the chart and write down your partner's opinions on who is best suited (or not) to do them. Also show why she or he thinks this. (Information from Unit 6 may help you with this part.)

1. In _____ 's opinion, _____ (should/should not)

   _____ because _____

   _____.

2. She or he also thinks that _____ ought to

   because _____.

3. In addition, she or he believes that _____

   because _____.

4. Finally, _____

   _____.

Focus 3

USE

Advice and Opinions

USE

- *Should/should not* and *ought to/ought not to* express the speaker's opinion about a situation. Therefore, they are usually used when you need to give advice to somebody or when you want to give your opinion about a topic or situation.

Exercise 2

In the United States, many "self-help" books are published every year. These books give people advice on what they should do in order to improve their lives in specific ways. Look at the list of book titles and the extracts below. Match each extract to the book you think it probably comes from.

BOOK TITLES

How to Stay Married for a Long Time   Lose 30 Pounds in 30 Days
Caring for a Neurotic Cat   Live Longer, Eat Better
How to Dress For Success   How to Attract Women
Getting along with Your Coworkers   Ways to Save the Planet

EXTRACTS

1. You should try not to surprise him or her. Any kind of change should be introduced gradually and slowly. Take things slowly, and he or she will soon be happy to accept whatever you propose.

2. As an important first step, you really ought to eliminate red meat. This may be hard at first, but you will be amazed at how many healthy alternatives exist.

3. Honesty is not always the best policy. In some situations, you should not say exactly what you think; the truth might cause more trouble than it is worth. For example, you should try to be tactful and diplomatic when called upon to settle an argument, by trying to show that you value both points of view.

4. Learn to cook! You ought to learn some unusual and exotic dishes that you can prepare in advance. Pretend that it was easy and effortless to prepare so you can focus your attention on *her* and not on the meal. Wait for her to compliment you on your skill as a chef. Remember you should never beg for compliments!

5. Organize the people in your office! The office manager ought to arrange special bins for different types of paper, for bottles, and for cans. Make everybody at work feel they have a part to play.

6. You should never settle into a regular routine. Surprise each other with fun activities, like picnics after work or moonlight barbecues on the beach.

7. You should try to motivate yourself to keep going on. Buy a dress that is just a little bit too small and hang it in your closet. You should look at it every day and dream of the day when it will really fit you.

8. You should not draw attention to yourself. Choose conservative but becoming styles because you ought to look competent and professional at all times.

Exercise 3

Choose three of the book titles from Exercise 2 and write other appropriate pieces of advice. Use *should, ought to,* and *should not* as necessary.

Focus 4

Should versus *Must*

USE

- *Should* shows that something is a good idea:
  - **(a)** A: I can't sleep at night.
    B: You **should** drink a glass of milk before you go to bed.
    B is giving advice, but *A* is not obliged to follow that advice. *A* is free to do what she or he pleases.

- *Must* is much stronger:
  - **(b)** A: I don't have a driver's license.
    B: You **must** get a license before you drive.
    B is giving advice, but in this situation, it is obligatory for *A* to follow the advice. *A* is not free to do what she or he pleases.

- Refer to Unit 8 for more information on *must*.

Exercise 4

Oscar has just bought a used car. Complete the following, using *should, shouldn't, or must,* as appropriate. Different people may have different opinions about some of these, so be ready to justify your choices.

1. He _____ get insurance as soon as possible.

2. He _____ take it to a reliable mechanic and have it checked.

3. He _____ get registration.

4. He _____ drive it without insurance.

5. He _____ drink and drive.

6. He _____ wear a seat belt.

7. He _____ lock the doors when he parks the car.

8. He _____ keep a spare key in a safe place.

Focus 5

Should and *Ought To* versus *Had Better*

USE

- You can also use *had better* to give advice.
  - *Had better* is much stronger than *should* and *ought to,* but not as strong as *must*:
    - **(a)** You **should** go to school tomorrow. (I think it's a good idea for you to do this.)
    - **(b)** You **had better** go to school tomorrow. (If you don't go, something bad will happen.)

    In this situation, *had better* suggests that there will be a negative result if you do not follow the advice.
  - *Had better* also expresses more urgency than *should:*
    - **(c)** You **should** see a doctor about that. (It's a good idea.)
    - **(d)** You **had better** see a doctor about that. (It's urgent.)
    - **(e)** You **must** see a doctor about that. (It's obligatory.)
  - *Had better* is often used in situations in which the speaker has power or authority over the hearer:
    - **(f)** Teacher to student: If you want to pass this class, you **had better** finish all your assignments.
    - **(g)** Student to teacher: If you come to my country, you **should** visit Kyoto.
- In situations in which there is a power difference between speaker and hearer, *had better* sounds like an order or a command. Therefore, if you are not sure about the relationship between the speaker and the listener, it is always "safe" to use *should* or *ought to.*

Focus 6

Had Better

- *Had better* refers to the present and the future. It does not refer to the past, even though it is formed with *had:*
    - **(a)** You **had better** finish this tomorrow.
    - **(b)** I **had better** leave now.
    - **(c)** He **had better** pay me for this.
- *Had* is often contracted to *'d:*
    - **(d)** You**'d better** leave me alone.
- To form the negative, use *had better not:*
    - **(e)** You**'d better not** leave me alone.
    - **(f)** You **had better not** finish this late.

Exercise 5

Complete the following with *should, ought to, must,* or *had better* as necessary.

1. Inez: How can I register to take the TOEFL?

   Patsy: First you _____ complete this application form.

2. Naoko: I want to get a good score on the TOEFL, but I'm not sure how to do that.

   Kate: I think you _____ take every opportunity to practice your English.

3. Yu-shan: I'm sorry I haven't been coming to class recently.

   Advisor: You _____ start attending regularly if you want to stay in this

   program.

4. Herbert: I think I'm getting the flu.

   Eleanor: You _____ go to bed and drink plenty of orange juice.

5. Claudia: I've lost my credit card.

   Rafael: You _____ report it immediately.

6. Doctor: You _____ take these pills four times a day.

7. Mother: Time for bed!

   Calvin: Just five more minutes.

   Mother: No! You _____ come here at once or else I won't read you a bed-

   time story.

8. Carmen: I'd love to visit Poland.

   Carol: Well, first of all, you _____ get a special visa.

9. Debbie: I've got a sore throat.

   James: You _____ try not to talk too much.

10. Lois: You _____ clean up your room immediately. If you don't, there

    will be trouble.

Exercise 6

Circle the *best* response in the following:

1. You (should not/must not) smoke when you are in a movie theater in the United States.
2. While you are in Los Angeles, you (had better/should) try to visit Disneyland.
3. In the state of Michigan, people under the age of 21 (should not/must not) purchase alcohol.
4. Children (should/had better) wear helmets when they ride bicycles.
5. Look, the bus is coming! We (should/had better) run if we want to catch it.
6. Everybody who comes into the United States (must/should) show a valid passport or I.D.
7. I've just spilled coffee on the new rug. I (should/had better) clean it up right away before it stains.
8. Professor Katz gets really angry when students chew gum in class. You (had better/should) get rid of your gum before we get to class.
9. Tourists visiting my hometown in the spring (had better/should) bring cameras, as it's very beautiful at that time of year.
10. My brother is looking for a new girlfriend. He (must/should) take cooking classes, and maybe he'll meet someone there.

Focus 7

USE

Should versus *Could*

USE

- You can also use *could* to express opinions or to give advice. However, *could* is much weaker than *should* because it only expresses possible options or possibilities for action in a situation; it does not show that the speaker necessarily thinks this a good idea or that it is right:

    (a) You **should** see that movie. (I think it is a good idea for you to see it.)

    (b) You **could** see that movie. (It is possible for you to see that movie if you want to.)

- We often use *could* when we want to suggest all the possiblities that are available to somebody, without saying which one we think is best:

    (c) If you want to improve your Spanish, you **could** take classes, you **could** listen to Spanish-speaking stations on the radio, you **could** find a conversation partner, or you **could** take a vacation in Mexico.

Exercise 7

Look back at the occupations in the Task at the beginning of the unit. Are there any occupations that are usually done by men that you think are possible for women to do and vice versa? Write your answers below, using *could*. Share your ideas with the rest of the class.

Men could _____ , but usually they don't.

Women could _____ , but _____

_____

_____

_____

Can you think of any other occupations that men could do but usually do not? Can you think of any that women could do but usually don't?

Exercise 8

Look at the following situation and respond to the questions below.

A woman went shopping. First she bought a large piece of cheese. Then she stopped at a pet store to buy a white mouse for her nephew's birthday. Just as she was leaving the store, she saw an adorable black and white cat. She couldn't leave the store without it, so she bought the cat as well.

Unfortunately, her car is parked a long way from the pet store, and she can only carry one thing at a time. What could she do in order to get everything to her car? How many solutions can you find?

She could _____

_____

_____

_____

There are no parking areas near the pet store, so she cannot move her car, and there is nobody around to help her. Unfortunately, cats eat mice and mice eat cheese. This means that if she leaves the cat with the mouse, the cat will eat the mouse and if she leaves the mouse with the cheese, the mouse will eat the cheese.

What should she do? What is the best solution to her problem?

She should _____

_____

You can find the solution to this problem at the end of the unit.

Focus 8

USE

Should and *Ought To* versus *Could, Had Better,* and *Must*

USE

As you have seen, although all these modal auxiliaries express opinions and give advice, they express different degrees of strength:

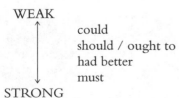

WEAK

could
should / ought to
had better
must

STRONG

Activities

Activity 1

Read the following situation and follow the instructions given:

Jennifer is an American student. She is planning to major in international business and has decided that it would be advantageous if she knew how to speak Japanese. Therefore, she borrowed some money from her father and went to Japan for six months. She has been in Tokyo for three months, taking classes in Japanese language and conversation. When she first arrived, she was overwhelmed by culture shock, so she quickly made friends with other Americans she met. Instead of living with a Japanese host family, she decided to move in with two other American women. Now she spends all her time with her new friends. She takes Japanese classes every day, but she talks only to the other English-speaking students and she seldom spends any time with the students who do not speak any English. As a result, she rarely speaks any Japanese and has not made much progress in the language; she has not learned much about Japanese culture either. She is having a lot of fun in Tokyo with her friends, but now she has a serious problem. Her father has just called to tell her that he will be coming to Tokyo on business, and he wants her to help him while he is there. He wants her to help interpret for him, and he also wants her to help advise him on the culture and customs. She is feeling very anxious about meeting her father.

First, brainstorm and write a list of all the *possible* solutions to Jennifer's problem that you can think of in two minutes. Then get together with two or three other students and share your solutions. Look at all the possibilities you can think of and then select from these the three *best*. Be ready to share these with the rest of the class and to justify them as necessary.

Activity 2

Get together with another student and choose one of the following topics. How many different ideas can you come up with?

How to get a traffic ticket
How to get rid of your boyfriend / girlfriend
How to avoid learning English
How to get an *F* in this class
How to annoy your roommate

With your partner, make a poster presentation on the topic you chose. Take a large poster-sized sheet of paper or card and use it to make a poster that expresses your ideas. You can use graphics, pictures, and diagrams to make your poster informative and eye-catching. Display your poster and use it to explain your ideas to the rest of the class.

Activity 3

Many American newspapers have advice columns to which people write and for help with their problems. Three famous ones are "Dear Abby," "Ann Landers," "Miss Manners." Clip any advice columns you can find in various newspapers and bring them to class. Circulate the letters without their replies. In groups, try to come up with helpful advice. Share your responses with the rest of the class. Compare your advice with the advice the professionals gave.

Activity 4

In groups, write a letter to "Dear Abby," asking for advice on a particular problem. Exchange your problem letter with another group and write solutions to their problem. Share both problem and solution with the rest of the class.

Activity 5

Write a short report, giving advice to someone who is planning on visiting your hometown, your country, or the community where you grew up. Advise him or her on places to visit, clothes to wear, things to bring, things to do, and how to act. When you finish writing, check your report and see how you have used the language discussed in this unit. It is not necessary to use a modal auxiliary in every sentence, as this would sound very unnatural! Remember to start your report with an introductory statement. For example: my hometown/country, (name), is very interesting, and if you follow my advice, I am sure that you will have an enjoyable and rewarding visit....

Activity 6

Read the following and circle *should* or *should not* to express the point of view that is closest to your own opinion on the topic.

1. School uniforms should/should not be obligatory.
2. Animals should/should not be used in laboratory experiments.
3. Doctors should/should not reveal the identity of AIDS patients.
4. Mothers should/should not work outside the home when their children are young.
5. A woman should/should not take her husband's family name when she marries.

   Choose the topic that interests you the most and then go around the room until you find one or two other students who share your opinion on that topic. Form a group with these students and brainstorm all the reasons and examples you can think of to support your point of view and then write them down. Choose the strongest ones, with the best examples, and use them to make a short report (oral or written) presenting your opinion. Share your report with the rest of the class and be ready to justify your position as necessary.

Solution To The Problem In Exercise 8

This is a version of a well-known logic problem. First, the woman should take the mouse to the car, leaving the cat with the cheese. Next, she should return and pick up the cat and take it to the car. As soon as she gets to the car with the cat, she should remove the mouse and take it with her, leaving the cat in the car. When she gets back to the shopping area, she should pick up the cheese and leave the mouse. Then she should take the cheese to the car and leave it there with the cat. Finally, she should return to collect the mouse and bring it with her to the car.

   There are many different versions of this problem. Do you know one? Share it with the rest of the class.

Phrasal Modals and Modals of Necessity

Have To/Have Got To, Do Not Have To, Must/Must Not, Should

Task
Entering the United States

A friend of yours from Japan is planning a short trip to California. She is going to fly directly from Tokyo to San Francisco. She doesn't have room for too many things because she wants to take only a backpack with her. Here are some of the things she is thinking of taking.

	a visa traveler's checks	
a camera	a lot of clothes	a gun
	a passport drugs skis	
a dictionary	photographs of her hometown	food
an international driver's license		10 bottles of cognac
a map of the U.S.	books about her country	a credit card
	fresh fruit	

Can you help her? Look at the categories below. With a partner, try to put all the things she wants to take in the appropriate categories.

#1 It's prohibited.	#2 It's OK, but it isn't necessary.	#3 It's a good idea.	#4 It's necessary and obligatory—you can't enter the U. S. without it.

Focus 1

Obligation, Necessity, and Prohibition

MEANING

- To show something is necessary and obligatory, you can say:
  - **(a)** You **must have** a passport.

    OR
  - **(b)** You **have to have** a passport.

    OR
  - **(c)** You **have got to have** a passport.
- To show something is a good idea, you can say:
  - **(d)** You **should bring** a camera.
- To show something is permitted but isn't necessary, you can say:
  - **(e)** You **don't have to bring** a lot of clothes.
- To show something is prohibited and absolutely not permitted, you can say:
  - **(f)** You **must not (mustn't) bring** drugs into the United States.

Exercise 1

Underline the sentences that have the same meaning.

1. **a.** When you visit India, you should have a visa.
   b. When you visit India, you have to have a visa.
   c. When you visit India, you must have a visa.

2. **a.** Chan wants to go to graduate school, so he has to get a good TOEFL score.
   b. Chan wants to go to graduate school, so he has got to get a good TOEFL score.
   c. Chan wants to go to graduate school, so he must get a good TOEFL score.

   What differences can you see between the *forms* of 2a and 2c? Between 2b and 2c?

Focus 2

Modals and Phrasal Modals
of Necessity

- *Must* is a modal and does not change in form to agree with the subject:

  (a) I **must** go now and he **must** go too.

- *Have to* and *have got to* are phrasal modals. They are different from modals because they contain more than one word and end in *to*. Phrasal modals change in form to agree with the subject:

  (b) I **have to** go now and he **has to** go too.

- Modals versus phrasal modals: statements

Modal *must*	Phrasal Modal *have to*	*have got to*
I must go. She must go.	I have to go. She has to go.	I have (I've) got to go. She has (She's) got to go.

- Modals versus phrasal modals: questions

Modal *must*	Phrasal Modal *have to*	*have got to*
Must I go? Must she go?	Do I have to go? Does she have to go?	Have I got to go? Has she got to go?

Exercise 2

What do the following road signs mean? What happens if you do not obey them? Make a statement for each sign that explains what you have to do when you are driving and you see this sign. The first one has been done for you as an example.

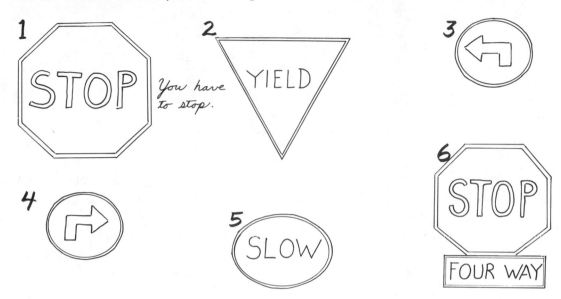

1. STOP — *You have to stop.*
2. YIELD
3.
4.
5. SLOW
6. STOP — FOUR WAY

Focus 3

MEANING

Advice versus Necessity

MEANING

- Modals and phrasal modals have many different meanings. In exercise 2, you were expressing **necessity**: When drivers see a stop sign like the one in #1, it is **necessary** for them to stop or they will break the traffic law. As you saw in the Task, we can express necessity with the modal *must* or with the phrasal modals *have to* and *have got to*.
- The modal *should* is not as strong as *must, have to,* and *have got to*.
  - As you saw in the Task, *should* shows that something is a good idea and expresses advice but not necessity.
- For more information on the use of *should* to give advice and opinions, see Unit 7.

Exercise 3

Turn back to the Task. Find the things that are necessary for your friend to take. Write statements about them below.

NECESSARY

_____

_____

_____

Exercise 4

Decide which of the following are _necessary_ to do if you want to get a driver's license in the United States.

speak English very well

know how to drive

practice before the test

take an eye test

take a written test

have a medical examination

own a car

pass a driving test

drive on the right

study the information booklet from the Department of Motor Vehicles (the department that issues driver's licenses)

Exercise 5

Your friend wants to know what he has to do to get a driver's license. Make statements to explain what it is necessary for him to do if he wants to get a driver's license in the United States; then explain what it is necessary for him to do if he wants to get a driver's license in your country.

Focus 4

USE

Have To versus Have Got To

USE

- Generally, _have to_ is more neutral than _have got to_. In other words, _have got to_ is very strong; use this when you want to emphasize that you feel something is very important and very necessary:

  (a) Joe **has got to** follow a very strict diet because he has a serious heart condition.

86

Exercise 6

Make a statement for each situation below. For each one, decide which you would use, *have to* or *have got to*.

1. Your sister's four-year-old son takes a nap every day and goes to bed at 8:00 every night. But today he didn't take a nap, and it's now 10:00 P.M.

   She says to her son, "You _____ go to sleep now."

2. The last time your friend went to the dentist was four years ago. He doesn't think he has any problems with his teeth, but he feels he should probably go to the dentist for a checkup.

   He says, "I _____ make an appointment to see the dentist sometime soon."

3. You haven't been reading the assignments for your history class, and you did very badly on the first two quizzes. You are afraid that you'll fail the course.

   You tell your classmate, "I _____ study every day if I don't want to fail my history class."

4. Your roommate is making dinner. She has just put a loaf of bread in the oven. Suddenly she realizes that she doesn't have an important item that she needs for dessert.

   She says, "I _____ go to the store. If I'm not back in ten minutes, can you take the bread out of the oven? It _____ come out at 7:00."

Focus 5

MEANING

Expressing Prohibition:
Must Not / Mustn't

- When you want to show that something is not permitted or is prohibited, you can use *must not* or the contracted form *mustn't*:

   (a) You **mustn't** smoke in here.

- *Must not* and *mustn't* are often used as a strong command in situations where the speaker definitely wants the listener to obey:

   (b) You **must not** have any more!

Exercise 7

Look at the cartoon. Write statements using *must not* to describe each prohibited activity.

1. _____

2. _____

3. _____

4. _____

5. _____

6. _____

7. _____

8. _____

Exercise 8

Look at the photos. With a partner, try to figure out what the signs mean in each one. What is the difference between the two photographs? Work with your partner and try to complete the summary below.

PHOTOGRAPH A

PHOTOGRAPH B

Reprinted with permission from Mark Chester, *No in America*, Taylor Publishing Co, Dallas (1986).

In Photograph A, you _____,

but in Photograph B, you _____.

Focus 6

Necessity, No Necessity, and Prohibition

 MEANING

- **Must, have to,** and **have got to** versus **do not have to:**
  - *Must, have to,* and *have got to* show that it is necessary to do something:
    - **(a)** If you want change, you **must** buy something.
    - **(b)** If you want change, you **have to** buy something.
    - **(c)** If you want change, you **have got to** buy something.
  - *Do not have to* shows that it is not necessary to do something:
    - **(d)** If you want change, you **don't have to** buy anything.
- **Must not** versus **do not have to:**
  - *You must do it* and *You have to do it* have the same meaning:
    - **(e)** You **have to** have a valid passport to travel overseas.
    - **(f)** You **must** have a valid passport to travel overseas.
  - However, *You must not do it* and *You do not have to do it* do NOT have the same meaning.
  - *You do not have to do it* means it is not necessary for you to do it:
    - **(g)** There aren't any classes on Saturday, so you **don't have to** come to school.
  - *You must not do it* means it is prohibited:
    - **(h)** You **mustn't** smoke in the movie theater.

Exercise 9

Turn back to the Task. Find three things that are prohibited and three things that (in your opinion) are not necessary. Write statements about them below.

PROHIBITED

1. _____ .

2. _____ .

3. _____ .

NOT NECESSARY

1. _____ .

2. _____ .

3. _____ .

Exercise 10

Turn back to Exercise 4. Find three things that are not necessary to do to get a driver's license and write statements about them below.

1. _____ .

2. _____ .

3. _____ .

Exercise 11

Peter is an athlete. Every week his coach gives him a different training schedule. Read his current schedule and complete the sentences below, using *have to, do not have to,* and *must not.*

TRAINING SCHEDULE					
	M	**T**	**W**	**T**	**F**
Necessary	lift weights	run 15 miles	cycle 50 miles	rest and eat high-calorie food	run 20 miles
Not Necessary	run	swim	lift weights	take a sauna	cycle
Prohibited	drink coffee	eat meat	eat dairy products	exercise	drink milk

1. Peter has to _____ on Monday.

2. He doesn't have to _____ .

3. He must not _____ .

4. _____ . (drink milk)

5. _____ . (swim)

6. _____ . (run 20 miles)

7. _____ . (rest/ take a sauna)

Now make your own sentences about Peter's training schedule. Do not use information from sentences 1–7.

8. _____ .

9. _____ .

10. _____ .

Focus 7

FORM

Talking about the Past: *Have To* and *Must*

FORM

- "He **has to** exercise every day, but he **doesn't have to** swim" refers to regular habits, so you use the present.
- To talk about the past, change *have* and *has* to *had:*

  He had to exercise last week, but he **didn't have to swim.**
- There is no past tense form of *must* when it is used to express necessity. When you want to express necessity in the past, use *have to.* Do not use *must* to talk about past necessity:

Present	Past
We **have to** go. We **must** go.	We **had to** go.

Exercise 12

Maggie is telling her friend Jan about a terrible job she had last year. Complete their conversation with *must, have to,* and *do not have to* in the present or in the past, as appropriate.

Maggie: My worst job was when I worked as a waitress last summer.

Jan: What was so terrible about it?

Maggie: First, I (1) _____ get up at 5:00 A.M.

Jan: Did you drive to work?

Maggie: No. I didn't have a car then, so I (2) _____ walk two miles.

Jan: What time (3) _____ be at the restaurant?

Maggie: 6:00.

Jan: 6:00. How awful! Did you wear a uniform?

Maggie: No, we (4) _____ wear a special uniform or anything, but the work was really hard.

Jan: What about your present job?

Maggie: Oh, I *love* my present job. You see, I start work at 11:00 A.M., so I (5) _____ get up early, and the people are really nice.

Jan: (6) _____ work on weekends?

Maggie: No, I (7) _____ work on weekends, but that's not so good.

Jan: Why?

Maggie: My boyfriend (8) _____ work on weekends, so I never see him.

Jan: That's no problem—find a new boyfriend!

Focus 8

Talking about the Future: *Must* and *Have To*

FORM

- To talk about necessity in the future, use *will (not)* before *have to:*
  - **(a)** **We will (we'll) have to** repaint the house in a couple of years.
  - **(b)** **We will not (won't) have to** paint the house again for a couple of years.
- You can also use *must* to talk about future necessity or prohibition:
  - **(c)** We **must** go to the bank tomorrow.
  - **(d)** You **must not / mustn't** park here tomorrow.
- Do NOT use *will* with *must:*
  - **(e)** I **must** call him next week,
    NOT: I will must call him next week.

Exercise 13

Complete the following, using *will have to* and *won't have to* in the appropriate places.

Some people are pessimistic about life in the future because it will be necessary to do many different things. They think that we (1) _____ (change) our habits. For example, to protect the environment, we (2) _____ (develop) materials that do not cause pollution. In addition, we (3) _____ (drive) less, and we (4) _____ (try) to develop different methods of transportation. If we continue to use the automobile as much as we do today, in the future we (5) _____ (wear) oxygen masks to protect us from the polluted air.

However, other people are optimistic about the future because they think it won't be necessary to do many of the things we have to do today. For example, we (6) _____ (leave) home to shop because we will buy everything by computer. Furthermore, we (7) _____ (work) every day and also, we (8) _____ (cook) because we will use pills instead of food.

Can you add ideas of your own about things we will have to do in the future and things we will not have to do? Share your ideas with the rest of the class.

Exercise 14

Read the conversations below carefully and complete the missing parts.

CONVERSATION A

Ann has just finished talking on the phone with Tom. When she hangs up the phone, her friend Bill wants to know about their conversation.

Bill: You sound worried. Is Tom having problems?

Ann: Tom's landlord sold the apartment house, so Tom (1) _____ find another place to live.

Bill: Oh, that's too bad. When (2) _____ (he) move out of his apartment?

Ann: I think he (3) _____ move out by the end of the month.

CONVERSATION B

Emily, a five-year-old, is playing in the street. Her mother, who is watching from the house, suddenly runs out to her. A big car zooms by.

Emily's mother: Emily! You (4) _____ be more careful! Don't cross the street

without looking for cars!

Emily: But I didn't see the car!

Emily's mother: You (5) _____ look in both directions before you cross the street.

CONVERSATION C

Outside the classroom, you hear a conversation between your teacher and Wang, one of your classmates.

Your teacher: Wang, I'm afraid this is the last time I'm going to tell you this. You

(6) _____ hand in your homework on time.

Wang: I know, I know. But—

Your teacher: No more excuses! You really (7) _____ try to keep up with the class

if you want to pass.

CONVERSATION D

It's the end of the school year. Ron and Marion have just had their last class of the term.

Ron: It's vacation time at last! We (8) _____ work for two months!

Marion: Not me. My grades were very bad, so I (9) _____ study all through the

summer.

Ron: I know how that feels. I failed physics two years ago, and I (10) _____

read physics books all summer—and my friends just went to the beach every day. They

(11) _____ study at all.

Activities

Activity 1

In Exercise 8, you saw some examples of signs. The purpose of this activity is to create signs of your own and have your classmates guess what they mean. Come up with some ideas for "prohibited" signs. Here are some possibilities, but there are many more:

You mustn't feed the ducks.   You mustn't eat in class.
You mustn't sleep in class.   You mustn't drink this water.

When you have thought of something, draw a sign to represent it. Do not write the command next to the sign—your classmates must guess what it is. Look at their signs and write down what you think they mean.

Activity 2

In this activity, you will be comparing your childhood memories with your classmates'. Think back to when you were a child. Think of five things you had to do then that you do not have to do now. Then think of five things you did not have to do then that you have to do now. Next, compare your list with those of two or three other classmates and be ready to report on your findings to the rest of the class.

You		Your Classmates	
Childhood	**Now**	**Childhood**	**Now**

Activity 3

What about children in this country today? Do they have to do things that you did not have to do? Are there any things that children in this country today do not have to do?

Use the lists you and your partners made and interview two or three different children (or parents of children) to find out if they have to or do not have to do these things too. Write a report on your findings, entitled, "Children's Lives: Past and Present." Make sure that your report has a brief introduction and that all your ideas relate to the topic. When you finish, read your report carefully and check to see how you have used the language practiced in this unit.

Activity 4

Do you know how to get a driver's license in any other countries in the world? What do you have to do to get a license there? In what ways is it different here? Talk to your classmates and find out what they know. Be ready to report on your findings.

Activity 5

Do you know what a person has to do in order to get any of the following?

a green card (for permanent residence in the United States)
a Social Security number
a marriage license
a license for a gun

Choose *one* and find out as much information as you can. If possible, ask a native speaker to tell you what he or she knows about the topic and record his or her answers. Be ready to share your information with the rest of the class.

Activity 6

A friend of yours is interested in studying at a North American university. Write him/her a letter, explaining what he or she will have to do in order to enter a university.

Expressing Likes and Dislikes
Rejoinder Phrases, Hedges, Gerunds as Subjects and Objects

Task

In this task, you will be exchanging opinions about different kinds of food and comparing your findings.

Work with a partner. One of you is *A*, the other is *B*. Complete the chart together. In the top left-hand box, write three kinds of food that *A* likes and *B* likes too. Next, in the top right-hand box, write three kinds of food that *A* does not like, but *B* does. After that, in the bottom left-hand corner, write three kinds of food *B* doesn't like, but *A* does. Finally, in the last box, write three kinds of food that *A* does not like and *B* does not either.

		A	
		I like	**I don't like**
B	**I like**	(*A* likes and *B* likes too.)	(*A* doesn't like, but B does.)
	I don't like	(*B* doesn't like, but *A* does.)	(*B* doesn't like and *A* doesn't either.)

Focus 1

Expressing Similarity

FORM
MEANING

- **Affirmative sentences:**
  - These sentences express similarity:
    - **(a)** I like fruit. Roberta likes fruit.
    - **(b)** I like fruit and Roberta does too.

    In each example, the subjects are different (*Roberta* and *I*), but everything else expresses similarity between us.
  - To form:
    - **(c)** I like fruit. Roberta likes fruit. ⟶ I like fruit **and** Roberta **does too.**
- **Negative sentences:**
  - **(d)** I don't eat meat. Roberta doesn't eat meat.
  - **(e)** I don't eat meat and Roberta doesn't either.
  - To form:
    - **(f)** I don't eat meat. Roberta doesn't eat meat. ⟶ I don't eat meat, **and** Roberta **doesn't either.**
  - Be careful with subject / verb agreement:
    - **(e)** NOT: I like chocolate and Roberta **do** too.
    - **(f)** NOT: I don't like hot dogs and Roberta **don't** either.

Exercise 1

Turn back to the information you shared in the Task. Write sentences using *too* and *either* as appropriate.

Focus 2

FORM ● MEANING

Expressing Similarity: Inverted Forms

FORM
MEANING

- **Affirmative sentences:**
    - **(a)** I like dancing and David **does** too.
    - **(b)** I like dancing and so **does** David.
        NOT: and so David does.
    - These sentences all have the same meaning.
    - **(c)** I like dancing and so **do** David and Rena.
        NOT: and so David and Rena do.
- **Negative sentences:**
    - **(d)** I don't like country music and Bruce **doesn't** either.
    - **(e)** I don't like country music and neither **does** Bruce.
        NOT: and neither Bruce does.
    - These sentences all have the same meaning.
    - **(f)** I don't like country music and neither **do** Gary and Bruce.
        NOT: and neither Gary and Bruce do.
    - *Neither* is a negative word; therefore, do not use *not* with the second verb.

Exercise 2

Use the information you shared in the Task to write sentences using *so* and *neither*.

Exercise 3

Now work with a different partner and share the information on your charts in the Task. Use this information to complete the following report. Make sure that your statements are not only grammatical but also true.

My classmates and I have strong opinions about the kinds of food we like and dislike. For example,

_____ and so _____ .

_____ and neither _____ .

_____ too.

_____ either.

We also found other similarities in our taste in food. _____

either. _____ neither _____ .

_____ so _____ .

_____ too.

Focus 3

FORM

Expressing Similarity

FORM

When the verbs are the same but the subjects are different, do not repeat the second verb; instead, do one of the following:

- Use *do:*
  (a) I speak French and so **does** my mother.
    OR
- Use an auxiliary verb if the first verb is an auxiliary verb:
  (b) I **can** speak French and so **can** she.
  (c) I **have** seen it and so **have** you.
    OR
- Use *be* if the first verb is *be:*
  (d) I **am** happy and so **is** he.
  The second verb takes the same tense as the first verb.

Exercise 4

Match the first half of the sentences in Column A with the second half in Column B. Draw an arrow to show the connection. The first one has been done for you.

She is late ———
We saw it last night
They've never eaten there
She'll call you tomorrow
Barbara was looking sad
The children have seen that movie
You didn't do the right thing
I can't play tennis
Her bike wasn't cheap
Scott doesn't have any money
The secretary speaks Spanish

and so have I.
and Peter didn't either.
and my brother can't either.
and so is her boyfriend.
and we do too.
and her friend was too.
and so will I.
and neither do we.
and we haven't either.
and they did too.
and neither was her car.

Focus 4

USE

Rejoinder Phrases

USE

- Rejoinder phrases (*so do I, neither does he, I do too, he doesn't either*) are very common in conversation. We use them when we want to show agreement with somebody else's opinions or ideas:

    (a) Tina: I love going to the movies.
    Rob: **So do I.**

    (b) Tina: I never go to violent movies.
    Rob: **Neither do I.**

    (c) Tina: I can't stand watching violence.
    Rob: **I can't either.**

    (d) Tina: I prefer comedies.
    Rob: Really? **I do too.**

- *Neither do I* and *so do I* emphasize the speaker's feelings about the topic.
    I do too and *I don't either* are more neutral because they do not emphasize the speaker's feelings as strongly.

102

Exercise 5

Read the comic strip. Can you find the missing parts of the conversation in the list below? Write the numbers in the appropriate cartoon bubble.

Focus 5

Hedges

USE

- In conversation, rejoinder phrases show agreement with the speaker:
  - **(a)** Stacey: I love ballet.
    - Jeff: **So do I!**
- However, if you do not agree strongly with the speaker's opinion, you can use a hedge:
  - **(b)** Stacey: I love ballet. What about you?
    - Jeff: **Sort of.**
  - **(c)** Stacey: Do you like opera?
    - Jeff: **Kind of.**
    - Jeff does not like opera or ballet very much.
- *Sort of* and *kind of* are used in informal conversation. In fast speech, they are often reduced to *kinda* and *sorta*.
- Rejoinder phrases follow a statement:
  - **(d)** Stacey: I like basketball.
    - Jeff: **I do too. OR So do I.**
  - **(e)** Stacey: I don't like football.
    - Jeff: **I don't either. OR Neither do I.**
- Hedges follow a question:
  - **(f)** Stacey: Do you like soccer?
    - Jeff: **Kind of. OR Sort of.**

Exercise 6

Claire and Chris have just met at a party and are finding out how much they have in common.

Look at the chart showing their likes and dislikes and complete the conversation below, using appropriate information from the chart. The first one has been done for you.

✔✔ = A LOT ✔ = A LITTLE

	Likes		Dislikes
CHRIS	swimming✔✔ cats✔✔ cooking✔✔	hiking✔✔ music✔ Chinese food✔✔	TV✔✔ getting up in the morning✔✔ rap music✔✔
CLAIRE	cats✔ eating in✔✔ restaurants Chinese food✔✔	cooking✔ music✔✔ swimming✔✔ hiking✔	rap music✔✔ getting out of bed✔✔ staying home✔✔ watching TV✔✔

Chris: Well, let me see . . . what are some of my favorite things? The ocean . . . I love swimming in the ocean.

Claire: (1) So do I. Maybe we should go for a swim sometime.

Chris: Yes, that'd be great! Do you like hiking too?

Claire: (2) _____ . In general, I prefer to be active. I mean, I don't like sitting home and watching TV.

Chris: (3) _____ . But I don't like getting up in the morning.

Claire: Well, (4) _____ . Most people don't like getting out of bed in the morning! What about music? Do you like music?

Chris: (5) _____ . I don't know too much about it, actually.

Claire: Really? I love all kinds of music, except for rap. I hate rap!

Chris: (6) _____ . We certainly agree on that one! What else? I love cooking; do you?

Claire: (7) _____ . I really prefer eating out in restaurants, especially in Chinatown. I really love Chinese food.

Chris: (8) _____ . I've heard that the new Chinese restaurant on Grant Avenue is supposed to be really good.

Claire: (9) _____ . Why don't we give it a try?

Chris: That sounds good. By the way, I have six cats. Do you like cats?

Claire: Well, (10) _____ .

Chris: That's OK—as long as you don't *hate* them. . . .

Exercise 7

One way to meet people is through personal ads in newspapers or magazines. These personal ads appeared in a local newspaper. Read them quickly and then read the statements that follow. Circle *T* (true) if you think the statement is true and *F* (false) is you think it is false.

(A) COULD THIS BE YOU?

You are attractive, slim, and athletic. You like dancing, eating candlelit dinners, and walking on the beach by moonlight. Like me, you also enjoy camping and hiking. You love dogs and you don't smoke. If you are the woman of my dreams, send a photo to Box 3092.

(C) I'VE GOT YOU ON MY WAVELENGTH

Athletic, professional, DF-animal lover seeks active man who knows how to treat a lady. Box 4021.

(B) BEAUTY & BRAINS

Warm, humorous, well-educated SWF loves walking on the beach, dancing, cycling, and hiking. Seeks intelligent life partner with compatible interests. PS - I'm allergic to cats, dogs, and smokers. Box 875.

(D) A FEW OF MY FAVORITE THINGS:

Cooking for my friends; cycling; walking on the beach with my dog; wise and witty women.
I can't stand: snobs; cheap wine; jogging; people who smoke; women who wear makeup.
DM looking for a special woman. Box 49

1.	*A* likes walking on the beach and so do *D* and *B*.	T	F
2.	*B* does not like smokers and neither do *A* and *C*.	T	F
3.	Cooking for friends is one of *B's* favorite pastimes.	T	F
4.	*D* does not like women who wear makeup.	T	F
5.	*D* likes dancing, and *A* does too.	T	F
6.	*A* wants to find someone who likes hiking, and so does *D*.	T	F
7.	Jogging and cycling are two of *B's* favorite sports.	T	F

Do you think any of these people would make a good couple? If so, why? If not, why not?

Focus 6

Gerunds as Subjects and Objects

FORM

- *Smoking, drinking,* and *dancing* are **verbs**; however, you can also use them as **nouns**.
    - **(a)** He is **smoking** a cigarette right now. (part of a verb phrase)
    - **(b)** **Smoking** is bad for your health. (noun: subject of a sentence)
    - **(c)** Brian stopped **smoking** last month. (noun: object of a sentence)
- Gerunds are formed from verbs: **verb + -ing**: *Reading.* Gerunds work like nouns; therefore, they can be
    - **(d)** the **subject** of a sentence: **Cooking** is his favorite hobby.
    - **(e)** the **object** of a verb: He likes **cooking**.
    - **(f)** the **object** of a preposition: He talked about **cooking**.
    - **(g)** the **complement** of a sentence: His favorite hobby is **cooking**.

Exercise 8

1. Underline all the gerunds in Exercise 7.
2. Underline (with a broken line) all the gerunds that are subjects and circle the gerunds that are objects / complements in sentences 1, 3, 5, 6, and 7.

Activities

Activity 1

THINGS IN COMMON

The purpose of this activity is to share information with one other person and then to report to the rest of the class on what you find. In sharing information with your partner, try to find out *how many things you have in common*. Some ideas for starting your conversation are given below. When you have nothing more to say on this topic, decide on another one and find out what you have in common connected to that. Use the chart for your notes.

Topic	Notes
family	some ideas . . . brothers and sisters?/ grandparents alive?/father older than mother?

Activity 2

Form teams. Your job as a team is to find as many similarities as possible among the pairs of things listed below. The team that finds the most similarities is the winner.

1. an apple and an orange
2. learning a foreign language and learning to ride a bike
3. tennis and golf
4. hiking and jogging

Activity 3

Form pairs or groups of three.

1. Think of 15–20 statements using *so / too/ either/ neither*. Make sure they are meaningful. Write each statement on two cards, like this:

   A   **B**

   My parents live in Paris   and so does my sister

   I don't like broccoli   and they don't either

   Therefore, if you have 20 statements, you will have 40 cards.

2. Get together with another pair or threesome.

3. Place all the *A* cards in one pile and all the *B* cards in another pile. Shuffle each deck of cards carefully.

4. Put the *A* pile facedown on the table.

5. Distribute the *B* cards among the players. Do not look at the cards and place them facedown on the table in front of you.

6. The first player turns over the first card from the *A* pile on the table and puts the first card from his or her *B* pile beside it. The player must not look at his or her card before putting it down on the table. The object of the game is to create meaningful sentences. If the two cards on the table do not make a meaningful match, the next player puts his or her *B* card down. The game continues in this way until a meaningful match is created. The first player to spot a match shouts "Match" to stop the game. If the match is acceptable, he or she collects all the *B* cards on the table. The next *A* card is then turned over and the game continues.

7. The player with the most cards at the end is the winner.
   This game should be played as quickly as possible.

Activity 4

Make a survey similar to the one in the Task and find out more about your classmates' likes and dislikes. You can ask about movies / movie stars / types of music / singers / musicians / sports, and so on. Make a report on your findings.

> Recently I made a survey of my classmates' likes and dislikes. I asked them their opinions on several different topics and would now like to share some of my findings with you. . . .

Activity 5

Write a personal ad for yourself like the ones in Exercise 7. Display the ads that the class writes and try to guess who wrote each ad.

Want and *Need*

Reprinted with permission of Chronicle Features, San Francisco

Task

You are shipwrecked on a desert island. Complete the list below.

Things I Need (because they are necessary for survival on the island)

1. _____

2. _____

3. _____

4. _____

5. _____

6. _____

Things I Want (because they will make me happy on the island)

1. _____

2. _____

3. _____

4. _____

5. _____

6. _____

Get together with a partner and compare your lists. Together make a new list, reflecting *both* your ideas.

1. _____   1. _____

2. _____   2. _____

3. _____   3. _____

4. _____   4. _____

Focus 1

MEANING

Want versus *Need*

MEANING

- *Want* expresses desires, things that would be nice to have, things that would make your life happier or more comfortable. (Unfortunately, we can sometimes only dream about the things we want in life!)
- *Need* is used for something that is necessary and essential.

Focus 2

FORM

Forming Statements with *Want* and *Need*

FORM

- *Want* and *need* are followed by a noun or a noun phrase:
  - **(a)** I **want** a radio.
  - **(b)** Anthony **needs** some medicine.
  - **(c)** We **want** several good books.
  - **(d)** Carole **needed** a cup of coffee.
- *Want* and *need* are also followed by an infinitive:
  - **(e)** Jack **needed** to sleep.
  - **(f)** Delphine **wanted** to go.
  - **(g)** They **need** to eat more vegetables.
  - **(h)** We **want** to build a house.

Exercise 1

Share your final list from the Task with the rest of the class, using *want* and *need* as appropriate. (We want . . . / We need. . . .) Be ready to justify your choices.

Exercise 2

It is your birthday. Your family wants to buy you things that you really need. Make a list of three things that you really *need* right now. Beside each item, write a short description of the kind or type you really *want*. (You can specify color, make, size, material, etc.)

EXAMPLES: I *need* some warm clothes for winter.

I *want* a black leather jacket and a pair of dark brown boots.

WHAT I NEED   **THE TYPE I WANT**

1. _____   1. _____

2. _____   2. _____

3. _____   3. _____

Exercise 3

Look at the statements and decide what the person needs or wants, as appropriate. The items in the list at the end will help you, but you probably have better ideas of your own.

1. Help!!! I just cut my finger!

   She needs a Band-Aid.

2. I'm going to Hawaii next week, and I really don't like any of my summer clothes.

   She _____ .

3. I have a terrible toothache.

   You _____ .

4. I can't pick this pan up. It's too hot.

   He _____ .

5. Ugh! This grapefruit is too sour.

   I _____ .

6. This class is very boring!

   The students _____ .

7. I can't read the instructions on this bottle because the print is too small.

   He _____ .

8. No, thanks, I don't like red wine. Do you have anything else?

   He _____ .

9. Oh, no! The button has just come off my blouse, and I don't have time to fix it.

   She _____ .

10. Oh, no! The flowers are dying!

   They _____ .

a pot holder	a Band-Aid	new eyeglasses
a safety pin	a pair of binoculars	some new clothes
some salt	change classes	a needle and thread
some sugar	go to the dentist	some water
something to drink		

Focus 3

FORM

Negative Statements

FORM

- For negative statements, add
  - *do not (don't)* or *does not (doesn't)*:
    - **(a)** I **don't** want to go.
    - **(b)** They **do not** need to tell her.
    - **(c)** She **doesn't** want to drive.
  - *did not (didn't)*:
    - **(d)** We **didn't** need your help.
    - **(e)** He **didn't** want to see us.
- In negative statements with plural count nouns or with non-count nouns, *some* changes to *any*:
  - **(f)** They **need some** new books.
  - **(g)** They **don't need any** new books.
  - **(h)** She **wants some** sugar in her coffee.
  - **(i)** She **doesn't want any** sugar in her coffee.

Exercise 4

Estella is having a garage sale. These are some of the things she is selling. With other students, discuss whether or not you need or want any of these things.

picture frames	garden furniture	kitty litter
sofa cushions	rugs	candles
dishes	a bed	baby clothes
laundry soap	computer software	a washer and dryer
garden tools	computer paper	bath towels
fertilizer for houseplants	a stereo	old magazines

Exercise 5

Alessandro is going to cook dinner. The recipe requires:

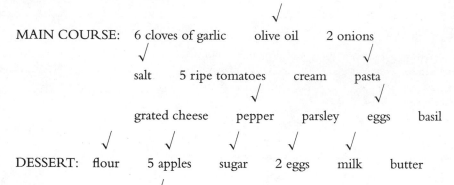

MAIN COURSE: 6 cloves of garlic   olive oil ✓   2 onions

salt ✓   5 ripe tomatoes   cream   pasta ✓

grated cheese   pepper ✓   parsley   eggs ✓   basil

DESSERT: flour ✓   5 apples ✓   sugar ✓   2 eggs ✓   milk ✓   butter

Alessandro has checked (✓) the items he has already got in his kitchen. What does and doesn't he need to buy before he can start cooking?

Exercise 6

Use *want* or *need* to describe each situation below.

1. Peter realizes that it is necessary for him to borrow $100 to pay the rent this month.
2. Dan has a toothache. Suddenly he remembers that he has not been to a dentist in five years.
3. Hannah told her parents all the things she would like for her birthday next month: a doll, a bicycle, a teddy bear, and a cat.
4. Francisco is in class. He is bored, he does not like the teacher, and he does not like his classmates. He misses his girlfriend, who lives in Acapulco. Unfortunately, he is a long way from Acapulco.
5. I asked Ben if he wanted to buy some of my computer paper, but he had already bought some.
6. Mary offers her friend Karl some more wine, but he says he has a headache, and wine is bad for a headache.

Activities

Activity 1

Choose *one* of the following and with a partner, make a list of what you need to do in order to achieve it. Do other people agree with you?

1. get an *A* in this class
2. speak English fluently
3. become a citizen
4. keep in touch with old friends
5. get in better physical shape

Activity 2

"You Can't Always Get What You Want" is the the title of a Rolling Stones song. Interview different people outside the classroom to see how many people know the song and if they can remember any of the lyrics. Write down any words they can remember. Compare your findings with your classmates. If possible, try to get hold of the song and see if you can follow the words. What do you think the song means?

Activity 3

WHAT DO MEN AND WOMEN WANT?

If possible, divide into groups of the same sex (women work with women and men work with men). In your group, make a list of the characteristics you think are most important in your ideal partner. What things do you need and what things do you want?

What We Need	What We Want

Compare lists. Do men and women want and need the same things? Why or why not?

Activity 4

Some people who study literature believe that every character in every story has a clear motivation: They *want* or *need* something. To see if you agree with this, think of a short story or folktale or a movie that you know. Summarize the story and then, if you can, say what the main characters need or want.

11

Present Perfect

Since and *For*

Task

Quickly read the following:

MEDICAL HISTORY

NAME: Michael James Harris   SEX: Male   DATE OF BIRTH: 5/13/56

MARITAL STATUS: Single   HEIGHT: 5 ft 11 in   WEIGHT: 185 lbs

SERIOUS ILLNESS(ES): None   TIME IN HOSPITAL: May 1973. Broke

SMOKING: Stopped 10 years ago   both legs in traffic accident

EYESIGHT: Wears glasses for   DRINKING: 1 glass of wine with dinner

reading; started in 1987   ALLERGIES: None

PRESENT PROBLEM: Headaches   WHEN PROBLEM STARTED: 2 months ago

---

Work with a partner and find details from Michael Harris's medical history to complete the following list. Find two things that relate to the past, two things that relate to the present, and two things that started in the past and continue to the present. The first one has been done for you.

PAST

1. *He broke his legs.* _____

2. _____

PRESENT

1. _____

2. _____

FROM PAST TO PRESENT

1. _____

2. _____

Focus 1

USE

USE

Present Perfect:
Connecting Past and Present

- We use the present perfect to show a connection between something in the past and something in the present. The present perfect shows the result or relevance now of a past action, event, or experience.

PAST	PRESENT
February:	September:
(a) I **moved** to New York. (simple past)	**(b)** I **live** in New York now. (simple present)

FROM PAST TO PRESENT
(c) I **have lived** in New York since Febuary.
(d) I **have lived** in New York for seven months. (present perfect)

- In this situation, the simple past tells us only about the past; the present tells us only about the present. One use of the present perfect is to tell us about **something which began in the past and continues to the present**. For information about a different use of the present perfect, see Unit 12.

Focus 2

FORM

Forming the Present Perfect

FORM

- *have/has* + past participle *

Statement	Negative	Question
I You \} **have gone.** We \} **('ve)** They	I You \} **have not gone.** We \} **(haven't)** They	**Have** {I you we they} **gone?**
She \} He \} **has gone.** It \} **('s)**	She \} He \} **has not gone.** It \} **(hasn't)**	**Has** {she he it} **gone?**

*See Appendix 1 for the past participles of irregular verbs.

Exercise 1

Use the information about Michael Harris from the Task to complete the doctor's report about him. Use the simple past, simple present, or present perfect of the verbs in parentheses.

REPORT ON MICHAEL HARRIS

Michael Harris spoke with me yesterday about serious headaches. He (1) _____ (have) these headaches for two months. His previous medical history is good. He (2) _____ (not have) any serious illnesses. In 1973, he (3) _____ (be) in the hospital for three weeks, when he (4) _____ (break) both legs in a car accident. He (5) _____ (not smoke) now; he (6) _____ (stop) smoking ten years ago, and he (7) _____ (not smoke) since that time. He (8) _____ (wear) glasses for reading, and he (9) _____ (wear) them since 1987. He (10) _____ (drink) a little wine with dinner every night. I examined Mr. Harris and took several tests. I asked him to return next week.

Exercise 2

Write the questions that the doctor asked Mr. Harris in order to get these responses.

EXAMPLE: 1. *Do you drink?*
Yes, a little. I drink a glass of wine with dinner every night.

2. _____?

Yes, I do. I wear them for reading.

3. _____?

I started wearing them in 1987.

4. _____?

Yes, I've worn them since 1987.

5. _____?

No, I don't smoke now.

6. _____?

I stopped ten years ago.

7. _____?

No, I haven't smoked since that time.

8. _____?

Yes, I have had these headaches for two months.

Exercise 3

Go back to Exercises 1 and 2. Look for the words *since* and *for*.

In the boxes below, write down the word or words that directly follow them. We have done the first one for you.

Since	For
	two months

What does this tell you about the use of *since* and *for*?

Focus 3

For versus *Since*

MEANING

- You can use *for* to talk about the **length** of a period of time (for two weeks; for ten years; for five minutes).
- You can use *since* to talk about **when** a period of time **began** (since 1985; since my birthday; since Monday; since April).

Focus 4

For and Since

- You can use *since* to introduce a time clause:

Main Clause (from past to present)	Time Clause (past)
(a) He has worked here	**since** he graduated from high school.

- You can also use *since* with a phrase referring to a specific time:
  - **(b)** He has worked here **since** April.
  - **(c)** He has worked here **since** the beginning of the month.
- You can use *for* with a phrase that refers to a quantity of time, but not with a time clause:
  - **(d)** He has worked here **for** several years.
- It is possible to omit *for*:
  - **(e)** I've lived here five months.
  - **(f)** I've lived here **for** five months.

  Both **(e)** and **(f)** are correct; **(e)** is more informal.
- It is also also possible to omit *for* in questions:
  - **(g)** (**For**) how long have you lived here?
- It is not possible to omit *since*:
  - **(h)** I've lived here **since** January.
    NOT: I've lived here January.
  - **(i)** **Since** when have you lived here?
    NOT: When have you lived here?

Exercise 4

What difference in meaning (if any) is there in these statements?

1. He lived here for ten years.
   He has lived here for ten years.
2. (It is May. He moved here three months ago.)
   He has lived here for three months.
   He has lived here since February.
3. They have worked for the same company for a long time.
   They worked for the same company for a long time.

4. She has known them many years.
   She has known them for many years.

5. (It is July.)
   Anthony hasn't smoked for six months.
   Anthony stopped smoking in January.

Exercise 5

Look at the hotel register. How many people are staying in the hotel right now? Who has stayed there the longest?

Hotel Beresford Arms

701 Polk Street ▪ San Francisco, CA 94109
(415) 493-0443

Date: *3/11*

Guest	Check-In	Check-Out
Mr. Cruise	3/3	
B. Simpson	3/1	
Mr. and Mrs. Kowlowski	3/8	
Mr. and Mrs. Gordon	3/2	3/5
Ms. Chapman	3/2	
Mr. Nixon	3/2	3/8
Maria da Costa	3/6	
Yee Mun Ling	3/4	

Use the information from the register to make statements with the words given below.

1. Mr. and Mrs. Gordon / for
2. Maria da Costa / since
3. Yee Mun Ling / since
4. Mr. B. Simpson / for
5. Mr. and Mrs. Kolowski / for
6. Ms. Chapman / since
7. Mr. Cruise / for
8. Mr. Nixon / for

121

Exercise 6

Read the following statements and decide if they are referring to an action that is finished or unfinished. If you think it is finished, write *F* beside it; write *U* if you think it is unfinished.

1. He has lived here 20 years.
2. We have studied English for a few months.
3. I saw him last week.
4. My friends worked there for six months.
5. He's worn glasses since he was a child.
6. She slept ten hours.

Focus 5

USE

Actions Continuing Up to Now

USE

- When you talk about the duration of an action or situation that began in the past and that continues to the present, you can use **present perfect + for**.

    (a) They **have studied** martial arts **for** a long time.

    (b) Carrie **has been** a member of the tennis club **for** six months.

- Some verbs are not used in this way because the actions they describe cannot continue from past to present.

    (c) Shin **started** to smoke on his eighteenth birthday, so he has smoked **for** three years.

    (d) NOT: He has started to smoke for three years.

    In **(c)**, we understand that it is the smoking that continues, not the starting. *Start* refers to something that happens at one time only, or at several different times, but not to an action that continues over time.

- For the same reason, the following verbs are not usually used with **present perfect + for** to express the duration of an action or situation that continues from past to present:

start	leave
arrive	meet
begin	stop

Exercise 7

Rewrite these sentences using the present perfect and *since* or *for*.

    EXAMPLE: Karen wears glasses. She started to wear glasses when she was a child.
        Karen has worn glasses since she was a child.

1. He works for the TV station. He started working there eight years ago.
2. They are married. They got married in 1962.
3. She knows how to fix a car. She learned how to do it a long time ago.
4. Tom rides his bike to work. He started to do it when his car broke down.
5. I wanted to go to China several years ago. I still want to go now.
6. My brother stopped smoking when he was in college, and he doesn't smoke now.
7. I was afraid of bats when I was a child, and I am afraid of them now.
8. My mother is in France. She went there last week.
9. My sister runs two miles every morning before breakfast. She started to do this when she was 15 years old.
10. They go to Cape Cod every summer. They started to do this 12 years ago.

Exercise 8

Complete the following. Put in the empty blanks *since* or *for* or the appropriate form of the verb in parentheses.

    Leroy and Paula are having a party. Two of their guests, Lee and Bob, have just met.

Lee: (1) *Have you known* _____ (know) Leroy and Paula (2) *for* _____ a long time?

Bob: I (3) _____ (know) Paula (4) _____ my senior year in college. I first (5) _____ (meet) Leroy at their wedding two years ago. What about you?

Lee: I'm a colleague of Leroy's. We (6) _____ (work) together (7) _____ several years.

Bob: Oh, Leroy (8) _____ (show) me some of your work last week. It's great.

Lee: Thanks. What do you do?

Bob: I (9) _____ (teach) French (10) _____ ten years, but I

(11) _____ (quit) a couple of years ago. Now I'm an actor.

Lee: An actor! I thought you looked familiar.

Bob: Well, not really. I (12) _____ (not work) as an actor (13) _____ last

October. In fact, last night I (14) _____ (start) to work as a waiter at the

Zenon.

Lee: Really? I (15) _____ (eat) there last night. *That's* why you look familiar!

Exercise 9

Look at the following and underline the sentences that you think are correct.

My sister is very good at languages.

1. She studies Italian; she started studying Italian in 1991, so . . .

   she has studied Italian for several years.
   she studies Italian several years.
   she studied Italian for several years.
   she is studying Italian since 1991.

2. When she was a child, she wanted to learn Russian; she still wants to learn it.

   She has wanted to learn Russian when she was a child.
   She wants to learn Russian since she has been a child.
   She has wanted to learn Russian for she was a child.
   She has wanted to learn Russian since she was a child.

3. Two years ago she started taking courses at the local community college. Unfortunately, she doesn't have a car, so . . .

   she takes the bus to school for two years.
   she have taken the bus to school for two years.
   she has taken the bus to school since two years.
   she has taken the bus to school for two years.

Activities

Activity 1

Work in pairs or groups of three. Complete the following with information about your partner(s). You will need to decide on appropriate questions to ask before you start. For example:

How long have you studied English?
How long have you lived in this town?

1. _____ for _____ hours.

2. _____ since _____.

3. _____ for _____.

4. _____ for _____ years.

5. _____ since _____.

Activity 2

Work with a partner. Read the statements below and try to match each statement to people in your class. Write the name in the column marked *Guesses*. Next, verify your guesses by asking people if your guess is right or wrong.

GUESSES	WHO ...	FACTS
_____	has studied English the longest time?	_____
_____	has been married the longest time?	_____
_____	has owned his or her watch the longest time?	_____
_____	has known how to drive the longest time?	_____
_____	has known how to drive the shortest time?	_____
_____	has had the shoes she or he is wearing today the longest time?	_____
_____	has smoked the longest time?	_____
_____	has worn glasses the longest time?	_____
_____	has worn glasses the shortest time?	_____
_____	has had the same hairstyle the longest time?	_____

Activity 3

Political Power

In this activity, you will be finding out how different countries are governed. Get together with a group of classmates from different countries, if possible. First use the chart to think about your own country or a country you are familiar with. When you have all had enough time to think, begin sharing your information. Use the chart to take notes on what your classmates tell you. In the first part of the chart, check (✔) the appropriate box or write in the box marked *other*. In the second part of the chart, write notes. Be ready to share this information with the rest of the class.

Country	Type of Leadership				
	President	Monarch*	Prime Minister	Military	Other
Great Britain		✔	✔		

*king, queen, emperor, etc.

Country	How Current Leader Came into Power			
	Election	Succession	Coup	Other
Great Britain	✔ *(Prime minister)*	✔ *(Queen)*		

126

Country	Length of Time the Current Leader Has Been in Power	Best Thing She or He Has Done While in Power	Worst Thing She or He Has Done While in Power**

**If you don't want to talk about your country's leader, you can talk about the President of the United States.

Present Perfect and Simple Past
Ever and *Never*

Task

Work with a partner and quickly read this page from Max's passport. How many different countries has Max visited? When did he visit each one?

Now use Max's passport to complete the following:

Max has visited (1) _____ countries in Asia, Europe, and North America. He has

been to (2) _____ different countries in Asia. He went to (3) _____

and Malaysia in (4) _____ . He went to Singapore in (5) _____,

and he went to Indonesia in (6) _____ . He has been to (7) _____

twice. The first time he went there was in (8) _____ , and the second time

was in (9) _____ . He also went to Taiwan in (10) _____ .

In addition, he has visited (11) _____ countries in Europe. He went to

(12) _____ in 1985 and England in (13) _____ . Max has also been

to (14) _____ ; he went there in (15) _____ . Although he has

been to many different countries in his life, he hopes to visit many more in the future.

Focus 1

Present Perfect versus Simple Past

USE

- To talk about a completed action, experience, or situation at a **specific time** in the past, you can use simple past to show that you are thinking about the **past**, not the present:

    (a) Last year, she **graduated** from high school.

LAST YEAR

NOW

(b) He **lived** in this house from 1980 to 1988.

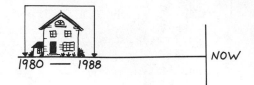

- To talk about a completed action, experience, or situation in the past when **you do not refer to when it happened**, use present perfect:

(c) He **has been** to Mexico.

(d) They **have run** a marathon.

- Here we show that something happened in the past, but we do not show **when** it happened. We show only that it happened **at some time before now**; we are thinking about the past in relation to the present:

  (e) I **drank** champagne last night. (**simple past** because I want to show **when** it happened)

  (f) I **have drunk** champagne. (**present perfect** because I want to show that **the experience** is more important than when I did it)

- We often use the present perfect to introduce the general idea and then continue with the simple past to give specific details about it:

  (g) **I've been** to Thailand. I **went** there about ten years ago and traveled all over the country. I **had** a great time, and I **enjoyed** meeting the friendly Thai people.

Exercise 1

Turn back to the Task. Circle every marker of past time (in 1975, 10 years ago, and so on) you can find. Now draw a line connecting this time word with a verb. Is the verb simple past or present perfect? Why do you think this is so?

Focus 2

FORM

Forming the Present Perfect

FORM

- You form the present perfect with *has/have* + past participle:

  (a) Rob and Barbara **have seen** that movie.

  (b) Carolyn **hasn't written** to me.

  (c) **Have** you **eaten** oysters?

  (d) Tessa **has visited** a lot of different countries.

- For more information on forming the present perfect, see Unit 11, Focus 2.

Exercise 2

There is a "classic" film festival in town featuring a number of famous American movies. Robert loves classic movies, and so he is is planning to invite some friends to a movie on Saturday night. Naturally, he wants to suggest a movie that nobody has seen. Use the information below to help him choose.

FILM FESTIVAL

BALBOA
38th & Balboa 221–8184
- HIGH NOON
  4:55   8:30   10:55
- ROMAN HOLIDAY
  6:50   10:25
- PSYCHO
  12:30   4:45   8:40   11:15

CORONET
Geary & Arguelio, 752–4400
- ON THE WATERFRONT
  1:20   3:30   5:37   7:30

GALAXY
Van Ness & Sutter 474–8700
- THE GODFATHER
  6:10   8:30   10:55

METRO
Union-Webster 931–1835
- CASABLANCA
  1:00   3:15   5:30   10:00

REGENCY
Van Ness & Sutter 585–6773
- THE GRADUATE
  4:40   7:40   10:30

---

1. Ann has seen the movie at the Coronet.
2. Patty and Mark went to the Metro last night.
3. Karen went to the Balboa on Tuesday to see the movie that started at 8:30.
4. Tom went to the Galaxy last weekend.
5. Carolyn and Terry have seen the movie at the Regency.
6. A couple of days ago Robert went to the Balboa and saw the movie that started at 8:40.

Which movie should they go and see?
Have **you** seen any of these movies?
Find out how many of your classmates have seen these movies.

Exercise 3

Use the information from the last exercise to make appropriate questions for the following responses.

EXAMPLE: *Did Carolyn & Terry go to the movies yesterday*_____?
Yes, they did. They went to see *The Graduate* yesterday.

1. _____?

Yes. Tom has seen *The Godfather*.

2. _____?

No, Patty and Mark haven't seen *High Noon*.

3. _____?

No, she didn't see it last weekend. She saw it on Tuesday.

4. _____?

No, they didn't see *Psycho*. They saw *Casablanca*.

5. _____?

Yes, he has. He saw it a couple of days ago.

6. _____?

No, they haven't seen *Roman Holiday*, but they have seen *The Graduate*.

7. _____?

No, he didn't. He saw it last weekend.

Exercise 4

Alice is on vacation in New York City. Complete her postcard home, using either simple past or present perfect with the verbs in parentheses.

Hi folks!

Having a great time! I (1) _____ (walk) at least 50 miles, but

I (2) _____ (see) lots of interesting things. Yesterday I

(3) _____ (take) the Staten Island Ferry, and on Thursday

I (4) _____ (go) to the top of the Empire State Building.

I (5) _____ (see) several shows. Two nights ago I

(6) _____ (go) to see Cats: I (7) _____ (have) great

tickets. Wonderful food!!! I (8) _____ (eat) some delicious

meals. Yesterday I (9) _____ (try) sushi for the first time.

See you next week.

Love, Alice

P.S. I (10) _____ (spend) lots of money!

The Murphys
1403 Eastwood
Ann Arbor,
MI 48103

Exercise 5

Read this job advertisement:

What kind of job do you think this is?

EXCITING OPPORTUNITY
for the right person
Are you independent
and adventurous?
Requirements:
* knowledge of other cultures
* ability to speak at least one
foreign language
* flexibility
* must enjoy working with other
people and like travel.
Interested?
This is a difficult but
well-paying job.
Write Box 392,
giving a short description of your
previous experience.

This is one of the letters the company received in answer to the advertisement. Complete the blanks with the appropriate form of the verb in parentheses. The first one has been for you.

Dear Sir,

I am writing about the job advertised in today's paper.

I (1) _graduated_ (graduate) from high school in 1978. I (2) _____ (have) experience in many different fields. I (3) _____ (work) as a typist, receptionist, sales assistant, and teacher. I (4) _____ (travel) extensively and (5) _____ (learn) Spanish, French, and Italian.

In 1979, I (6) _____ (go) to Europe. First I (7) _____ (work) as a tour guide and (8) _____ (help) American tourists in Paris, France. After that, I (9) _____ (move) to Italy, where I (10) _____ (live) with an Italian family and (11) _____ (look after) their three children. In 1984, I (12) _____ (work) in Barcelona, Spain, for three months and (13) _____ (teach) English conversation to children. In 1985, I (14) _____ (return) to the United States, and I (15) _____ (be) a receptionist at a beauty salon for six months. In 1986, I (16) _____ (leave) the United States again, and for two years I (17) _____ (give) sailing lessons on charter yachts in the Caribbean. I finally (18) _____ (come) home to the United States in 1989 and (19) _____ (take) a job at City Bookstore.

As you can see, I (20) _____ (work) with a lot of different people, and I (21) _____ (experience) different cultures. In all my jobs, I (22) _____ (enjoy) meeting other people. I believe this experience makes me a good candidate for the job.

Sincerely,

Nancy Martin

Nancy Martin

Do *you* think Nancy Martin is a good candidate for the job? Why do you think so?

Focus 3

MEANING

Ever and Never

- *Ever* with the present perfect tense means "at any time before now." It is usually used in questions and negative statements. It is not usually used in affirmative statements:

    (a) Have you **ever eaten** Mexican food?

    Yes, I **have eaten** Mexican food.

    NOT: I have ever eaten Mexican food.

    (b) I **haven't ever** eaten Mexican food.

- *Never* with the present perfect tense means "at no time before now":

    (c) I **have never eaten** Mexican food.

- *Not* versus *never*

    - These sentences have similar meanings:

        (d) I **have never eaten** Mexican food.

        (e) I **have not eaten** Mexican food.

    - *Never* means *not* + *ever*. In sentence (d), *never* emphasizes the fact that I have not had this experience in my life before the present moment. It is therefore stronger than *not*.

Exercise 6

Read the conversation. Underline and correct any mistakes.

Mick: Have you ever <u>visit</u> Europe?   *visited*

Dave: Yes. I've been there several times, in fact. Three years ago I've gone to France.

Mick: Really? Where did you go?

Dave: I went to Paris, of course. And then I rode my mountain bike in the Pyrenees. Last year I've ridden my bike in Germany and Switzerland. Have ever you been there?

Mick: I've never been to Germany, but I've ever been to Switzerland.

Dave: When was that?

Mick: I've studied German there about eight years ago.

Focus 4

Present Perfect versus Simple Past: Questions

USE

- When you ask the question, "Have you ever eaten frogs' legs?" you are interested in knowing about the experience, not about when it happened. You expect the answer: "Yes, I have," "No, I haven't," or "No, I've never done that."
- When you ask, "When did you eat them?" you are more interested in when it happened, and we expect the answer to tell us about that: "Two years ago" or "I ate them two years ago."

Exercise 7

Complete the conversations, using the present perfect or the past simple of the verbs in parentheses. The first one has been done for you.

1. **A:** Excuse me, sir, we're doing a survey. Can I ask you a few questions?

   B: Sure, go ahead.

   A: <u>Have you ever used</u> WonderWhite detergent? (you/use/ever)

   B: No, _____ it. (I/try/never)

   A: Why not?

   B: _____ laundry in my life. (I/do/never) My wife always does it.

   A: What about you, sir? _____ your clothes with WonderWhite?

   (you/wash/ever)

   C: Yes, _____ it. (I/try)

   A: When _____ it for the first time? (you/try)

   C: _____ it for the first time about six months ago. (I/use)

137

2. **A:** _____ any books by Latin American writers? (you/read/ever)

   B: Yes, I _____ . I _____ a great novel by a Colombian writer a few years ago. (read)

   A: Which one?

   B: I _____ his name.(forget) He _____ the Nobel Prize several years ago. (win)

   A: Oh, you mean Gabriel Garcia Marquez.

3. **A:** My brother is coming to stay with us for a few days next week. Do you have any ideas about how we can entertain him?

   B: _____ here before now? (he/be/ever)

   A: Yes. He _____ (come) once about three years ago.

   B: _____ to Chinatown then? (he/go)

   A: No _____ Chinatown (he/be/never), but _____ a lot in China and in the Far East. (he/travel)

   B: Maybe you'd better not take him to Chinatown then! _____ him to Greektown when he was here three years ago? (you/take)

   A: No, and _____ Greece (he/visit/never).

   B: Great! Why don't you take him there?

4. **A:** _____ last night? (you/ go out)

   B: Yes. _____ to that new Italian restaurant. (we/go)

   A: What's it like? _____ there. (I/be/never)

   B: It's O.K., but _____ better Italian food in other restaurants. (I/eat)

   A: _____ the one on Main Street? (you/try/ever)

   B: Yes. _____ great meal there last weekend. (we/have)

Exercise 8

Complete the following, using the words in parentheses.

My friend and I (1) _____ (decide) to take our next vacation in Bali. Yesterday we (2) _____ (go) to a travel agent and we (3) _____ (pick up) lots of different brochures. We (4) _____ (take) them home and (5) _____ (read) them all very carefully. We want to go there because my friend (6) _____ (travel) in Southeast Asia, but she (7) _____ (never be) to Bali and I (8) _____ (read) many books about the customs and culture of the Balinese people. My brother (9) _____ (be) there several times. He (10) _____ (go) there for the first time about 15 years ago, and he (11) _____ (stay) there for six months. He (12) _____ (return) to Bali last year and according to him, life there (13) _____ (change) a lot because there are so many tourists now. I don't care! I (14) _____ (hear) so many different things about Bali, but now I want to find out for myself!

Activities

Activity 1

In this activity, you will be finding out about some of the things that your classmates have done. Look at the list below. Move around the class and ask questions to see if you can find anyone who has ever done any of these things.

First you need to find who has had the experience (name); then you need to get specific details about the experience (when) (where) (how/why). Take notes below; it is not necessary to write full sentences at this point. In the box marked ★★★, you can add a question of your own if you want to.

Be ready to share your findings with the rest of the class. Finally, you will use this information to make a written report.

HAVE YOU EVER ...?

Experience	Name	When	Where	How/Why
met a famous person				
climbed a mountain				
seen a shark				
felt really frightened				
flown in a hot-air balloon				
★★★				

Now use the information you collected to complete this report on your findings.

A few days ago I interviewed some of my classmates about things they have done before now, and I learned some interesting things about their past experiences. For example,....

Activity 2

Move around the class and ask questions to find out if the following statements are true or false. If the statement is true, write *T* beside it; if it is false, write *F*.

1. Somebody in this room has appeared on TV.
2. Everybody here has eaten tacos.
3. At least three people have never ridden on a motorcycle.
4. Somebody has swum in more than two oceans.
5. Several people have seen a ghost.
6. At least three people have been to Disneyland.
7. Nobody has been to Paris.
8. Somebody has run a marathon.
9. Half the class has never played soccer.
10. Somebody has never smoked a cigarette.

Activity 3

The purpose of this activity is to confuse your classmates. You will tell the class about three things you have done in your life. Two of these things are true, but one is false. Your classmates will try to guess which one is false. For example:

I have ridden a bicycle from San Francisco to Los Angeles.

I have traveled by boat up the Amazon.

I have broken my leg twice.

Which statement is false?

In order to decide which one is false, your classmates can ask you questions about the specific details of each experience. For example, "When did you ride your bike to Los Angeles?" "How long did it take?" "Which leg did you break?" and so on. After they have listened to your answers, the class will vote on which experience is false.

Take turns talking about your true and false experiences until everyone has taken part.

Activity 4

You have probably had many different experiences since you came to this country. In this activity you will be finding out the best and the worst experiences your classmates have had since they came here. First go around the room and get as much information as you can from at least three different people. Use the chart to take notes on the information your classmates give you.

Name	Country	Length of Time She or He Has Been Here	Best Experience	Worst Experience

You have been asked to write a short article for your college newspaper on the experiences of foreign students.

Review the information you collected and choose the two most interesting or surprising "best" experiences and the two most interesting or surprising "worst" experiences. Organize your article so that you talk first about the bad experiences and then about the good experiences. Start your article with a brief introduction to the topic and to the students you interviewed. For example:

> What is it like to be a foreign student? I will try to answer this question by telling you about both the good and bad experiences of some of my classmates. Recently I interviewed (number) students in my class and they told me about the best and the worst times they have had since they came here. I would like to share with you some of the things I learned.

Activity 5

Write a letter to a family member or a friend and tell him or her about the best and the worst experiences you have had since you left home.

UNIT

13

Present Perfect Progressive

Task

Read the statements below. Why do you think they were said? What had probably happened just before?

STATEMENT	RECENT ACTIVITY
1. **A:** Ugh. . . . your hands are covered with oil and grease! **B:** Sorry.	_____
2. **A:** Are you O.K.? Your eyes are all red.	_____
3. **A:** You look terrible. **B:** I didn't get much sleep last night.	_____
4. **A:** That's enough for tonight. Give me your car keys. **B:** Why? **A:** I'll take you home. You can't drive like this.	_____
5. **A:** Why is your hair wet?	_____
6. **A:** Hey, kids! Stop right there! **B:** What for? **A:** Take your shoes off at once! I don't want mud all over the carpet.	_____

Now look at the activities in the list. Try to match each of the statements above to an appropriate activity in the list. Write the activity in the space beside the statement.

ACTIVITIES

baking bread   drinking
swimming   studying for a test
chopping onions   running
eating garlic   fixing a car
playing in the yard   watching TV

Focus 1

Present Perfect Progressive: Recent Activity

MEANING

- The present perfect progressive connects the past with the present in two slightly different ways. You can use the present perfect progressive to talk about an activity which was in progress very recently in the past:

(a) Why are your hands green?
   I've **been painting** my room.

- The activity is so recent that its effect or result is often still visible or apparent in the present.

Focus 2

Present Perfect Progressive

FORM

- *has/have* + *been* + verb + *-ing*:

Statement	Negative	Question
I You We They } **have been sleeping.** (**'ve**)	I You We They } **have not been sleeping.** (**haven't**)	**Have** { I you we they } **been sleeping?**
She He It } **has been sleeping.** (**'s**)	She He It } **has not been sleeping.** (**hasn't**)	**Has** { she he it } **been sleeping?**

Exercise 1

Turn back to the Task and write appropriate statements, using the present perfect progressive in response to statements 1–6. The first one has been done for you:

1. *She has been fixing a car*_____.

2. _____.

3. _____.

4. _____.

5. _____.

6. _____.

Exercise 2

You are riding the subway in a big city, late at night. There are several other people in the same car. You observe them carefully and try to figure out what they have been doing recently. Probably you will be able to think of several possibilities for each one.

1. A young man with a black eye and ripped clothing:

   He _____.

2. A man with lipstick traces on his face and on the collar of his shirt:

   He _____.

3. Two young women with many bags and packages from well-known department stores:

   They _____.

4. A couple wearing shorts and walking shoes and carrying backpacks. They seem very tired:

   They _____.

5. A young woman with a bookbag full of chemistry textbooks. She has a book open in her hands and she is asleep:

   She _____.

6. A woman with red stains on her hands:

She _____.

7. A man with white hairs all over his clothes and scratches on his hands.

He _____.

Focus 3

Actions Continuing to the Present

USE

- We also use the present perfect progressive to describe actions or situations starting in the past and continuing up to and including now.

(a) He has been waiting for 20 minutes (and he is still waiting).

20 MINUTES AGO   NOW

Exercise 3

Complete the following sentences, using the "scrambled" verb in parentheses. We have done the first one for you.

1.   **Lee:**   What are you doing?

Mary Lou: I'm waiting to make a phone call. This woman *has been talking* _____ on the

phone for the last 20 minutes. (katl)

2. Dan: Haven't you finished writing that book yet?

Heidi: No, we're still working on it.

Dan: You _____ it for almost a year! (retwi)

Heidi: I know, but it's nearly finished now.

3. **Sky:** What's up? You look miserable.

   Tom: I am. I want to go for a bike ride, but it _____ since eight o'clock this morning. (anir)

4. **Gin:** What do you want to do tonight?

   Bruce: I want to go out and have fun. I _____ here all day. (krow)

5. **George:** Excuse me, but is this your dog?

   Barbara: Yes. Is there a problem?

   George: I can't get to sleep because that dog _____ for hours! Please keep it under control, or I'll call the police. (krab)

6. **Julie:** Have you seen Patsy recently?

   Jan: No. She's got a new boyfriend, and she _____ all her time with him. (psned)

7. **John:** Are these your glasses?

   Betty: Yes! Thank you so much. I _____ for them everywhere! (oklo)

8. **Mike:** How are things going in New York?

   Dave: We don't live there anymore.

   Mike: Really?

   Dave: Yes. We _____ in Philadelphia since January. (lvei)

9. **Diane:** Why are Kemal and Cynthia so depressed?

   Marianne: They _____ grammar for ages, but they still don't understand how to use the present perfect progressive. (yusdt)

10. **Pam:** Aren't you ready yet?

    Andrew: No. I've lost my keys and I _____ to find them for the last half hour. (ytr)

Focus 4

Present Perfect Progressive versus Present Perfect

USE

- The **present perfect** and the **present perfect progressive** can both describe actions or situations starting in the past and continuing up to and including now. In this case, it is necessary to add a time adverbial to show how long the activity has been in progress:

  (a) Jim has worked here **for ten years.**

  (b) Jim has been working here **for ten years.**

  In both sentences, we understand that Jim still works here.

- The following verbs are commonly used with both present perfect and present perfect progressive to describe an unfinished action:

  live   work   teach   study

- You can also use the present perfect progressive to **emphasize** an activity that started in the past and that continues **without interruption** to the present:

  (c) We **have been working** on this for a long time.

- You can express the same meaning with the present perfect:

  (d) We **have worked** on this for a long time.

- The present perfect progressive emphasizes the fact that the activity has continued without stopping.

- The present perfect **without a time adverbial** shows that an activity finished sometime before now in the past, but we are not sure when:

  (e) They **have painted** their house.

- As you saw in Focus 1, the present perfect progressive without a time adverbial is often used to talk about an activity that finished very recently before now:

  (f) They **have been painting** their house.

- See Unit 12 for more information on this use of the present perfect.

Exercise 4

Look at each group of statements and discuss the differences in meaning. Think of a possible situation in which you could use each statement.

1. **a.** Bill has read that book.
   b. Bill has been reading that book.
   c. Bill has been reading that book for three weeks.
2. **a.** Sally has eaten frogs' legs.
   b. Sally has been eating frogs' legs.
3. **a.** I've been riding a motorcycle.
   b. I've ridden a motorcycle.
   c. I've ridden a motorcycle since I was a teenager.
4. **a.** We've been studying English grammar.
   b. We've studied English grammar.
   c. We've been studying English grammar for a long time.
   d. We've studied English grammar for a long time.

Focus 5

USE

Recent Habits

USE

- You can also use the present perfect progressive to talk about a regular habit or activity that someone started recently and which she or he continues to do. In this situation, you can add a time adverbial to emphasize that the action started recently:
  (a) They've been eating out a lot **recently.**
  (b) He's been working a lot **lately.**
  (c) I've been walking to work **recently.**
  (d) I've walked to work.
- In (c), we understand that "walking to work" is a recent habit. I started to do this a short time ago and will continue in the future.
- In (d), we understand that I did this at some time in the past, but I do not do it at the moment. In this situation, you do not usually add a time adverbial.

Exercise 5

Barbara is talking with her old friend, Janet. They have not seen each other for several months, and Janet is surprised by some of the changes in Barbara's appearance. Complete their conversation, using verbs from the list below.

happen	sail	cook
do	feel	take
go	study	eat
ride	date	ski
talk		

Janet: Barbara, you look great! You've really lost a lot of weight.

Barbara: Well, I (1) _____ my bike to school recently and I

(2) _____ an aerobics class.

Janet: Is that all? No special diets or anything?

Barbara: Not really. I (3) _____ (not) to any fast-food restaurants, and I

(4) _____ at home instead. So I (5) _____ a lot of

fresh vegetables and salads and other healthy stuff like that. It really makes a difference. I

(6) _____ much better, with lots more energy.

Janet: Well, you seem to be very busy these days. You're never home when I call. What else

(7) _____ you _____ ?

Barbara: I (8) _____ this really cute guy. He has a boat, so we

(9) _____ a lot and he also has a cabin in the mountains, so we

(10) _____ too. And also, we (11) _____

about taking some trips together. So it's all pretty exciting. But what about you? What

(12) _____ with you?

Janet: Nothing. I (13) _____ for my final exams, but when they're over,

I'm going to start having fun!

Exercise 6

What would Holly and Don say in each situation below? The words in parentheses will help you, but you will need to add some other words of your own.

1. It's 4:00, and Holly's husband Don has been napping since 1:00. Holly is waiting for him to wake up. When he finally wakes up, she says: (I/wait/three hours)

   _____

   _____ .

2. Don has promised to change the oil in Holly's car. While he is sleeping, she decides to try to do it herself, but she can't. When Don wakes up, she says: (I/try/45 minutes)

   _____

   _____ .

3. Holly's mother calls to tell her that Holly's sister has had another baby. Her mother asks, "When are you and Don going to have kids?" Holly tells her: (we/discuss/ten years)

   _____

   _____ .

4. After his nap, Don is hungry and he wants Holly to go out with him to eat pizza. Holly doesn't want to go because she bought fresh fish for dinner and wants to try out a new recipe. She tells Don, "I don't want to go out to eat because (I/plan/dinner/all day)"

   _____

   _____ .

Exercise 7

Complete the dialogues, using present perfect progressive, present perfect, or simple past. Be prepared to explain your choice.

Jim: What's the matter? You look frustrated.

Jill: I am. I (1) _____ (try) to study all day, but the telephone never stops ringing. People (2) _____ (call) all day about the car.

Jim: That's great. I (3) _____ (hope) to sell that car for six months now. Maybe today's the day!

Maria: I'm sorry I'm so late. (4) _____ (you/wait) long?

Alex: Yes, I have! Where (5) _____ (you/be)?

Maria: I really am sorry. My watch is broken, and I didn't know what time it was.

Alex: Why didn't you ask somebody? I (6) _____ (stand) out here in the cold for at least 40 minutes.

Maria: Oh, you poor thing! But we'd better hurry to get to the movie theater.

Alex: It's too late. The movie (7) _____ (start).

Maria: Really?

Alex: Yes. It (8) _____ (start) 20 minutes ago.

Activities

Activity 1

You have just received a letter from the editor of your high school newspaper. She wants to include information about former students in the next edition of the paper. Write a letter to the editor, telling her what you have been doing recently. (Do not feel you have to use present perfect progressive in every sentence! To make this a natural letter, think about all the other tenses you can use as well.)

Activity 2

WHAT HAVE I BEEN DOING?
The purpose of this game is to guess recent activities from their current results.
Work in teams. Each team should try to think of four different results of recent activities. An example of one of these could be

Recent Activity   **Present Result**
You have been exercising and now you are exhausted.

When everyone is ready, each team takes turns to pantomime the results of the activities they have chosen. For example, Team A has chosen "being exhausted." Everybody in Team A gets up and pantomimes being exhausted. The rest of the class tries to guess what Team A has been doing. The first person to guess correctly, "You have been exercising and now you are exhausted," scores a point for his or her team.

Activity 3

This is another team game. Each team presents a series of clues, and the rest of the class try to guess what situation these clues refer to. For example, Team A chooses this situation: A woman has been reading a sad love story. The team tries to think of as many clues as possible that will help the other students guess the situation. When everyone is ready, Team A presents the first clue:

Team A: Her eyes are red.

The other teams make guesses based on this first clue:

Team B: She has been chopping onions.
Team A: No. She feels very sad.
Team C: She's been crying.
Team A: No. She's very romantic.
Team D: She's been fighting with her boyfriend.
Team A: No. She was alone while she was doing this.
Team C: She's been reading a sad love story.

You can choose one of the situations below or you can choose one of your own.

1. She or he has been crying.
2. She or he has been watching old movies.
3. She or he has been coughing a lot.
4. She or he's been training for the Olympics.
5. She or he has been chopping onions.
6. She or he has been feeling sick.
7. She or he has been losing weight.

The person who guesses the correct situation scores a point for his or her team.

Activity 4

Describe some things that you have been doing since you came to this country that you had never done before. Share your experiences with your classmates. Make a poster depicting everybody's experiences.

Activity 5

Listen to a news broadcast. What events have been happening in the world? What are some important events that have happened in the last five years?

Making Offers with *Would ... Like*

14

Task

Imagine that you are at a party. Your friend is on the other side of the room. You can see each other, but you cannot hear each other because the room is very crowded and the music is very loud.

For this activity, work in pairs. Student A: Communicate the problem (listed on the chart below) to Student B **without speaking or writing**. Student B: **Do not** look at the list of problems. Your job is to offer a solution to Student A **without speaking or writing**. You will both need to pantomime your responses to each other. That is, you will need to use gestures, facial expressions, and other nonverbal ways of communicating.

When you have finished, check the list to see if Student B correctly understood Student A's problems. Then write down an appropriate *offer* using *Would you like?* . . . on the Solutions side of the chart.

Problems	Solutions
Student A: **1.** You are thirsty and want something to drink.	
2. You have a headache.	
3. You are hot. You want your friend to open a window.	
4. You are hungry. Your friend is standing by a table with food on it. You want him or her to get you something to eat.	
5. You have to sneeze. You need a handkerchief.	
6. You need a light for your cigarette.	
7. You need an ashtray.	
8. You are tired. You want your friend to give you a ride home.	

Focus 1

USE
How to Make Offers

- When someone has a problem or needs something, there are several ways to offer help. The most polite way is to use *Would you like?* . . .

Focus 2

FORM
Different Ways to Make Offers

FORM

- There are several ways to make offers with *Would you like?* . . .
  - *Would you like* + noun phrase
    - **(a)** Would you like some more coffee?
  - *Would you like to* + verb phrase
    - **(b)** Would you like to sit down?
  - *Would you like me to* + verb phrase
    - **(c)** Would you like me to open the window?
- This form is also useful when you make an offer about someone else.
  - *Would you like* (person) *to* + verb phrase
    - **(d)** Would you like Sally to open the window?
    - **(e)** Would you like someone to open the window?

Exercise 1

Look back at the offers you wrote down in the Task. Are your offers formed correctly?

Focus 3

Would You Like?...
versus Do You Want?...

- *Would you like?...* is a polite way of asking *Do you want?.... Do you want?...* is an informal way of making an offer. Usually it is used with close friends and family. For example,

    (a) Would you like a cup of tea?

    is more polite than

    (b) Do you want a cup of tea?

    (c) Do you want me to help you with your homework?

    is more informal than

    (d) Would you like me to help you with your homework?

Exercise 2

Your new friend is having her first party in North America. She has invited some friends and their parents, but she has asked you to help her because she is nervous and does not know English very well. Change her following commands and questions into polite offers, using *Would you like?...*

1. Come in.
2. Sit down.
3. Give me your coat.
4. Want a chair?
5. Let me get you an ashtray.
6. Something to drink?
7. Cream in your coffee?
8. Want me to open that window for you?
9. More coffee?

DUANE GILLOGLY

Exercise 3

Look at the list below. Choose three things and make offers you hope your classmates will accept. Go around the class and make offers with *Would you like?...* to as many people as possible.

When you respond to an offer: a) be as polite as possible, and b) if you must refuse the offer, give a reason for refusing it.

1. listen to music
2. watch TV
3. eat something
4. drink something
5. borrow videos
6. read magazines
7. _____ (make up your own offer)

Exercise 4

Write down as many responses as you can remember to the offers that you made in Exercise 3. Write the responses of people who accepted your offer in the Accept column. Write the responses of people who refused your offer in the Refuse column. Then, for each column, rank these responses in order of politeness (Which responses seemed most polite? Which seemed least polite?)

Responses to Offers		
	Accept	Refuse
Most Polite ↑ ↓ Least Polite		

Focus 4

Politely Accepting and Refusing Offers

USE

- Using *please* along with *yes* is a polite way of accepting an offer.

Offer	**Polite Acceptance**
(a) Would you like something to drink?	Yes, please.

- Extra phrases that show that you appreciate the offer make your acceptance sound even more polite. But this is not always necessary in informal situations.

Offer	*Yes* + **Appreciation**
(b) Would you like me to help you?	Yes, please. That's very nice/kind of you.

- Using *thank you* or *thanks* along with *no* is a polite way of refusing an offer.

Offer	**Polite Refusal**
(c) Would you like some coffee?	No, thank you.
	No, thanks.

- Polite refusals can also include a reason why the offer cannot be accepted.

Offer	**Refusal** + **Reason**
(d) Would you like some coffee?	No, thank you. I've had enough.
(e) Would you like me to help you?	No, thanks. That's very nice of you, but I can manage.

Exercise 5

It is often difficult to refuse offers, especially when they are polite and sincere. Work with a partner for this exercise and take turns making offers and politely refusing them. Use the ideas in Exercise 3 to make offers, or make up your own. But this time all offers must be refused.

Exercise 6

Look at the following responses. What was the offer that was probably made? Write it down in the blank.

1. Offer: _____?

   Response: No, thanks. I've had enough.

2. Offer: _____?

   Response: Yes, please. It's delicious.

3. Offer: _____?

   Response: Oh, no, thank you. I've seen it already.

4. Offer: _____?

   Response: No, thanks. I'm warm enough.

5. Offer: _____?

   Response: Yes, please. It's very heavy.

6. Offer: _____?

   Response: Thanks, I'd love to. That sounds great.

7. Offer: _____?

   Response: Thanks, but I've already got one of my own.

Exercise 7

For each of the following situations, write a short dialogue in which one person makes a polite offer (using *Would . . . like*) and the other person either politely accepts or politely refuses the offer. Then find a partner and read your dialogues aloud, taking parts.

1. The English instructor, at the front of the classroom, is ready to show a video in class today. The switch to turn on the video player is right by Stefan, at the back of the room.

   Stefan says: _____?

   The instructor says: _____.

2. The dinner at Mrs. Black's house is almost finished. Mrs. Black notices that some of the guests ate their dessert—cherry pie—very quickly, and she thinks they might want another piece.

   Mrs. Black says: _____?

   A guest says: _____.

3. Alfredo has a seat at the front of the city bus. He notices that an old woman has just gotten on, but there are no more seats left.

   Alfredo says: _____?

   The old woman says: _____.

4. As Mary is about to leave for the post office, she sees that there are several envelopes on the desk, stamped and addressed by her roommate Judith.

   Mary says: _____?

   Judith says: _____.

5. Just as Thomas starts to drive away to work, he sees that his neighbor Rob is walking down the sidewalk to the bus stop. Thomas knows that Rob's office is not far from where he works.

   Thomas says: _____?

   Rob says: _____.

Activities

Activity 1

Your good friend is at home in bed, sick. You want to help out and make your friend feel better. Make a list of things that you might do to help and then make offers using *Would you like?* . . . . Your "friend" can accept or refuse your offers.

Activity 2

How do native speakers of English behave at parties? Is their behavior at formal parties different from their behavior at informal parties, where the guests are all close friends or relatives?

Complete the following chart and feel free to provide more information in the two blanks at the bottom. If you do not know the answers you need to complete the chart, find a native speaker of English or someone who has spent a long time in an English-speaking country. Interview him or her to get the information you need.

What Does the Host Do or Say When She or He:	Formal Parties	Informal Parties
(a) wants the guests to sit down		
(b) wants the guests to start eating		
(c) wants the guests to eat/drink more		
(d) wants the guests to start some activity (dancing/playing a game)		
(e)		
(f)		

Activity 3

How to Help Me

Take two pieces of paper. On each piece, write down one thing that a classmate could do for you that would be helpful. Write down something different on each piece. (If your class is a large group, one piece of paper is enough.) Hand in your pieces of paper and do not write your name on them.

Your teacher will give you two papers (one if it is a large class), which other students wrote, and you must decide who you think has written each request for help. Get up and go around the room to find that person. Make an offer to help him or her, using the *Would you like?* . . . form. If your offer is rejected, find someone else who you think wrote the original request for help.

You must accept an offer if it is about the help you requested (the thing you wrote down on your piece of paper). You must refuse all other offers for help, even if they sound good!

Activity 4

Without using any words, your group will mime a problem. (When you "mime," you use gestures, actions, and facial expressions to silently "act out" a situation. No words allowed!) Another group will try to guess what the problem is and make an appropriate offer to help solve the problem.

15

Requests and Permission

Can/Could, Will/Would, May

Task

You are about to start house-sitting for a friend of yours. Your friend has left you a note with instructions about what to do while she is gone. Unfortunately, someone has spilled coffee on the note, and now it is difficult to read. Try to find the missing parts of the note from the choices on the next page. Write the appropriate number in the spaces on the note.

I'm glad you'll be here to watch the house while I'm gone! My neighbors think that this neighborhood is not completely safe at night, so (A)

The cats eat twice a day, (B)
I don't want them to stay out at night so (C)

The plants need to be watered twice a week. (D)

I left some bills to mail on the kitchen table. (E)

My cousin from out of town said that he would call this week. (F)

The rent check is on the kitchen table. It's due at the end of the week. (G)

I told the landlord about the broken light in the bathroom. If he calls, (H)

Thanks for everything. (I)

1. . . . could you ask him to fix it as soon as possible?
2. . . . remember to lock the windows and doors when it gets dark. Thanks.
3. . . . so will you please give them water on Tuesday and Friday?
4. . . . See you next week!
5. . . . Would you mind mailing them for me tomorrow morning?
6. . . . please make sure they come in around 8:00.
7. . . . Would you take a message and tell him I'll be back on the 29th?
8. . . . so could you feed them in the morning and at night?
9. . . . Please mail it before Friday.

Focus 1

FORM ● USE

Making Polite Requests

FORM
USE

- Questions using the modals *can, could, will,* and *would* are ways of making polite requests. If you really want someone to say yes to a request, it is important to make the request polite.
  - The modals *could* and *would* sound more polite than the modals *can* and *will.*
  - Providing some good background or reason for why you are making the request and using *please* are also ways to make requests sound more polite. In questions, *please* **usually** comes between the subject *you* and the verb.

    (a) I left my notes at home. Could you **please** lend me yours?
  - The reason for making the request can also come **after** the question.

    (b) Could you please lend me your notes? I left mine at home.
  - Another way to make a polite request is to use the phrase *Would you mind* + verb + *-ing.*

    (c) Would you mind lending me your notes?

Exercise 1

Below are some situations in which requests are commonly made. For each situation, make a polite request.

1. You want to know what time it is. You find someone who is wearing a watch and you say: ____

_____ ?

2. When you pay for your groceries at the supermarket, you remember that you need some change. You hand the cashier a dollar and say: _____

_____ ?

3. You have been waiting in line at the bank for 15 minutes, but you need to get a drink of water. You turn to the friendly-looking person standing behind you in line, and you say: _____

_____ ?

4. You are watching a videotape in class. Your classmate in front of you is in the way. You want him or her to move his or her chair. You say: _____

_____ ?

5. Your teacher just showed the class a videotape. It is finished; your classroom is dark. Your instructor wants the student who is sitting near the light switch to turn on the lights, so she or he says: _____

_____ ?

6. There is a lot of noise outside your classroom. Your teacher wants the student who is sitting near the door to close it, so she or he says: _____

_____ ?

7. A classmate is giving a presentation, but she is speaking very quietly. You cannot hear her. You say: _____ ?

Focus 2

Making Polite Refusals

USE

- If you need to refuse a request, the refusal is more polite when: 1) you say **why** you have to refuse the request, and 2) you use a "softening" phrase.

Request	"Softening" Phrase + Reason
Can you lend me your notes?	**(a)** **I'm sorry**, but I need them to study for the test.
	(b) OR **I'm afraid** I didn't take any notes!
	(c) OR **I'd like to,** but I left mine at home too.

Exercise 2

Make requests of all your classmates and find someone who will grant your request (say yes) for the following things. For each request, try to find at least one person who will say yes. If a classmate says no, write down what the reason is for refusing your request (if a reason is given).

Request	Reason for Saying No
1. lend you some money	
2. buy you a cup of coffee	
3. tell you the name of a good bookstore	
4. give you a ride home after class	
5. teach you how to dance	

Focus 3

FORM

Responding to Requests

- To respond informally to requests, short answers are acceptable.

Request	Verbal Response
Can you lend me your notes?	**(a)** Sure.
	(b) You bet.
	(c) Yeah, no problem.
	(d) I'd be glad to.

- *Could* and *would* are usually not used in response to requests.

  Can/Could you lend me your notes? **(e)** Yes, I can
  NOT: Yes, I could.

  Will/Would you lend me your notes? **(f)** Yes, I will
  NOT: Yes, I would.

Exercise 3

Make polite requests for the following situations. Use *can, could, will, would,* or *would you mind* in these requests.

What is the response? How is the request politely accepted or refused?

1. You have a toothache. Your dentist asks you to sit back in the chair, open your mouth, and

   point to the tooth that hurts. The dentist says: _____

   _____ ?

   What do you do or say? _____

   _____ .

2. Your friend is helping you hang a picture on your wall. He is holding it up while you decide where it should go. You say: _____

_____ ?

What does your friend do or say? _____

_____ .

3. At your first exercise class, the instructor asks you to use the wall to get your spine in a straight position. The instructor says: _____

_____ ?

What do you do or say? _____

_____ .

4. There's a place on your back that suddenly begins to itch. You ask your close friend to scratch

it. You say: _____ ?

What does your friend do or say? _____

_____ .

But your friend is not quite getting the right place. So you say:_____

_____ ?

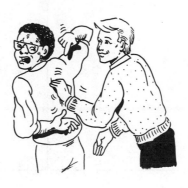

5. You are at a restaurant, and the people at the next table are smoking. You want them to stop, so

you say:_____

_____ ?

What do they do or say? _____

_____ .

Exercise 4

Place the following questions in the chart below, writing the number of each sentence in the appropriate box. The first one has been done for you.

Something the Speaker Wants to Do (request for permission)	Something the Speaker Wants Somebody Else to Do (general request)

1. Could I smoke?
2. Can you open the window?
3. May I ask a question?
4. Could you speak more slowly?
5. Would you mind lending me your dictionary?
6. Can I leave early?
7. Would you tell me the answer?
8. May we swim in your pool?
9. Could you show us how to do it?
10. Could I borrow your knife?
11. Would you mind if I handed in my assignment a day late?

Focus 4

Asking for Permission

- When you want **somebody** to do something, you can make a request. When **you** want to do something, and you want to find out if it is permitted or allowed, you can request permission:
  - **(a)** Could I leave early?
  - **(b)** Can I smoke in here? } Is it all right if I do this?
  - **(c)** May I ask a question?
- In formal situations, *may* or *could* are used in questions to request permission. If the speaker thinks that the listener has a lot of authority or power, she or he uses *may* or *could*.
- As with requests, *can* is used in informal situations to ask for permission. If the speaker and the listener know each other well and / or have an equal amount of power, *can* is used.
- You can also politely ask for permission using *Would you mind* + *if* +**simple past tense.**
  - **(d)** Would you mind if I asked you a question?

Exercise 5

For each answer, what was probably the question?

1. Question: _____?

   Teacher to student: No, I'd like you to hand it in on Friday. I announced the due date two

   weeks ago, so I'm afraid I won't be able to make any exceptions.

2. Question: _____?

   Friend to friend: Sure, it is a little cold in here.

3. Question: _____?

   Lecturer to member of the audience: Sorry, but I'm going to have to ask you to hold your

   questions until the end of my talk. We'll have 15 minutes for questions.

4. Question: _____?

   Secretary (on phone): Yes, may I tell him who's calling?

5. Question: _____?

12-year-old kid (on phone): Yeah, just a moment. I'll get him.

6. Question: _____?

Mother (to child): OK, you can have one more. But only **one**, because we're going to eat soon and I don't want you to spoil your appetite.

7. Question: _____?

Hostess to guest: Oh, of course, please help yourself. I'm glad you like them.

8. Question: _____?

Customer to salesperson: Yes, I want to look at the sweaters that are on sale. The ones that were advertised in the newspaper?

Focus 5

FORM ● USE

Responding to Requests for Permission

FORM USE

- As with responses to requests, you can verbally answer requests for permission with short, positive phrases:

    Sure.   OK.   Yeah.   Of course.   No problem.

- If you need to refuse a request for permission, the refusal is more polite when you say **why** you have to refuse the request, and you use a "softening" phrase such as *Sorry*.

Exercise 6

For each of the following situations, work with another classmate to make general requests and requests for permission, and then respond to these requests. Decide how polite you need to be in each situation and whether *can, could, will, would, may,* or *would you mind* is the most appropriate to use. There is more than one way to ask and answer each question.

1. You are at a friend's house, and you want to use the phone.
2. Your teacher says something, but you do not understand, and you want her to repeat it.

3. Your friend has asked you to pick her up at the airport. You want to know if her flight, #255 from Denver, is on time, so you call the airline.

4. You want to borrow your roommate's car.

5. Your roommate is going to the store, and you remember that you need some film.

6. You are the first one to finish the reading test in class. You want to find out from your teacher if you are allowed to leave the room now.

7. It is very cold in class, and the window is open.

8. You see that your teacher is in her office with the door partly open. You want to go in to talk to her.

9. You are on the phone with the dentist's secretary because you want to change your appointment time.

10. You are at a close friend's house, and you would like a cup of tea.

11. Your friends have arrived at your house for dinner, and you want them to sit down.

12. You want to hold your friend's baby.

Activities

Activity 1

Go to a restaurant or cafeteria and pay attention to the different kinds of requests that are used. Try to observe five different requests. Take notes on these, using the chart below.

Observation Sheet		
Place:		
Time:		
Day:		
Request	**Who Made It**	**Response**

Discuss the results of your observations with other classmates. Were their observations similar? What words were used most often in requests: *can, could, will, would,* or *would you mind*?

Activity 2

Play this game in a group of five or six students or with the whole class. You are sick and cannot go out of your house. Choose a classmate and ask him or her to buy you something at the mall when she or he goes. Pick a letter from the alphabet. Your friend must think of something to buy that begins with the letter you choose, and then she or he must tell you what she or he will buy. She or he then chooses the next student and so on.

> **EXAMPLE: Shelley:**   Bruno, would you please buy me something that begins with the letter *S*?
>
> **Bruno:**   Sure. I'll buy you some stamps. Sue, could you buy me something that begins with the letter *M*?
>
> **Sue:**   OK. I'll buy you a magazine. Hartmut, will you buy me something that begins with the letter *P*?

Activity 3

How do people request permission to speak with someone on the telephone? Are these ways different depending on the situation?

Make at least five observations to complete the following chart. If you cannot make direct observations, you can interview people about what they say in different situations.

Setting	Relationship	What They Say

Activity 4

Congratulations! You have just won a gift certificate for Easy-Does-It Maid Services. This entitles you to four hours of maid service for your home. First, make a list of what you want the maid to do in your home (clean your windows, do your laundry, scrub the toilet, etc.). Then, write these requests on a polite note to your "maid."

UNIT

16

Past Habitual

Used To with *Still* and *Anymore*, Adverbs of Frequency

Task

Work with several other students. Look at the photographs of these well-known people as they look today. If you are not sure who all these people are or why they are famous, try to find someone in the class who does.

Meryl Streep

Madonna

Diana Ross

Tina Turner

Bruce Springsteen

Warren Beatty

177

Look at the photographs of the same people. These photographs all came from their high school yearbooks. Match the old photographs with the current ones.

In your opinion, who has changed the most? Who has changed the least? Why do you think so?

Photographs from: *Yearbook, The Most Star-studded Graduating Class* by the Editors of *Memories Magazine*. Copyright 1990 by Diamandis Communications, Inc. Used by permission of Doubleday, a division of Bantam Doubleday Dell Publishing Group, Inc.

Focus 1

MEANING

Comparing Past and Present with *Used To*

- *Used to* shows that something was true or regularly happened in the past, but it does not happen now in the present:

    Tina Turner **used to** have short, wavy hair (but now she doesn't).

Focus 2

FORM

Used To

- *Used to* does not change form to agree with the subject:

Statement	Negative	Question
I You We They } used to work.	I You We They } did not use to work. (didn't)	Did { I you we they } use to work?
She He It } used to work.	She He It } did not use to work. (didn't)	Did { she he it } use to work?

Exercise 1

Make statements with *used to* about the changes in Madonna and Bruce Springsteen. Use the words in parentheses. You can add other ideas of your own.

1. Madonna

   a. (have a big nose) *She used to have a bigger nose; she didn't use to have a small one* _____.

   b. (be a dancer) _____.

   c. (be poor) _____.

   d. (live in Michigan) _____.

2. Bruce Springsteen

   a. (have straight hair) _____.

   b. (play football in high school) _____.

   c. (live in New Jersey) _____.

   d. (sing about blue-collar life) _____.

Focus 3

MEANING

Anymore

MEANING

- *Anymore* shows a change in a situation or activity that was regular or habitual in the past:

Past	Present

   (a) Madonna used to live in Michigan, but she doesn't live there anymore.

- It is not necessary to repeat the second verb phrase if it is the same as the first one:

   (b) Madonna used to live in Michigan, but she doesn't anymore.

- You can also use *anymore* without *used to*:

   (c) Madonna doesn't live in Michigan anymore.
   (From this sentence, we understand that she used to live there.)

Focus 4

FORM
Position of *Anymore*

- *Anymore* comes at the end of the sentence or clause:
    - **(a)** I don't live in Brazil anymore.
    - **(b)** They don't work here anymore.
    - **(c)** Alice doesn't live here anymore.
- *Anymore* is always used with a negative:
    - **(d)** We don't go there anymore.
    - **(e)** They never talk to me anymore.
    - **(f)** No one likes him anymore.

Exercise 2

Rewrite the statements you wrote in Exercise 1, using *anymore* and *used to* if appropriate. (The conjunction *but* may be helpful in these statements.)

> **EXAMPLE:** *Madonna doesn't have black hair anymore.*
>
> *Madonna used to have black hair, but she doesn't anymore.*

Focus 5

MEANING
Still

MEANING

- To show that someone or something has NOT changed, you can use *still*.
    - **(a)** She lived in New Mexico 15 years ago; she lives in New Mexico now:
        She **still** lives in New Mexico.
- *Still* means that the action or habit continues to the time of speaking.
    - **(b)** He smoked 20 cigarettes a day in the past; he smokes 20 cigarettes a day now:
        He **still** smokes 20 cigarettes a day.
        (From this sentence, we understand that he started this habit in the past and hasn't stopped.)

Focus 6

Position of *Still*

- *Still* is a mid-sentence adverb. It comes:
  - **before the main verb:**
    (a) He **still** lives in New Orleans.
  - **after the verb** *be* **or an auxiliary verb:**
    (b) He is **still** crazy after all these years.
    (c) I will **still** love you.

Exercise 3

Look back at the Task. Write statements using *still* about the people who you think have not changed very much. Use the words in parentheses, but also add other ideas of your own.

1. Meryl Streep

   a. (long, blond hair) _____ .

   b. (very slim) _____ .

2. Bruce Springsteen

   a. (house in New Jersey) _____ .

   b. (called The Boss) _____ .

Can you add anything else you know about these people? Now write about Diana Ross, Warren Beatty, and Tina Turner, showing how they have or have not changed. Use *still*, *anymore* or *used to* in your descriptions.

Exercise 4

Complete the following with *still* or *anymore* as appropriate.

1. **A**: Where's Jeff?

    B: He doesn't live here _____.

2. **A**: Is Gary home yet?

    B: No, he is _____ working.

3. **A**: Have you finished writing your book?

    B: No, I'm _____ working on it.

4. **A**: Do you want a cigarette?

    B: No, thanks, I don't smoke _____.

5. **A**: Where do you live?

    B: I _____ live at home with my parents.

6. **A**: Hurry up! We're going to be late!

    B: I'm _____ wrapping the gift.

7. **A**: How's your grandfather?

    B: He's doing pretty well, even though he can't go out much _____.

Exercise 5

Look at the maps of the island nation of Madalia. Work with a partner and use the information from the maps to complete the report below. Use *used to*; *didn't use to*; *still* and *anymore* as appropriate. Use the verbs in parentheses. The first one has been done for you as an example.

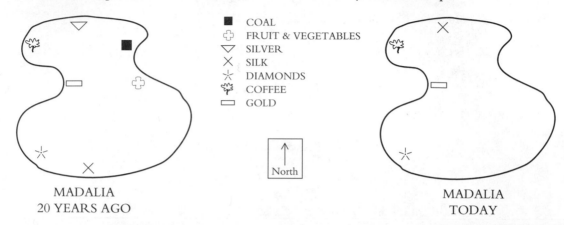

MADALIA
20 YEARS AGO

■ COAL
♣ FRUIT & VEGETABLES
▽ SILVER
✕ SILK
✲ DIAMONDS
☙ COFFEE
▭ GOLD

North

MADALIA
TODAY

EXAMPLE: Madalia is a small country that is rich in natural resources, and Madalians have exploited those resources for many years. However, in the last 20 years it is possible to note some changes in these resources. For example, 20 years ago, Madalians (1)*used to mine* (mine) *coal* in the Northeast.

In addition, they (2) _____ (grow) _____ in the East. Also, they

(3) _____ (mine) _____, but today, they (4) _____ (not

+ mine) it _____ . Furthermore, in the past, they (5) _____

(not+produce) _____ in the North; they (6) _____ (produce) it in the

_____ . On the other hand, some things have not changed. They (7) _____

(mine) _____ in the Southwest, and they (8) _____ (grow) _____

in the Northwest. Finally, they (9) _____ (mine) _____ in the West.

Exercise 6

Look at the words below. Arrange them as a list with *most frequent* at the top and *least frequent* at the bottom. Add any other similar words you can think of and put them in the appropriate place on the list.

| often | always | never | seldom |
| sometimes | hardly ever | usually | rarely |

Check your answers with Unit 1, Focus 3.

184

Focus 7

FORM

Position of Adverbs of Frequency

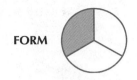

FORM

- Unit 1 showed how adverbs of frequency come **before** the main verb: **(a)** I usually get up at six and **after** the verb *be*: **(b)** They were rarely happy.
- Adverbs of frequency are also placed:
  - **Between an auxiliary verb and the main verb:**
    - **(c)** You will **sometimes** hear from them.
    - **(d)** I have **seldom** spoken to her.
  - **Before *used to*:**
    - **(e)** They **never** used to smoke.
    - **(f)** He **always** used to call her.

Exercise 7

Write a short article for your old high school magazine, reporting on your life and habits and how they have changed (or not) over the years since you left high school. Also describe your present life and habits and compare these with your past.

Try to include the following:

something you used to do but don't do anymore

something you used to do and still do

something you didn't use to do but do now

something you never do

something you seldom do

something you sometimes do

something you often do

something you usually do

Don't forget to include changes (or not) in your physical appearance. We have begun the article for you:

I left high school in _____ (year). As I look back on my life since then, I realize that some things have changed, and some things have stayed the same. Let me start by telling you about some of the changes. . . .

Activities

Activity 1

If possible, find an old photograph of yourself (as a baby, a child, or one taken several years ago). If you cannot find a photograph, draw a picture. Stick the photo or picture to a large piece of paper and write several statements about yourself, showing things you used to do and don't do now; things you didn't use to do and things you still do. Do not write your name on the paper. Your teacher will display all the pictures and descriptions. Work with a partner and try to guess the identity of each person. Who has changed the most in the class and who has changed the least?

Activity 2

Think of a place you know well—the place where you were born or where you grew up. Write about the ways it has changed and the ways it has not changed.

Activity 3

Interview a senior citizen. Find out about changes in the world or in customs and habits during his or her lifetime. What does she or he think about these changes? Report on your findings to the class.

Activity 4

The women's movement has helped change the lives of many women in different parts of the world. However, some people argue that things have not really changed and many things are still the same for most women. Think about women's lives and roles in your mother's generation and the lives of women today. Report on what has changed and what has stayed the same.

Activity 5

Create a new identity.

This activity gives you the opportunity to "become" a different person. Choose a new identity for yourself:

What is this person's name, age, sex, profession, habits, occupation, personality, and appearance? How does this new person differ from the "real" you?

Create a full description of this person and introduce the "new" you to the class, comparing him/her with the person you used to be. If you want to, make a mask or drawing to represent the "new" you.

> **EXAMPLE:** I want to introduce the new me. I used to be a mother and a housewife, but now I am a secret agent. I never used to leave home, but now I often travel to distant and exotic places. I used to wear practical clothes that I always bought on sale. Now I usually wear black leather jumpsuits, dark glasses, and big hats, but sometimes I wear elegant evening dresses and expensive jewelry. . . .

Activity 6

It is your job to write a profile of one of your classmates. Interview someone and find out something that your classmate:

1. never does
2. seldom does
3. sometimes does
4. often does
5. usually does
6. always does

When you have found this information, write a report on your findings, **without using your classmate's name**. Begin with an introduction; for example, "I am going to tell you some things about one of our classmates." End your report with a question: "Can you guess who this is?"

Display your report, along with all the other reports your classmates write. Can you identify the people described?

17

Past Perfect and *Before* and *After*

Task

Work with a partner and look at Family Tree A. It shows Tom's family when he left home to travel around the world for many years.　　(m) = married

A. THE BURTON FAMILY TREE: When Tom left home

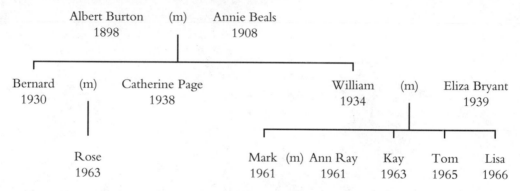

Albert Burton　(m)　Annie Beals
1898　　　　　　1908

Bernard　(m)　Catherine Page　　　　William　(m)　Eliza Bryant
1930　　　　　1938　　　　　　　　1934　　　　1939

Rose　　　　Mark　(m)　Ann Ray　Kay　Tom　Lisa
1963　　　　1961　　　1961　　1963　1965　1966

Now look at Family Tree B. It shows Tom's family after he returned home. How many differences can you find in his family between when he left and when he returned?

B. THE BURTON FAMILY TREE: When Tom returned home

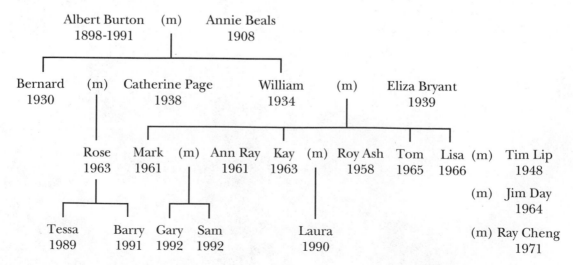

Albert Burton　(m)　Annie Beals
1898-1991　　　　1908

Bernard　(m)　Catherine Page　　　William　(m)　Eliza Bryant
1930　　　　　1938　　　　　　1934　　　　1939

Rose　Mark　(m)　Ann Ray　Kay　(m)　Roy Ash　Tom　Lisa　(m)　Tim Lip
1963　1961　　　1961　　1963　　1958　1965　1966　　　1948

(m)　Jim Day
1964

(m) Ray Cheng
1971

Tessa　Barry　Gary　Sam　　　　　Laura
1989　1991　1992　1992　　　　　1990

Number of differences: _____

According to the information in the family tree, how many of the following statements are true?

1. When Tom returned, his grandfather died.
2. Tom returned before his grandfather died.
3. Tom returned after his grandfather died.
4. When Tom returned, his grandfather had died.

Focus 1

Past Perfect and Simple Past

MEANING

- When two actions or events both happened in the past, the past perfect describes the action or event which happened **first**; the simple past describes the action or event which happened **second**:

(a) When I got there, he had eaten all the cookies. = **First**, he ate the cookies; **then**,
          2   1   I got there. (I didn't see him
                                                    eat the cookies!)

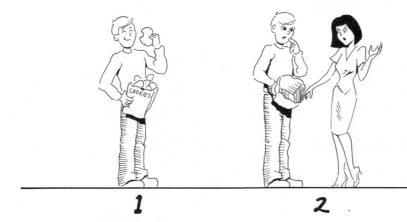

Focus 2

FORM

How to Form Past Perfect

- *had* + past participle

Statement	Negative	Question	Short Answer
I You We They } **had** arrived. **('d)**	I You We They } **had not** arrived. **(hadn't)**	**Had** { I you we they } arrived?	Yes, we **had.**
She He It } **had** arrived. **('d)**	She He It } **had not** arrived. **(hadn't)**	**Had** { she he it } arrived?	No, she **had not** **(hadn't).**

Exercise 1

Complete the following statements based on the family tree in the Task. Try to be as precise as possible. Use the past perfect as necessary; you can use any appropriate verb, except in the sentences where we have shown the verb to use in parentheses. The first one has been done for you.

EXAMPLE: 1. When he returned home, Tom found that his grandfather *had died* _____.

2. When Tom returned, his cousin _____ .

3. Tom arrived home to find that his sister Lisa _____ .

4. When _____ , his sister Kay _____ ;

   in addition, she and her husband _____ .

5. On his return home, Tom found that his brother and sister-in-law _____

   _____ .

6. When Annie Beals saw her favorite grandson, Tom, again, she had experienced both sorrow

and joy. On the one hand, her _____ ; but on the other hand, she

(gain) _____ .

7. Sam and Gary have never met their grandfather, because he _____ when they

_____ .

8. When Tom left home, he didn't have any _____ or nieces; when he got home,

he had _____ and two _____ .

9. By the time Tom got back home, his parents and his aunt and uncle (become) _____

_____ .

10. Tom also found that Rose _____ children, but she (not) _____ .

Lisa, on the other hand, _____ three times, but she (not) _____

any children.

Exercise 2

In the following pairs of statements, decide which event probably happened first. Write *1* beside
the event you think happened first and *2* beside the one you think happened second. The first one
has been done for you.

EXAMPLE: My legs ached. *2*
I played tennis. *1*

1. His car broke down.
He took the bus.

2. Charlotte was depressed.
She failed her English exam.

3. Tanya sat in the sun all afternoon.
Her skin was very red.

4. We didn't eat all day.
We were really hungry.

5. Brenda's clothes were too tight.
She didn't exercise for several months.

6. Neville couldn't sleep.
He drank several cups of very strong coffee.

7. We studied hard for three weeks.
We thought the test was easy.

8. The brothers fell asleep immediately.
They played soccer for several hours.

Now join the two statements to make one sentence, using *because* to connect them; change one
of the verbs in each sentence into past perfect. The first one has been done for you.

EXAMPLE: My legs ached. *2*
I played tennis. *1*
My legs ached because I had played tennis.

Focus 3

MEANING

Before, After, By, and *By the Time*

MEANING

- *Before, after, by,* and *by the time* show the order of actions or events:
  - *Before* introduces the event that happened second or more recently:

First Event		Second Event
(a) They were married	**before**	Christmas.
(b) She left	**before**	I arrived.

  - *After* introduces the event that happened first:

Second Event		First Event
(c) They were married	**after**	Christmas.
(d) She left	**after**	I arrived.

- When we use *before* and *after*, it is **not necessary** to use the past perfect because they make the order of events clear:

  (e) He **left before** I got there.

  It is possible to use the past perfect in this sentence, but it is not necessary:

  (f) He **had left before** I got there.

- *By* (+ noun phrase) and *by the time* (+ verb phrase) introduce an event that happened sometime before the second or more recent event:

First Event		Second Event
(g) They were married	**by**	Christmas.
(h) She had left	**by the time**	I got there.

- *By the time* is often associated with the past perfect.
- See Unit 4, Focus 4 for punctuation rules in time clauses.

192

Exercise 3

Look at the following statements; each one uses past perfect. Check (✔) the sentences where it is necessary to use past perfect to indicate the order of events.

1. My sister graduated from college after she had gotten married.
2. I didn't see Brad last night because he had left when I got there.
3. After I had finished my work, I took a long, hot bath.
4. Kozue had checked the gas before she started to drive to Houston.
5. When the party was over, they had drunk nine bottles of wine.
6. The teacher sent the student home before the class had ended.
7. The store had closed when I got there.
8. We didn't see the movie because it had started before we got to the movie theater.
9. Cathy never knew her grandparents because they had died before she was born.
10. When Shirley got to the library, she found that someone had borrowed the book she needed.

Exercise 4

Rewrite the following sentences by omitting the underlined words and using the word in parentheses. Underline the verb in each sentence where it is possible (but not always necessary) to use past perfect. The first one has been done for you.

> **EXAMPLE:** First Sue listened to the weather report and then she decided to go for a bike ride. (after)
>
> *After Sue listened to the weather report, she decided to go for a bike ride.*
>
> OR *Sue decided to go for a bike ride after she listened to the weather report.*

1. Sue studied several maps, and then she decided on an interesting route for her bike ride. (before)
2. She changed her clothes, and then she checked the tires on her bike. (after)
3. She put fresh water in her water bottle, and next she left home. (before)
4. She rode for several miles, then she came to a very steep hill. (after)
5. She rode to the top of the hill, and then she stopped to drink some water and enjoy the view. (before)
6. She rode for ten more miles, and then she got a flat tire. (after)
7. She fixed the flat tire quickly, and then she continued her ride. (before)
8. It started to rain, and then she decided to go home. (after)
9. Before she got home, she rode over 30 miles. (by the time)
10. She took a long, hot shower, and finally she ate a huge plate of pasta. (after)

Focus 4

Past Perfect versus Present Perfect

- The past perfect contrasts two actions or events in the past.

  (a) She **was** tired yesterday because she **had taken** a long bike ride.

- The present perfect connects the past with the present. It tells us that something happened sometime before now (see Unit 12) or that something started in the past and continues until now (see Unit 11).

  (b) She **is** tired **now** because she **has taken** a long bike ride.

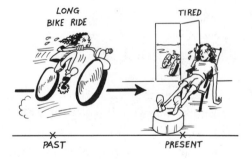

Exercise 5

Underline the mistakes in the following sentences and correct as necessary.

had

EXAMPLE: I wasn't tired yesterday because I <u>have</u> slept for ten hours the night before.

1. Nigel wasn't hungry last night because he has eaten a large fresh salmon for lunch.

2. Jan is really confused in class last Tuesday because she hadn't read the assignment.

3. Graham had gone home because he has a terrible headache today.

4. Howard is a lucky man because he had traveled all over the world.

5. Martha went to the hospital after she has broken her leg.

6. Before he has left the house, George locked all the doors and windows.

7. Professor Westerfield always returns our papers after she had graded them.

8. I didn't see you at the airport last night because your plane has left before I got there.

9. Matthew and James were late because they have missed the bus.

Exercise 6

In the story below, use the appropriate verb tense (simple past, past progressive, past perfect, present perfect) for the verbs in parentheses.

Some people attend all their high school reunions, but Al (1) _____ (go + not) back to his high school since he (2) _____ (graduate) ten years ago. Five years ago, he (3) _____ (make) arrangements to go to his five-year high school reunion, but two days before that reunion he (4) _____ (break) his leg. He (5) _____ (paint) his house on a tall ladder when he (6) _____ (lose) his balance. So he (7) _____ (not+go) to his five-year reunion.

Al (8) _____ (not+visit) his hometown for ten years and his new wife, Marta, (9) _____ (never+be) there. Al and Marta (10) _____ (get) married about a year and a half ago and they (11) _____ (not+be) married long when some of Al's high school friends (12) _____ (come) to visit them last year. So at least Marta (13) _____ (meet) a few of Al's old friends, even though she (14) _____ (not + be) to his hometown.

Activities

Activity 1

The purpose of this activity is to compare different events and achievements at different times in our lives. You will need to get information from five of your classmates to complete this.

The left-hand column in the chart below shows different ages; your job is to find three interesting or surprising things your classmates had done by the time they reached this age. If you don't want to talk about your life, feel free to invent things that you had done at those ages. Be ready to report on your findings.

	(Name)	(Name)	(Name)	(Name)	(Name)
By the time, she or he was 5 years old...					
By the time she or he was 10 years old...					
By the time she or he was 15 years old...					
By the time she or he was 18 years old...					
By the time ... ... *					
By the time ... ... *					

* you choose an age

Now choose *the three most surprising* pieces of information you found for *each age* (for example: The age of 15 is very interesting! By the time Roberto, Ali, and Tina were 15, they had done quite different things. Roberto had worked in his father's office, Ali had visited ten different countries, and Tina had won several prizes for swimming. . . .) Present this information as an oral or written report. Be sure to announce your purpose in an introductory sentence and to end with a concluding comment.

If you prefer, you can turn your information into a poster presentation. Take a large poster-sized sheet of paper or card and use this to make a poster that communicates the information you found. You can use graphics, pictures, and diagrams to make your poster interesting and eye-catching. Display your poster so that your classmates can enjoy it and be ready to answer any questions they might have about it.

Activity 2

Guess Who I Was

Work in teams. With your team, choose three famous people who are now dead. Make sure you choose famous people everyone has heard of. For each person, write three statements about what s/he had done before they died. Most people should be able to guess the identity of your person after they hear all three statements.

Team A presents the first statement about their first person. The other teams have to try to guess the identity of the dead person from the statements.

Each team can ask two yes/no questions after each statement. (The "trick" is to make your statements difficult, but not impossible!)

> **EXAMPLE:** Before she died, she had made several movies.
>
> She had had some famous husbands and some famous lovers.
>
> Some people believe she had been depressed before she died.
>
> (Marilyn Monroe)

Activity 3

The purpose of this activity is to compare and contrast important historical events in the development of different countries.

Use the chart below to record THREE events that you think were important in the history of your country (or of a country that you know about). Don't worry if you don't know the exact date. Just mark on the chart more or less when you think it happened.

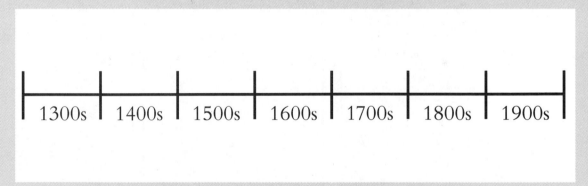

Now go around the class comparing your chart with your classmates' charts. Add to your chart significant dates from at least three other students. Where possible, try to get information from students who come from different countries. Can you add any important events from North American history too?

Use the information on your chart to compare and contrast what had happened in one country (or countries) when something else happened in another country. In addition, try to find different events that occurred at the same time in different countries. Present your findings as a written or oral report; don't forget to include an introduction and a conclusion. If you choose to make a written report, read the report carefully when you finish writing and check that you have chosen the most appropriate tenses. If you choose to make an oral report, record your presentation and afterward listen to yourself, checking specifically on your use of tenses. If you prefer, you can share your findings as a poster presentation (see Activity 1).

18

Quantity Classifiers with Food Items

Task

Jim has been invited to a potluck dinner (a meal where each guest brings a dish). The hostess has asked him to bring a salad for six people and some cookies. Jim wants to make everything himself and has asked for your advice and assistance. He has got the following ingredients in his kitchen; can you help him decide which ones he can use in each dish? Write them in the appropriate boxes below.

INGREDIENTS

mustard	sugar	salt	lettuce	hard-boiled eggs	cheese	vinegar
chocolate chips	tomatoes	flour	olive oil	butter	eggs	garlic

Salad	Salad Dressing	Chocolate Chip Cookies

Jim has no idea how much of each ingredient he should use. Can you help him? Write an appropriate amount beside each ingredient. Remember, there will be six people at the party.

Are there any *other* ingredients you would include? Add them to the boxes above, with suggested amounts.

Focus 1

Measure Words and Expressions

MEANING

- There are some very specific ways of counting and measuring food items. Some measure expressions refer to the **portions** or **containers** or to the **weights** and **measurements** used to quantify food. Other measure words refer to the **shapes** or **typical states** in which some food items (especially certain fruits and vegetables) can be found:

CONTAINERS

"Container" words usually describe food items as we buy them in a store:

a bottle of (beer, wine)

a jar of (peanut butter, mustard)

a box of (crackers, cereal)

a bag of (potato chips, flour)

a carton of (milk, eggs)

a can of (tuna fish, beer)

199

PORTIONS

"Portion" words usually describe items as we find them on a plate when we eat them:

a slice of (bread)

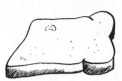

a scoop of ice cream

a piece of (candy, cake)

a pat of butter

MEASUREMENTS

In North America, these measurement words are common in recipes:

a cup (of rice, water, flour)

a tablespoon (of salt, sugar, water)

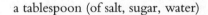

a teaspoon (of salt, sugar, water)

a pinch (of pepper, salt)

1 teaspoon (tsp) = approximately 5 milliliters
1 tablespoon (tbs) = approximately 15 milliliters
1 cup = approximately 1/4 liter
A pinch = a *very small* amount

- Many food items (meat, vegetables, cheese) are measured in pounds (lbs) and ounces (oz).
  1 ounce (oz) = approximately 30 grams
  1 pound (lb) = approximately 454 grams
- Some liquids (milk, whipping cream) are measured in pints, quarts, and gallons:
  1 pint = .4732 liters
  1 quart = .9463 liters
  1 gallon = 3.785 liters

SHAPES AND TYPICAL STATES

These expressions refer to the appearance or shape of specific items. (For example, cabbage grows in a shape similar to a "head"; therefore, we often say, "a head of cabbage.")

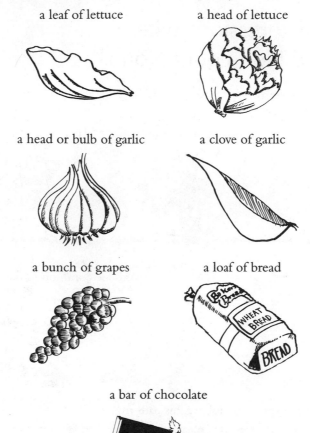

a leaf of lettuce   a head of lettuce

a head or bulb of garlic   a clove of garlic

a bunch of grapes   a loaf of bread

a bar of chocolate

Exercise 1

Turn back to the Task. Review the words you used to describe the amount of each ingredient and change them as necessary.

Exercise 2

Turn back to the Task and look carefully at the ingredients. Some of these are count nouns (tomatoes) and some are non-count nouns (flour). Write *C* beside each count noun and *NC* beside each non-count noun.

Focus 2

Measure Expressions with Count and Non-count Nouns

- Measure expressions help us to be more specific about quantity. They also enable us to make non-count nouns countable:

Three bottles of wine

Three cartons of milk

Two scoops of ice cream

Six pounds of coffee

- Most measure expressions follow this pattern:

a/an/One Two Three	+	Measure Word (Singular/Plural)	+ of +	Noun (Non-Count/ Plural)
a		cup	of	milk
a		pound	of	apples
two		cups	of	milk
two		pounds	of	apples

- Exception: specific numbers (including *dozen*):

    a dozen eggs   ten strawberries

       NOT: a dozen of eggs

Exercise 3

These are the recipes that Jim finally used. Complete the missing parts. (The picture may help you.)

A. Jim's Super Salad

1 large _____ of red leaf lettuce

1 medium-sized _____ of romaine lettuce

1 _____ of watercress

1 large cucumber, cut into _____

6 tomatoes, cut into quarters

1/2 _____ of Swiss cheese, cut into small strips

1 _____ cooked chicken, shredded into small pieces

1/2 _____ olives

2 hard-boiled eggs, shelled and cut into quarters

1. Line a large salad bowl with the red leaf lettuce leaves.
2. Tear the romaine lettuce leaves into medium-sized pieces.
3. Place in the bowl in layers, with the watercress, slices of cucumber and tomato, cheese, and chicken.
4. Garnish with olives and eggs. Cover and refrigerate for one hour. Toss with Jim's Super Salad Dressing just before serving.

B. Jim's Super Salad Dressing

1 _____ Dijon mustard

4 _____ red wine vinegar

1 _____ sugar

1/2 _____ salt

1/2 _____ pepper

1/2 _____ olive oil

1. Put the mustard into a bowl. Whisk in vinegar, sugar, salt, and pepper.
2. Slowly add the oil while continuing to whisk the mixture.

C. Jim's Granny's Old Time Chocolate Chip Cookies

1/2 _____ butter

1 _____ brown sugar

3/4 _____ granulated sugar

2 eggs

2 _____ flour

1 _____ baking soda

1 _____ vanilla extract

1 _____ salt

1 1/2 _____ chocolate chips

1. Preheat the oven to 350° F. Grease a cookie sheet.
2. Cream the butter and both the sugars together until light and fluffy. Add the eggs and vanilla and mix well.
3. Sift the flour, baking soda, and salt. Mix thoroughly.
4. Add the chocolate chips.
5. Form into cookies. Place on a cookie tray and put on the middle rack of the oven for 8–10 minutes.
6. Cool for 5 minutes.
7. Enjoy! (This recipe makes about 40 cookies.)

Turn back to the Task and look at the ingredients (and the amounts) you suggested for these dishes. How many differences can you find between your suggestions and Jim's recipes? Whose recipe do you think will taste better?

Exercise 4

Thomas is a chef at Legends Celebrity Diner, where each item on the menu is named for a famous person. Thomas has had to take the afternoon off and has asked you to substitute for him. He has left you detailed instructions about how to make some of the most popular items on the menu. Unfortunately, some of the instructions have gotten jumbled up. Can you sort them out? Write the ingredients under the appropriate heading.

ARNOLD'S "TERMINATOR" BURGER

_____

_____

_____

_____

_____

STING'S "WHOLE EARTH" SANDWICH

_____

_____

_____

_____

_____

_____

TINA TURNER'S HOT FUDGE SUNDAE

_____

_____

_____

_____

MARILYN MONROE'S ICE-CREAM SHAKE

_____

_____

_____

_____

2 slices of whole wheat bread
2 scoops of chocolate ice cream
1/2 lb of chopped steak (cooked rare)
6 spinach leaves
2 1/2 cups of hot fudge sauce
3 slices of avocado
a dozen strawberries
2 tbs of all-natural mayonnaise
1 1/2 cups of bean sprouts
3 tbs of hot mustard

2 cups of toasted almonds
1 cup of hot chili sauce
3 scoops of vanilla ice cream
1 white hamburger bun
6 tbs of whipped cream
1 scoop of strawberry ice cream
2 cups of onion rings
1 scoop of coffee ice cream
3 crisp lettuce leaves
1 sliced tomato

Exercise 5

Two friends went shopping for a big party. They made a list of some of their favorite foods, and then they went to Food Giant, the big supermarket nearby. Here's their list.

Add the measure words (and a plural if necessary). Different answers are possible, and some answers may not require measure words.

1 1/2 _____	ground beef	2 _____	wine
3 _____	bread	2 _____	corn chip
2 _____	orange	2 _____	tomato
2 _____	cheese	3 _____	ice cream
1 _____	milk	6 _____	coke

Exercise 6

Last week Matthew ate a delicious spaghetti sauce at his friend Nancy's house. He enjoyed it so much that Nancy lent him the recipe so that he could make a copy of it. However, Nancy has obviously used this recipe many times and it is quite difficult to read. Can you help Matthew figure out the recipe? Fill in the missing parts below.

Spaghetti Sauce

(from Nancy's kitchen)

First, cut 3 _____ of bacon into small pieces and cook over a very low heat. Stir in 1/2 _____ of ground meat along with 4 _____ garlic and 2 _____ onion, chopped up very finely. Add 1 _____ salt, a pinch of cayenne pepper and 2 _____ of fresh herbs. Mix in two 8-ounce tomato sauce. Let it cook on low heat for about 30 minutes. Serve over fresh pasta.

If you were making this recipe yourself, would you change or add anything? Share any changes or additions with your classmates. Try to be as precise as possible.

206

Activities

Activity 1

Below is a blank Bingo card. Your teacher will read a list of food items that each require a measure word. When you hear the food item, write the measure word for that item in a box—*any* box. For example, if your teacher says "bread," you can write *slice* or *loaf* in a box. Don't start in the upper left corner; fill your boxes in any order you want. Your card should look different from your classmates'.

How to Play

When everyone has filled in their boxes, your teacher will read a food item. Write the item in a box with a matching measure word. For example, if your teacher says "bread," you will write *bread* in the box that says *loaf* or *slice*. Sometimes it may be possible to write one food item in more than one box. When this happens, *choose only one box*.

When you complete a line (diagonally, vertically, or horizontally) call out "Bingo." The first person to correctly fill a line and call out "Bingo" wins the game. Good luck!

Exercise 5,6 Activity 1: Idea by Wendy Asplin

Activity 2

In Exercise 4, you saw some of the items on the menu at Legends Celebrity Diner. Get together with a classmate and create some new items for the menu at this diner. Choose three people that you think everyone in the class will know (for example, movie stars, singers, politicians, your classmates, etc.). Create a dish named for this person. Be precise about the quantity of each ingredient in the dish. Share your "dishes" with the rest of the class.

Activity 3

The purpose of this activity is to do some research about various dishes and their recipes. The dishes below are very popular in North America, but different people sometimes have quite different recipes for the same dish. Your goal is to discover some of these variations.

Brownies   Potato Salad   Cheesecake   Cranberry Sauce

Divide into groups and choose **one** of these dishes. (If you prefer, you can select a dish that isn't on this list, preferably one that you don't know how to make.) Interview several different native speakers by asking them to tell you how to make the dish you have chosen. If possible, tape-record your interview. Get together with your group and compare the directions you have gathered. How many differences can you find? Be ready to share your findings with the rest of the class.

Activity 4

This "recipe" was written by an English teacher:

"Recipe" for the Perfect Student
Ingredients:
1 cup of motivation
1 cup of determination
1/2 cup of patience
1/2 cup of tolerance
1 cup of laughter
1 cup of imagination
1 1/2 cups of willingness to makes a guess
1 cup of independence
1 1/2 cups of cooperation with others
1 pinch of fun
Combine ingredients and stir gently to bring out the best flavor.

What do you think the teacher means by this?

Get together with a partner and create a "recipe" of your own. Here are some ideas, but you probably have plenty of your own:

Recipe for a long-lasting marriage
Recipe for the perfect boyfriend/girlfriend/husband/wife
Recipe for the perfect teacher
Recipe for the perfect house
Recipe for the perfect mother/father

Share your recipes with the rest of the class.

Activity 5

Your class has been given $5 per person to spend on food and drink for a party. Divide into groups and draw up a list showing how you will spend this money. Be specific about the quantities you will buy.

Activity 6

Think of your favorite recipe, preferably a typical dish from your country. Write it on a piece of paper and give it to your teacher. Your teacher will distribute the recipes among the class so that everyone receives somebody else's recipe. Try to cook the recipe according to the instructions you were given. Bring the results to class.

Activity 7

Organize an international potluck. Everyone in the class should prepare a dish, preferably from his/her country. Bring the dish to class to share and enjoy with your classmates. Be ready to tell your classmates how to make your dish. If possible, try to arrange your potluck at somebody's house, so you can watch each other cook. After the meal, collect all the recipes for an international cookbook. Make copies and distribute them to the class.

19

Articles
Definite, Indefinite, and ∅

Task

Put the following sentences in order so that they make a logical story. When you have finished, check to see if other students have the story in the same order.

a. Esinam found a real-estate agent to help them.

b. They finally decided to buy the house, remodel the kitchen, and take out the old kitchen cabinets.

c. Even though the house was little, it had a big, old-fashioned kitchen and two bathrooms.

d. Next they viewed a pretty house by a lake, but the house was too expensive.

e. Finally they saw a little house at the end of a dead-end street.

f. When I last talked to them, they were happy with their decision, and they liked the house a lot.

g. Esinam and Stuart decided to buy a house.

h. The real-estate agent then showed them a house near some apartment buildings, but the house was too big, and the apartment buildings were too ugly.

i. The little house was just right—not too expensive, not too far away from work, not too big.

j. First they looked at a nice house in the suburbs, but the house was too far away from work.

k. They told the real-estate agent that they wanted to live in a quiet neighborhood. They also said that they preferred small houses.

Focus 1

Articles

**FORM
MEANING**

- There are four articles in English, one definite and three indefinite forms.

DEFINITE

- *The* is used with specific nouns. Nouns are specific when the listener knows what specific thing or person the speaker is talking about.

    (a) Father to son: Where did you park **the** car?

INDEFINITE

- *A* (or *an* before nouns that start with a vowel sound) is used with singular count nouns that are non-specific.

    (b) I need **a** new car.

- *Some* is used for plural count and non-count nouns that are indefinite.

    (c) I need **some** pencils.

    (d) Would you like **some** rice?

- ∅ is used for plural count and non-count nouns that are indefinite and when the speaker wishes to talk about things in general.

    (e) Pencils are made with lead.

    (f) Rice is eaten in Africa.

Focus 2

USE

The Definite Article: Second Mention

USE

- *The* is used when the listener knows what specific thing or person the speaker is talking about. The speaker is thinking, "you know what I mean" when he or she uses *the*.
- The speaker thinks that the listener knows what she or he means in different situations:
  - when the noun has already been mentioned = second mention

    (a) She used to have a cat and a dog, but **the** cat got run over.
  - when a related noun has already been mentioned, it is called related second mention

    (b) He bought a suit yesterday, but **the** jacket had a button missing, so he had to return it.
        (**Jacket** is part of a **suit**: the listener knows which jacket since **suit** was already mentioned.)

    (c) I had a lock but I lost **the** key for it.

Exercise 1

Underline all the uses of *the* in the statements in the Task. For each one, describe why it is used based on the rules in Focus 2 regarding second mention or related mention. If neither of these rules helps to explain why *the* is used, circle *the*. You will return to this later, in Exercise 3.

Exercise 2

Each time *the* is underlined in the sentences below, decide **why** it is used. If it is used because it is the second mention of the noun following it, circle *S* (for Second mention). If it used because a related noun has been mentioned, circle *R* (for Related mention).

1. Jerry was late for his appointment, so he went into a telephone booth near the bus stop to make a phone call. It looked like someone was living in the telephone booth.   Ⓢ R

2. There was a small blanket covering the window of the telephone booth like a curtain.   S R

3. The floor of the telephone booth was swept clean with a broom.   S R

4. The broom was hung on a little hook in the corner of the telephone booth.   S R

5. By the telephone, there was a pen and a notepad with a short list of names and telephone numbers.   S R

6. The names and telephone numbers were each written in a different color ink.   S R

7. Jerry also noticed that there was a coffee mug and a toothbrush sitting neatly by the telephone directory.   S R

8. The coffee mug looked like it had recently been rinsed. There were still drops of water in it.   S R

9. Jerry had such a strong feeling that he was in someone's living space that he decided to find another place to make the phone call.   S R

Focus 3

The Definite Article: Uniqueness

USE

- We also use the definite article *the* when the noun is **unique**. In other words, there is **only one** possible reference because
  - the place where you are speaking makes it clear.
    - **(a) The** flowers are beautiful. (said in a garden)
    - **(b)** Who painted **the** ceiling? (said in a room) or
  - there's only *one* of the thing mentioned.
    - **(c) The** sun is shining today. (unique reference—there's only one sun) or
  - the adjectives used with the noun make only one reference possible (examples of these kinds of adjectives: *same, only, right*; numbers like *first, second, last*; and superlatives like *best, happiest, hardest*).
    - **(d)** We'll have to wait for **the** next bus. (There's only one possible next bus.)
    - **(e)** That's **the** hardest test I've ever taken. (There's only one possible hardest test.)
    - **(f)** She's **the** first person I met here and **the** only friend I have.

Exercise 3

In Exercise 1, you circled all the uses of *the* in the Task that could not be explained by either a) the second mention rule, or b) the related mention rule. For each time you circled *the*, use the rules from Focus 3 (above) to explain why *the* was used. (Make a list on a separate sheet of paper.)

Focus 2 and 3, and Exercise 3: Idea from Roger Berry, 1991, Rearticulating the articles, *ELT Journal* 45:3, 252-299.

Exercise 4

For each of the following sentences, answer the following questions:

a. Where would you hear this sentence spoken?

b. Who do you think the speaker is?

c. What do you think happened **before** or **after** the sentence was spoken? What do you think the conversation was about **before** or **after** the sentence was spoken?

Use the answers to these questions to discuss in class why *the* was used in each case.

1. Turn on *the* TV.
2. Could you change *the* channel?
3. We need some more chalk. Would you mind checking *the* blackboard in *the* back?
4. *The* rosebushes are lovely.
5. Could you pass *the* salt, please?
6. Excuse me, where's *the* women's restroom?
7. *The* sky is so blue today. I don't think you'll need *the* umbrella.
8. Have you seen *the* dog?
9. What a surprise! We live on *the* same street.

Focus 4

USE

The Indefinite Article

USE

- The indefinite article *a* (or *an* before nouns that start with a vowel sound) is used when the speaker first mentions a thing or person.

  (a) I read **a** great book yesterday.

  (b) Martha just bought **a** new backpack.

- It can also be used when the speaker is not talking about a specific thing or person but is making a generalization.

  (c) I'd like to get **a** ticket to the concert on Friday.

  (d) He is hoping to find **a** new wife.

- *Some* is used for the same purposes with plural or non-count nouns.

  (e) I would like to read **some** more books.

  (f) We need **some** more chalk.

Exercise 5

Fill in the blanks in the story below with *a/an*, *some*, or *the*.

1. Esinam and Stuart had _____ friend, Mel, who was also looking for _____ house to buy.

2. Mel was especially interested in finding _____ house with _____ view.

3. Mel thought that _____ best views were from _____ hills east of town.

4. There were _____ houses for sale in that area, but they were all very expensive.

5. Mel decided to ask for _____ loan from his parents so that he could afford to buy _____ house with his favorite view.

6. First he looked at _____ big old house with four bedrooms.

7. He liked _____ house very much, but it was too big for just one person.

8. So he decided to ask _____ friends to live with him and pay rent.

9. He bought _____ house, even though it was _____ only house he had looked at!

Exercise 6

Now look back at the completed story (Exercise 5) and tell why you used each article (*a/an*, *some*, or *the*).

Exercise 7

Fill in the blanks in the story below with *a/an, some,* or *the.*

1. Last fall Anita worked in _____ apple orchard, picking apples.

2. _____ work was not easy.

3. She had sore muscles _____ first week of work, and every night she slept very

   soundly.

4. _____ first orchard she worked in was considered small, with only 50 trees.

5. It was owned by _____ old, retired couple, who worked in the orchard as

   _____ hobby.

6. _____ next orchard Anita worked in seemed huge, about 20 acres.

7. In this orchard, _____ of the trees had yellow apples, which were called "Golden

   Delicious."

8. Every day Anita ate _____ apples for breakfast and for lunch.

9. Even though _____ weather was beautiful, and _____ hard work

   made her feel very healthy, Anita was relieved when _____ apple-picking season

   was over.

Focus 5

USE

The ∅ Article

- When we talk about things in general (all trees, all literature), we can use a plural noun or non-count noun with zero article (∅).
  - **(a)** There are many uses for trees.
  - **(b)** Literature, art, and music are considered "the fine arts."

Exercise 8

Circle the errors in article usage in the sentences below. Specifically, should you use *the* or the zero (Ø) article?

1. The love is a very important thing in our lives.
2. Without the love, we will be lonely and confused.
3. I believe that the money is not as important as love, although some people don't feel this way.
4. If the money is too important, then we become greedy.
5. When we get old, the health becomes almost as important as love.
6. My grandmother says, "Just wait and see. Work you do and the money you earn are important now, but when you're old . . .
7. . . . love that you feel for your family and friends, health of your loved ones—these are the things that will be most important."

Exercise 9

Fill in the blanks in the story below with *the*, zero (Ø) article, *a/an* or *some*.

1. Berta likes _____ books. She has two rooms full of books in her house.

2. In general, she finds that _____ books are expensive, although _____ paperback books are still fairly inexpensive.

3. Usually _____ used books are about a third of the price of _____ new books.

4. _____ textbooks are pretty expensive.

5. _____ romance novels and _____ mysteries are usually pretty cheap.

6. _____ cheapest books of all are at Al's Second-hand Bookstore in the University District.

7. At Al's, _____ used books in the back room are all three dollars or less.

8. Once she bought _____ book that cost $75. This book was _____ atlas, with pages and pages of beautifully colored maps.

9. Berta feels that _____ books are a good thing to spend money on these days even though they might seem kind of expensive when you buy them.

10. The nicest thing about _____ books, according to Berta, is that you can always keep them, to look at or read again and again.

Activities

Activity 1

TIC-TAC-TOE/Arranging Objects—Choose a small common object that can be moved around. It can be something that you are wearing (a ring, a watch) or carrying with you (a pencil, a book). It is all right if some people choose the same object. All of you will give your objects to one student.

Form two teams. Each team will tell the student who has the objects to arrange them according to their directions, one sentence at a time. (For example, "Put a book under the ring. Put the red pencil next to the book.") If the article usage in the sentence is correct (and the person is able to follow the directions), then the team gets to put an *X* or *O* in any of the tic-tac-toe squares. If it is not correct, then the team must pass. The first team to get three *X*'s or three *O*'s in a row or diagonally wins the game.

Activity 2

Find a photograph or drawing to bring to class. First describe the picture, and then work together to tell the class a story about it. This will be a "chain story." The first person says one thing about the picture, the second repeats that and adds another sentence, etc., until each student has contributed at least one sentence to the story. Concentrate on using articles correctly as you compose the story orally.

Activity 3

Now without the help of your classmates, write a short description of the picture that you described in Activity 2. It doesn't have to be exactly the same as the story you made, but again, try to use the articles correctly.

Activity 4

Here are some things that people say contribute to their happiness: love, romance, success, wealth/money, fame, popularity, health, religion. Interview three people about what they think is most important for their happiness. (Tape-record people's answers, if possible.) Be sure to get information about the people you are interviewing, such as age group, gender, occupation.

Summarize the results of your interviews and see if there is agreement in people's answers.

Activity 5

Find at least four headlines in a newspaper. Copy them down or cut them out and bring them to class. Put in articles (*the*, ∅ article, *a/an* or *some*) wherever you think they are appropriate, in order to make the headline into a more complete statement. (Note: You might need to add main verbs or auxiliaries too, such as a form of *be* or *do*.)

With the headlines you have chosen, is it possible to use more than one of these choices of articles? If so, does the meaning of the statement change?

> **EXAMPLE:** RIOT IN L.A. ALARMS NATION
>
> Adding articles: The riot in L.A. alarms the nation.
>
> Explanation: *The* riot is used because it is a specific riot (April 1992) that we have all heard about. It is not possible to choose another article.
>
> *The* nation is used because we all know **which** nation they are talking about; this is from a United States newspaper, so *the* nation refers to the United States. Thus, this is the only article choice that makes sense.

Task

How much geographical information do your classmates know? Move around the classroom to collect information to complete the chart below. Write down all the **different** answers you get in each category. When you have spoken to five other students, decide on the correct answers. Use a recent edition of an almanac to check your answers.

WHAT IS . . . ?

the largest continent in the world	
the longest river	
the largest country (in size, not population)	
the biggest island	
the highest mountain range	
the highest mountain	
the biggest desert	
the largest ocean	
the largest lake	
the largest planet	

Focus 1

Geographical Names

- Geographical names are proper nouns, and **usually** you don't need an article with them:
  (a) He lives in China.
  (b) Lake Superior is in North America.

Exercise 1

Look at the categories below. For each category (1–10), put the correct answers from the Task in either Column A or B. (Don't worry about Column C; you will complete this later.) For example, the highest mountain is **Mt. Everest**, which does not use *the*, so this would go in column B for #6.

Category	(A) Use *the*	(B) Don't Use *the*	(C) Exceptions
1. rivers			
2. continents			
3. countries			
4. islands			
5. mountain ranges			
6. mountain peaks		**Mt. Everest**	
7. deserts			
8. oceans			
9. lakes			
10. planets			

Now check your answers with Focus 2. Can you now add more examples to each column, and can you also find some examples for Column C?

Focus 2

Articles with Geographical Names

FORM

- We do **not** use *the*:
  - With the names of
    continents (South America)
    planets (Mars) (Exception: *the* earth, which can also be simply *Earth*)
    parks (Yosemite National Park)
    streets and most highways (First Avenue, Interstate 90)
    cities
  - Before individual (rather than plural)
    islands (Jamaica)
    mountain peaks (Mt. Shasta) (Exception: the Matterhorn)
    lakes (Lake Union)
  - With the names of countries (France, Australia), **except** when they are viewed as unions or federations, as in the United Kingdom, or are plural, as in the Philippines
- We use *the*:
  - With chains or groups (plural rather than singular) of
    islands (the Hawaiian Islands)
    mountains (the Andes)
    lakes (the Great Lakes)
  - With the names of
    rivers (the Yellow River)
    deserts (the Gobi Desert)
    oceans and seas (the Arctic Ocean, the Caspian Sea)
    regions, when the direction word acts as the proper noun (the West, the Midwest; but not Southeast Asia, where the continent is named)
  - With nouns with *of* in them, such as the Republic of China, the Bay of Bengal
- Note: These are the **regular** patterns for using articles with geographical names. Occasionally you will come across other exceptions.

Exercise 2

Fill in the blanks with *the* or ∅ (article not required).

(1) _____ Myanmar is sandwiched between (2) _____ India and (3) _____ Bangladesh on one side and (4) _____ China, (5) _____ Laos, and (6) _____ Thailand on the other, while to the south is (7) _____ Andaman Sea and (8) _____ Bay of Bengal. Myanmar has several important river systems including (9) _____ Irrawaddy, which runs almost the entire length of the country and enters the sea in a vast delta region southwest of (10) _____ Rangoon, the capital. (11) _____ Mekong River forms the border between Myanmar and Laos. (12) _____ Himalayas rise in the north of Myanmar, and (13) _____ Hkakabo Razi,

on the border between Myanmar and Tibet, is the highest mountain in (14) _____

southeast Asia, at 5881 meters (19,297 feet).

> (Adapted from *Burma, A Travel Survival Kit*, by Tony Wheeler, 1982. Lonely Planet Publications)

Now use the information from this exercise to complete the map.

Exercise 3

Look at these conversations. Underline all the geographical names, names of institutions, and names of famous buildings or places.

Dialogue 1

A: My brother is a freshman at the University of Washington.

B: Really? I thought he was at Louisiana State.

A: He was. He didn't like the climate in the South, so he decided to move to the Pacific Northwest.

Dialogue 2

A: How long did you stay in Washington, D.C.?

B: Not very long. We had just enough time to see the White House, the Capitol, and the Washington Monument.

A: Did you get to any museums or art galleries?

B: We wanted to go to the Smithsonian and the National Gallery, but we didn't have time.

A: Too bad!

In these examples, when is the definite article used and when is it **not** used? List all the examples from the conversation if that is helpful.

Focus 3

FORM

Articles with Institutional Terms

FORM

- We do **not** use *the*:
  - when the name of a university or college comes directly **before** the word *university* or *college* (Boston College), or when *university* or *college* is implied. (Louisiana State [University]).
- We do not **usually** use *the*:
  - with the names of parks (Central Park, Discovery Park).

- We use *the*:
  - when the phrase *University of* comes before the rest of the name (the University of Northern Iowa);
  - with the names of tourist attractions, monuments, or famous buildings (the Space Needle, the Golden Gate Bridge) (Exception: Disneyland);
  - with museums and libraries (the Museum of Natural History).

Exercise 4

The following conversation is between Sheryl Smith, a real-estate agent, and the Joneses, who are considering buying a house in the city of Golden Oaks. Fill in the blanks with *the* (when the definite article is required) or ∅ (when no article is required).

Sheryl Smith: I'm sure you'd like the area. It borders (1) _____ Discovery Park, which has free outdoor concerts at (2) _____ Rutherford Concert Hall, and also there's (3) _____ Whitehawk Native American Art Museum, which you've probably heard of. It's quite well known.

Mike Jones: Yes, yes.

Donna Jones: What about schools?

Sheryl Smith: Well, there's (4) _____ Smith College of Architecture, of course—

Donna Jones: I mean public schools. For our children.

Sheryl Smith: Oh, well, (5) _____ Golden Oaks Elementary School is only a few blocks away, on (6) _____ First Avenue. And there's a high school about a mile north of the park.

Mike Jones: (pointing): Aren't those (7) _____ White Mountains?

Sheryl Smith: Yes. On clear days, you can even see (8) _____ Mt. Wildman, the tallest mountain in the range.

Mike Jones: Oh, yes. I heard about a good fishing spot there, on (9) _____ Blue Lake.

Sheryl Smith: Yes, my husband goes there and to (10) _____ Old Man's River to fish. He could tell you all about it.

Mike Jones: Mrs. Smith, I think you might have made a sale today.

Exercise 5

Fill in the blanks with *the* or ∅ (article not required).

SAN FRANCISCO MUST SEE'S FOR FIRST-TIMERS

Once considered impossible to build, (1) _____ Golden Gate Bridge, a 1.7-mile-long single-span suspension bridge, was opened in 1937. A walk across offers a fantastic view of the city, (2) _____ Marin Headlands, and (3) _____ East Bay. Experience a taste of (4) _____ Orient in (5) _____ Chinatown, the largest Chinese settlement outside (6) _____ Asia. Originally only sand dunes, (7) _____ Golden Gate Park owes its existence to Scottish landscape architect John McLaren. In addition to the beauty of its landscape, the park contains: a conservatory modeled after (8) _____ Kew Gardens; (9) _____ Asian Art Museum with its well-known Brundage collection; (10) _____ Strybing Arboretum with its worldwide plant collection; and (11) _____ California Academy of Sciences, which includes a planetarium and aquarium.

(Adapted from *San Francisco*, TESOL Convention 1990, Leslie Reichert)

Activities

Activity 1

It is often said that Americans do not know very much about geography, compared to people from other countries. The purpose of this activity is for non-native people living in the United States (or near Americans if you are in a country other than the United States), to conduct a small survey to see to what extent this is true.

Take the questions from the Task and draw up a chart of your own. Add other items to the chart if you want. Then use this chart to get information from as many Americans as you can—ideally from five to ten different people. Compare the answers you receive with those that your classmates gave you, and share your findings with the rest of the class.

On the basis of the findings from everyone in class, is it true that Americans know less about geography than people from other countries? Are there any reasons to explain your results?

Activity 2

With the help of your teacher, form teams. Each team will have five minutes to think of as many names of islands, mountains, and lakes as possible. Each name, with correct article use, will be worth one point. The team that has the most correct names + articles wins.

Activity 3

Think of a city or region you know and like. What places are the "Must See's For First-Timers"? Write a short description of the tourist attractions and special features. If time allows, draw a map giving the relative locations of these places.

Activity 4

Rita and Ray were planning an overnight backpacking trip into the mountains, so they asked their friend Bill to give them directions to a nice camping spot where he had camped many times. Bill told Ray the directions over the phone. Below are the notes that Ray took:

> Round trip — Fire Mountain — 14 miles
> 1 mile before Fire Mountain — Crystal Pass (great
>   camping spot)
> To trailhead:
> north from seattle — Interstate 5 through Mt. Vernon
> east — Highway 65 to Darrington
> 1 1/2 miles past Darrington left on road — Smokey Peak
>   Road or Smoke Peak??
> about 2 miles down road — left — parking area (Fire Mt.
>   trail sign, elevation 2000 feet)
> steep trail — Lake Megan (about 1 1/2 miles)
> trail splits off (3 miles?) — right — across Southfork
>   River — not downhill
> up to Crystal Mountain (elevation 4500 feet?) and
>   campsite
> great view of Fire Mt.
> cold, take warm clothes!

Instructions: "Translate" this note into complete directions and a description of the route to Bill's special camping spot.

226

Indirect Objects with *For*

Task

Match the pictures to the pieces of dialogue below. Write the number of the picture beside the appropriate piece of dialogue.

A: Is this yours? You left it on that table over there.

B: Let *me* take those; they're much too heavy for you.

C: I'll pay! I insist.

D: Sit down and relax. Dinner will be ready in a few minutes.

E: Hey! Don't forget your keys! Catch!

F: I hope this is going to fit you.

Now match the description to each picture. Write the letter beside each picture.

a. He carried her books to her.
b. She handed the keys to him.
c. She bought lunch for him.
d. He carried her books for her.
e. He cooked dinner for her.
f. She threw the keys to him.
g. He handed a wallet to her.
h. She knitted a sweater for him.

Focus 1

FORM

Direct and Indirect Objects

FORM

  (a) He wrote a letter.
    Letter is the direct object. It tells us **what** he wrote.

• Sometimes we use two objects:

  (b) He wrote a letter to his mother.
    His mother is the indirect object. It tells us **whom** he wrote to.

  (c) He cooked dinner for his wife.
    His wife is the indirect object. It tells us **whom** he cooked for.

Exercise 1

Look at sentences a–h in the Task. <u>Underline</u> the direct object and (circle) the indirect object in each sentence.

Focus 2

For versus *To*

MEANING

- When we use two objects, *for* and *to* add important information to the sentence:

  (a) Jim gave the books to Jean.   *To* tells us about the **direction** of the action: the books went **from** Jim *to* Jean.

  (b) John cooked dinner for Betty.   *For* tells us that the action **helps** and **pleases** the person who "receives" it. In this situation, John did something that helped and pleased Betty.

- We often use these verbs with *for* to show that the action helps and pleases someone else:

build	do	cook
prepare	buy	carry
clean	get	make
keep	fix	knit
save		

Exercise 2

Match Column A with Column B to complete the sentences that begin in A. The first one has been done for you.

A

Bruce cleaned the house for his neighbor

Graham made a cheesecake for Lara

They prepared a picnic for their children

Dan bought those earrings for Jane

Her friends prepared a surprise party for her

Susan built a bookshelf for her parents

Alan bought a blue scarf for his aunt

Sean fixed his sister's car for her

B

because she already had a blue dress.

because she didn't know anything about engines.

because it was her birthday.

because she was too tired to do it herself.

because they had too many books and not enough space for them.

because they wanted to eat at the beach.

because she wanted them.

because it was her favorite dessert.

229

Exercise 3

Read this conversation:

Barbara: Happy birthday, Joan!

Joan: Oh, Barbara! A necklace! Thank you!

Barbara: So, are you having a good birthday?

Joan: Oh, yes. The kids cooked me breakfast, and then they gave me some great presents. Joey made me a vase. He made it at school. And Julie knitted me a scarf.

Barbara: What about Jim? What did he give you?

Joan: I couldn't believe it! Jim gave me a pair of diamond earrings!

Barbara: Diamond earrings!! You're lucky. On my birthday, my husband bought me tickets to a Giants game. And I don't even like baseball!

Now complete the chart below, showing who did what for Joan on her birthday.

Joan's Birthday Treats: Who Did What For Joan on Her Birthday?

Her Son Joey	Her Daughter Julie
Her Friend Barbara	**Her Husband Jim**

<u>Underline</u> the direct objects and (circle) the indirect objects in the following parts of Joan's conversation.

The kids cooked me breakfast.

Joey made me a vase.

Julie knitted me a scarf.

Jim gave me a pair of diamond earrings.

Compare these with the sentences you worked on in Exercise 1. What differences do you notice? Write down a few of them.

230

Focus 3

Using *For* to Highlight New Information

USE

- "The kids made me breakfast" means the same as "The kids made breakfast for me." However, when **the thing** is new information and **the person who receives it** is not, you can make these changes:

  (a) He bought me a *diamond ring.*   You emphasize the **ring**, not the person who received it.

- When you think the person who received it is the more important or new information, you can use *for:*

  (b) He bought a diamond ring *for me.*   You emphasize the **person** who received the ring.
  (not you)

- In both cases, the part of the message you want to emphasize comes last.

Focus 4

FORM

Deleting *For*

FORM

	Subject	Verb	Direct Object	Indirect Object
(a)	He	bought a	diamond ring for	me.

	Subject	Verb			Indirect Object	Direct Object
(b)	He	bought a	diamond ring ~~for~~ (me) → He bought		me	a diamond ring.

- Omit *for* and put the indirect object **in front of** the direct object.

231

Exercise 4

Answer the following questions, using the words in parentheses. Use *for* when you think it is more important to emphasize **who** benefits from the action; omit *for* when you think it is best to emphasize **what** they receive.

EXAMPLE: 1. Who did you buy that for?

I bought it for Cathy. (Cathy)

2. What did you buy for your friend—a blouse or a sweater? _____

(a blouse)

3. Who did he build the house for? _____ (his mother)

4. Did Sue cook that for Josh or for Larry? _____ (Josh)

5. What did she cook for him—pasta or fish? _____ (pasta)

6. Did you make that for Nina or for Chloe? _____ (Nina)

7. What did you get for your sister—a book or a record? _____

(a book)

Focus 5

FORM

Verbs That Do Not Omit *For*

FORM

- It is not possible to omit *for* and move the indirect object in front of the direct object with **all** verbs. For example, you can say:

  (a) He cooked dinner for me.   OR   He cooked me dinner.

- However, with some verbs, you can't usually omit *for*. For example, you can say:

  (b) She solved the problem for me.

  NOT: She solved me the problem.

Some Verbs That Can Omit *For*		Some Verbs That Usually Can't Omit *For*	
buy	build	explain	repair
cook	save	open	do
make	bake	carry	prepare
knit	get	fix (= repair)	solve
sew		clean	

Exercise 5

Read the following carefully. Where you think it is possible, rewrite the sentences without using *for*.

1. My suitcase was very heavy, but my friend carried it for me.

   _____

2. Gloria cooked a fabulous dinner for Harvey.

   _____

3. Gary was cold, so Karen knitted a scarf for him.

   _____

4. If I win the lottery, I'll buy a house by the ocean for you.

   _____

5. Chuck left his wallet at home, so Ross bought dinner for him.

   _____

6. The teacher was carrying a lot of books, so the student opened the door for him.

   _____

7. On your birthday, I'll bake a cake for you.

   _____

8. George doesn't know anything about machines, so Erica always fixes his car for him.

   _____

Exercise 6

Read the sets of sentences below. Decide which sentences, if any, are incorrect in each set. Change any incorrect sentences to correct ones.

1. Tomorrow is my father's birthday, and...
   a. I'm going to get him a present.
   b. I'm going to get a present him.
   c. I'm going to get a present for him.

2. Because it's his birthday,...
   a. I'm also going to fix him his car.
   b. I'm also going to fix him for his car.
   c. I'm also going to fix his car for him.

3. He likes to eat and drink, so....
   a. my sister is going to bake a cake him.
   b. my sister is going to bake a cake for him.
   c. my sister is going to bake him a cake.
   d. my mother is going to make him his favorite dessert.
   e. my aunt is going to cook him a special meal.
   f. my aunt is going to cook him a special meal for him.
   g. my brother is going to prepare him his favorite cocktail.
   h. I'm also going to buy him some wine.
   i. I'm also going to buy some wine for him.

Activities

Activity 1

When people have problems, they sometimes write letters to magazines or newspapers, asking for advice. Can you help solve one of these problems? Read the following letter to "Dear Arby." Then work with a partner and make a list of all the things "Confused" could do for her grandfather. Compare your ideas with those of your classmates and then complete Arby's answer.

DEAR ARBY....

Please, can you help? My grandfather will be 85 in July. We don't have a lot of money, and we want to do something really special for him. He's very independent and has many interests, but we can't think what to do. Any suggestions?

He likes movies, but he doesn't like to go out to movie theaters, and his TV gets very bad reception. He really loves Italian food, but there aren't any good restaurants around here. He enjoys music, but his stereo doesn't always work very well. He's also interested in other countries, but he can't travel anymore. His house is big and hard to clean, but he won't move to a new one.

Arby, please give us some ideas.

CONFUSED Cleveland, Ohio

Dear Confused,

   Your grandfather sounds like a very special person. Here are some ideas to help you. Why don't

you _____

_____

   Here are some other things you can do: _____

_____

_____

   You can also _____

_____

   Good luck!

   Arby

Activity 2

Congratulations! You've just won $100,000, but there is one condition: You have to spend one half of the money ($50,000) on your classmates.
   Work with a partner to make a list here, giving the reason for each gift beside it.
   When you are ready, tell the class what gifts you have decided on.

Gift	Person	Reason

Activity 3

A famous United States President, John F. Kennedy, once said, "Ask not what your country can do for you; ask what you can do for your country." Discuss the meaning of this statement.
   (Kennedy used the more formal "Ask not" rather than "Do not ask" or "Don't ask." Why do you think this is so?)

Activity 4

Form a group of at least five people. It is lunchtime and you are very hungry. A member of your group has volunteered to go to the local fast-food restaurant to pick up a hamburger, a chicken sandwich, or a hot dog for you. Look at the menu below and decide on your order.

MONSTERBURGERS

Hot dog, chicken sandwich, or burger with any of the following:

ketchup	cheese	mustard
tomatoes	mayonnaise	lettuce
pickles	bacon	avocado
onions	French fries	coleslaw

The first person in the group will give his or her order:

Carmen: I'm ordering a hot dog with mustard and ketchup and French fries for me.

The second person repeats the last order and adds his or her own.

Lu: I'm ordering a hot dog with mustard and ketchup and French fries for Carmen and a chicken sandwich with lettuce, tomato, and avocado for me.

The third person repeats Carmen and Lu's orders and adds his or her own. Continue like this until you have remembered everybody's order.

Finally, try to do this with the whole class!

Activity 5

Work in a group.

Choose one of the verbs from the list below. Prepare to act out a skit or short situation that demonstrates the verb. You can speak, but **you must not use the verb itself**. Your classmates will try to guess the verb you chose.

Your teacher will demonstrate this for you first.

give to	buy for	carry to	carry for
open for	make for	cook for	knit for
fix for	hand to	send to	sell to

Now, choose one of the statements from the list below. With your group, prepare to act out a skit or short situation to demonstrate the statement, **but do not use the statement itself.** Your classmates will try to guess which one you chose. Your teacher will demonstrate this for you first.

He/She bought him/her (something).
He/She cooked him/her (something).
He/She made him/her (something).
He/She carried (something) for him/her.
He/She built (something) for someone.
He/She bought (something) for him/her.
He/She cooked (something) for him/her.
He/She made (something) for him/her.
He/She opened (something) for him/her.
He/She built him/her (something).

22

The Passive

Task

You are gathering information for a book on Campinilea, an island located off the coast of Peru. The first chapter of the book is called "The Products and Natural Resources of Campinilea." Use the map to match the resources with the places they are found:

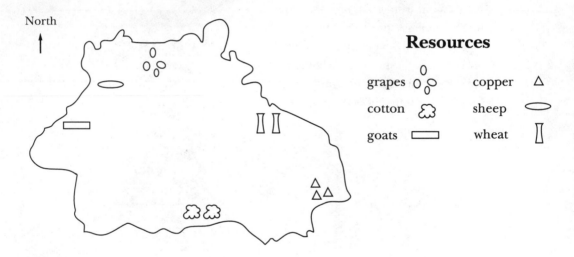

They cultivate   wheat in the East.
They raise   copper in the Southeast.
They grow   sheep in the Northwest.
They grow   grapes in the North.
They mine   goats in the West.
They raise   cotton in the South.

Which of the following statements sounds better for your chapter on the products and natural resources of Campinilea?

Grapes are cultivated in the North. OR They cultivate grapes in the North.

Why do you think this is so?

Focus 1

Passive versus Active

USE

- The active voice emphasizes *the person* who performs an action:

  (a) Farmers cultivate grapes in the North.

- When you want to emphasize *the action or result of the action* and not the person who performs it, you can use the passive:

  (b) Grapes are cultivated in the North.

- We often use the passive when we do not know exactly who performed an action or when it is not important to know who performed it.

- The passive is more formal than the active and is therefore more common in writing, particularly scientific and technological writing, than in conversation. The passive is also very common in news reports.

Focus 2

FORM

How to Form the Passive

FORM

- To form the passive, use the appropriate tense of *be*, followed by the past participle (pp):

Simple Present	am/is/are	+ pp	Beer **is produced** here.
Present Progressive	am/is/are being	+ pp	Beer **is being produced** here right now.
Simple Past	was/were	+ pp	Beer **was produced** here.
Past Progressive	was/were being	+ pp	Beer **was being produced** here ten years ago.
Present Perfect	have/has been	+ pp	Beer **has been produced** here since 1900.
Past Perfect	had been	+ pp	Beer **had been produced** here when the island was discovered.
Future (will)	will be	+ pp	Beer **will be produced** here next year.
Future (be going to)	am/is/are going to be	+ pp	Beer **is going to be produced** here.

- Present perfect progressive and past perfect progressive are rarely used in the passive.

Exercise 1

Change the statements about the natural resources of Campinilea in the Task so that they more appropriately fit a chapter on the topic of products and natural resources. The first one has been done for you.

1. *Grapes are cultivated in the North* .

2. _____ .

3. _____ .

4. _____ .

5. _____ .

6. _____ .

Exercise 2

The second chapter of the book on Campinilea is called "The People of Campinilea and their Customs." Look at the following statements about Campinilea; write *1* beside those which you think belong to Chapter 1 (Products and Resources) and *2* beside those which you think belong to Chapter 2 (People and Customs).

1. In the West, unmarried women leave their family homes at the age of 25 and raise goats in the mountains.
2. Miners mined silver throughout the island during the last century.
3. They will plant the first crop of rice in the South next year.
4. In the Southeast, fathers take their oldest sons to the copper mines on their 12th birthday in a special ceremony to teach them the legends and rituals associated with Campinilean copper.
5. Easterners are more traditional than Southerners; for example, farmers in the East have harvested wheat in the same way for hundreds of years, while those in the South are constantly exploring new techniques for growing cotton.
6. They have produced grapes in Campinilea for only a few years.

Do you think it would be appropriate to use the passive in any of these statements? Why do you think this? Rewrite those statements here:

_____

_____

_____

Exercise 3

Complete the following report about the products of Campinilea, using the appropriate form of the passive.

Campinilea is well-known for a number of products that are popular with tourists. For example, traditional sweaters (1) _____ (make) from the wool that (2) _____ (produce) in the South. This wool (3) _____ also _____ (send) to the Southwest region of the island, where it (4) _____ (weave) into colorful rugs. These rugs (5) _____ (sell) all over the world. Another popular product is jewelry. Rings and necklaces in traditional designs (6) _____ (make) from the copper that (7) _____ (mine) in the Southeast. The wine that (8) _____ (serve) in restaurants in the capital (9) _____ (make) from grapes that (10) _____ (cultivate) in the North. Visitors also enjoy Campinilean cheeses and bread, all of which (11) _____ (produce) locally.

Exercise 4

Complete the following, using appropriate tenses.

Adventurous tourists are beginning to discover Campinilea, and the island is hard at work getting ready to welcome more visitors. A new airport (1) _____ (build) last year, and at the moment, hotels (2) _____ (construct) along the southern beaches. A new road (3) _____ (finish) next year so visitors will be able to reach the northern region. Five years ago, very little (4) _____ (know) about Campinilea; but last year, three books (5) _____ (write) about the island, and several guide books (6) _____ (publish). At the moment, these books (7) _____ (translate) into different languages. English (8) _____ (teach) in schools so many Campinileans know a little English, but not many other foreign languages (9) _____ (speak).

Tourism has brought many changes to this small island, and people are afraid that it will have a negative effect on the traditional customs and culture of the people. For example, last month in the capital, several young Campinileans (10) _____ (arrest) for being drunk in public, and some tourists (11) _____ (rob) near the beach. However, if you leave the tourist areas and go up to the mountains, you will find that life is still the same as it was hundreds of years ago. For example, since the sixteenth century, the same tribal dances (12) _____ (perform) to celebrate the Campinilean new year, and the same type of food (13) _____ (serve). For centuries, visitors (14) _____ (invite) to join Campinileans in the celebration of festivals, and you will find traditional Campinilean hospitality in these regions has not changed at all.

Focus 3

USE

Including the Agent

USE

- We can include the agent (the person who performs an action) in the passive in the following situations:
  - To add new information:
    - **(a)** Tribal dances are performed every night. During the week, they are performed **by women**, and on weekends they are performed **by men**.

  In this case, it is necessary to include the agents *by women* and *by men* because they add **new** information to our knowledge of tribal dances.

  Compare these two statements:

  (b) Wheat is grown in the East.

  (c) Wheat is grown in the East by farmers.

  Sentence (c) sounds strange because **we already know** or **understand** the identity of the agent (farmers) from the context. Therefore, when you know or understand the identity of the agent, the *by* + agent phrase is unnecessary.

- With proper names or well-known people:

  (d) Campinilea was discovered by Francisco Pizarro.

  The agent is important here because Pizarro is well known. The *by* + agent phrase is commonly used to talk about works of art, well-known inventions, discoveries, historical events, and famous achievements:

  (e) *Hamlet* was written **by William Shakespeare**.

  (f) Many South American countries were liberated **by Simón Bolívar**.

- When the identity of the agent is unexpected or surprising:

  (g) I can't believe it! This novel was written by **a fourteen-year-old.**

- It is important to keep in mind, however, that in most of the situations where the passive is used, the *by* + agent phrase does not occur.

Exercise 5

Decide if the *by* + agent phrase is necessary in all of the following. Cross out the *by* phrases that you think are unnecessary.

1. Copper has been mined by miners for hundreds of years in Campinilea.
2. Campinilea was described by Jules Verne in one of his novels.
3. Cotton is grown by Campinileans in the south of Campinilea.
4. Hotels are being built by builders along the southern beaches.
5. Campinilea was colonized by the Spanish for many years.
6. English is taught by teachers in Campinilean schools.
7. Wheat is grown by Campinileans in eastern Campinilea. It is planted by men, and it is harvested by women and children.
8. Next year several new hotels in Campinilia will be built by American developers.
9. Rugs have been produced by people in Campinilea for centuries. They are woven by women from the mountain tribes and are then transported to the capital by mule and are sold in the markets by relatives of the weavers.
10. In restaurants in the city, fine Campinilean wines are served by waiters. These wines are rarely drunk by Campinileans, but they are much appreciated by foreign tourists.

Exercise 6

With the growth of tourism, petty crime has unfortunately increased in Campinilea. The Campinilean police are currently investigating a robbery that took place in a hotel room a few nights ago.

Work with a partner. One of you should look at page 245 (Picture A), and one of you should look at page 247 (Picture B). One of you has a picture of the room **before** the robbery, and the other has a picture of the room **after** the robbery. Seven different things were done to the room. *Without looking at your partner's picture,* find what these seven things were and complete the report below.

Last night the police were called in to investigate a robbery that took place at the Hotel Paraiso. The identity of the thief is still unknown. The police took note of several unusual occurrences. For

example _____

_____

_____

Members of the public have been asked to contact the police with any information about the identity of the thief. Any information leading to an arrest will be rewarded.

Activities

Activity 1

Work in pairs. Try to think of 20 different achievements (discoveries, inventions, or works of art), as well as the name of the person(s) who created them. For example:

    The telephone   Alexander Graham Bell

(There are some more ideas to get you going at the bottom of the page, but you probably have better ideas of your own.)

Write each name on an index card and then write each achievement on a *different* index card. You should have a total of 40 cards:

Hamlet

William Shakespeare

Now you are ready to play Achievement Snap:

1. Get together with another pair. Put all your "People Cards" in one deck and all your "Achievement Cards" in another deck. Shuffle each deck carefully.
2. Put the deck of Achievement Cards facedown on a table.
3. Deal the People Cards to the players. Each player should have several cards. Do not look at your cards.

4. The dealer turns over the first Achievement Card and puts down his/her first People Card. The object of the game is to make a correct match between Achievement and Person.

5. Keep taking turns at putting down People Cards until a match is made. The first person to spot a match shouts "snap" loudly and verbalizes the match: "The telephone was invented by Alexander Graham Bell." If everyone agrees that the match is factually correct **and** grammatical, the player takes the pile of People Cards on the table.

6. The winner is the person who collects the most People Cards.

(Note: It is still possible to continue playing after you lose all your People Cards. If you correctly spot a "match," you can collect the cards on the table.)

Some ideas:

Mona Lisa	Leonardo da Vinci
hydrogen bomb	Edward Teller
photography	Louis Daguerre
War and Peace	Leo Tolstoy
"Yesterday"	John Lennon and Paul McCartney
Psycho	Alfred Hitchcock
Mount Everest	Tenzing

Remember to use an appropriate verb in matching the person and the achievement. Common verbs include: *compose, write, discover, invent, climb, direct, sing, paint.*

PICTURE A

Activity 2

Make a presentation (oral or written) on your country or on a place that you know well. Describe the resources and products, any changes over time, and any predictions for the future.

Activity 3

It has been suggested that young people today do not have enough "general knowledge" and that they know less about the world than older people do. The purpose of this activity is to make a survey of your local community to find out if this is true. You will be interviewing North Americans of different ages and finding out about their levels of knowledge on a number of general topics.

The categories of the survey are as follows:

Discoveries   Inventions   Works of art

First, form specific project groups. One group will survey knowledge of discoveries, another, knowledge of inventions, and another, knowledge of works of art. In your group, decide on ten questions on your topic. For example, under the topic of discoveries, you could include:

Who was Brazil discovered by?
Who was radium discovered by?

You may need to research your topics in a library to be sure of your own answers. Next, share your group's proposed questions with the rest of the class to see what feedback and suggestions they give you. Decide on how many people you should all survey.

After that, administer your survey by asking native speakers the questions and noting their answers. You should also take note of their gender, their occupations, and their age category; for example, under 18 / 18 – 25 / 26 – 35 / 36 – 45 / 46 – 55 / over 55. (You need to be careful with this, because many people are sensitive about their ages.) Each person in the group is responsible for interviewing a specific number of different people.

When you have gathered all your information, meet with your group to share your findings. Put all your group's data together and decide how best to present your results. Use charts and diagrams as necessary. Present your group's findings to the rest of the class.

Finally, write a report of the results of the whole survey, showing the general conclusions. Remember to announce your purpose in writing the report; for example:

It has been argued that young people today do not have enough general knowledge and that they know less about the world than older people do. Our class was interested in finding out if this was true for people in our local community. In this report, I will describe the survey we designed and discuss the results we obtained.

Activity 4

Walk around your neighborhood or city. What is being done to make it a better place to live in?

Report on your findings to your classmates: While I was walking in the neighborhood, I noticed that. . . .

In what ways do you think your neighborhood/city will be a better place in the future?

PICTURE B

247

23

Get-Passive

Task

What do you think probably happened?

Now match the captions to the pictures.

a.

b.

c.

d.

e.

1. **A:** It's **your** fault. You broke it! _____
   B: No I didn't! **You** did it!
2. Your children broke my vase. _____
3. We're very sorry that we broke your vase. _____
4. This vase was broken by your children! _____
5. It was an accident! We were playing on the couch,
   and, somehow the vase got broken. _____

Focus 1

USE

Be-Passive versus *Get*-Passive

USE

- Unit 22 discusses the way you can emphasize an action or result over its agent by using the passive (*be* + past participle). Another way to do this is to use the *get*-passive:

  (a) Her car was stolen last night.

  (b) Her car got stolen last night.

- We usually use the *get*-passive to talk about unexpected actions or events—things which happen suddenly and without warning:

  (c) It suddenly started to rain and we all got soaked.

  (d) She got hit by a car while she was crossing the road.

Exercise 1

Look back at the statements in the Task. Why do you think the passive is used in some of these statements and not in others? Why do you think the *get*-passive is used in 5?

Focus 2

When to Use *Get*-Passive

USE

- *Get*-passives are more informal than passives with *be*. *Get*-passives are very common in conversation but are usually not appropriate in writing or in more formal spoken situations:

    (a) To a friend: Have you heard the news? Isao's car **got stolen**!

    (b) From a police report: A white Honda Civic **was stolen** last night.

- The agent + *by* phrase are not usually included in *get*-passive statements.

Exercise 2

Read the following situations. What do you think probably happened before each one? Match the situation with one of the previous events in the box below.

SITUATION	PREVIOUS EVENT
1. Oh, no! Not my clean white shirt!	_____
2. I'm sorry we're late. Terry refused to stop and ask for directions.	_____
3. It's so exciting to see my name in print.	_____
4. I told you not to leave it outside at night!	_____
5. When I came back to the parking lot, I found these dents on the side.	_____
6. They took him straight to the hospital by ambulance.	_____
7. Thank you for all your support. Now that I am mayor, I will work to improve our schools.	_____
8. The packet's empty, and there are only a few crumbs left!	_____

(a) They got lost.	**(b)** His car got hit.
(c) Someone got injured.	**(d)** Some wine got spilled.
(e) All the cookies got eaten.	**(f)** She got elected to public office.
(g) His book got published.	**(h)** Her bike got stolen.

Focus 3

FORM

How to Form the *Get*-Passive

FORM

- We can use the *get*-passive with a variety of tenses. (pp = past participle)

Present Simple	get	+ pp	Her cookies always **get eaten.**
Present Progressive	am/is/are getting	+ pp	Her cookies **are getting eaten.**
Past Simple	got	+ pp	Her cookies **got eaten.**
Past Progressive	was/were getting	+ pp	Her cookies **were getting eaten.**
Present Perfect	have/has gotten	+ pp	Her cookies **have gotten eaten.**
Past Perfect	had gotten	+ pp	Her cookies **had gotten eaten.**
Future (will)	will get	+ pp	Her cookies **will get eaten.**
(going to)	am/is/are going to get	+ pp	Her cookies are **going to get eaten.**

- QUESTIONS: Present and Past Simple:

| *Do/does* + | subject + | *get* + | pp | Do her cookies **get eaten?** |
| *Did* + | subject + | *get* + | pp | Did her cookies **get eaten?** |

- NEGATIVE: Present and Past Simple:

| subject + | *do/does* + (*don't/doesn't*) | *not* + | *get* + | pp | Her cookies **do not get eaten.** |
| subject + | *did* + (*didn't*) | *not* + | *get* + | pp | Her cookies **did not get eaten.** |

Exercise 3

Complete the following with *get*-passive and the appropriate tense.

1. **A:** I think I've prepared too much food for tomorrow's party.

   B: Don't worry. It _____ all _____ (eat).

2. **A:** Where's your car?

   B: It's _____ (fix).

3. **A:** How was your vacation last month?

   B: Terrible. We _____ (rob) and all our traveler's checks _____ (take).

4. **A:** Have you heard? Chuck _____ (invite) to dinner with the President at the White House!

   B: I don't believe it.

5. **A:** Please drive more slowly.

   B: Why?

   A: If you don't, we _____ (stop) by the Highway Patrol.

6. **A:** Are your assignments ready yet?

   B: Almost. We finished writing them last night, and now they _____ (type).

7. **A:** Do you know if Sid has moved?

   B: No. Why?

   A: I sent him a letter last week, but it _____ (return) yesterday with no forwarding address.

   B: That's strange.

8. **A:** Al's writing a novel.

   B: Really?

   A: Yes. He hopes it _____ (publish) next year.

9. **A:** Rosa quit her job.

   B: Why?

   A: She _____ (not/pay).

10. **A:** There was a terrible accident here last night.

    B: _____ anyone _____ (hurt)?

Focus 4

Using *Get*-Passive to Show Change

USE

- The *get*-passive emphasizes a **change** in a situation:

  (a) We were soaked to the skin.   (Emphasis on the result of the rain.)

  (b) We got soaked to the skin.   (Emphasis on the process of becoming wet in the rain.)

  (c) He was injured in a car crash.   (Emphasis on the result of the car crash.)

  (d) He got injured in a car crash.   (Emphasis on the **change**: He wasn't injured before, but now he is.)

- The *get*-passive is therefore used with verbs that express actions and processes, not with existing "states":

  (e) The answer was known. (**Known** = existing state.)
  NOT: The answer got known.

  (f) They are married. (Emphasis on existing state.)

  (g) They got married last year. (Emphasis on the change in their marital status.)

SOME COMMON STATIVE VERBS

We do not generally use these verbs with *get*-passive:

own	*see*	*understand*
like	*love*	*feel*
hate	*know*	*want*

- See Unit 2 for more information on stative verbs.

Exercise 4

Where possible, rewrite the underlined verbs with *get*-passives.

1. Last week, Mervin had a dinner party. He prepared lots of food, and everything <u>was eaten</u>. ___

   _____

2. This ring is very valuable because it <u>was owned</u> by Napoleon. _____

   _____

3. We are very sorry that Mr. Gordon is leaving our company—he <u>was liked</u> and respected by us

all. _____

4. What happened to your car?

It <u>was hit</u> by a truck. _____

5. Someone broke into her house, but surprisingly, nothing <u>was taken</u>. _____

_____

6. At the time of his arrest, that man was armed and dangerous, and he <u>was wanted</u> by police in

three different states. _____

7. We really hope our book <u>will be published</u> some day. _____

_____

8. I'm sorry I'm late; I had to go to the veterinarian's because my dog <u>was attacked</u> by a cat. ___

_____

9. Many beautiful houses <u>were</u> badly <u>damaged</u> in last month's earthquake. _____

_____

10. Marilyn Monroe <u>was loved</u> by many famous men. _____

_____

Exercise 5

Tabloid newspapers present sensational, but usually untrue, stories. Look at the following tabloid newspaper headlines and rewrite each one as a complete sentence. Use a *get*-passive wherever possible; use a *be*-passive where you cannot use a *get*-passive.

1. BABY KILLED BY GIANT COCKROACHES
2. ELVIS SEEN IN SUPERMARKET LINE
3. VICE-PRESIDENT KIDNAPPED BY SPACE ALIENS
4. BILL AND HILLARY TO DIVORCE?
5. WORLD'S WORST HUSBAND MARRIED 36 TIMES
6. FALSE TEETH STUCK IN MAN'S THROAT FOR SIX MONTHS

What do you think each headline is about? Why?

Activities

Activity 1

Look at the following tabloid headlines and ask a native speaker to explain what she or he thinks the headline means. Tape the conversation and then listen to the recording to see if she or he uses any passive forms in his or her explanation. Share your findings with the rest of the class.

    WOMAN HYPNOTIZED BY ALIENS

    MAN'S LIFE SAVED BY HITCHHIKING GHOST

    SUITCASE DROPPED 5,000 FEET BY AIRLINE

    HUBBY BURNS TO A CRISP AS WOODEN LEG TORCHED BY WIFE

    WOMAN PREGNANT WITH DAUGHTER'S BABY

Activity 2

In this activity, you will make a chain story about somebody's bad day—a day when everything went wrong. One student will start the story and will continue until she or he uses a *get*-passive. When she or he uses a *get*-passive, the next person will continue.

Student 1: Andy had a really bad day. First, he overslept. When he got dressed, he forget to put his pants on.

Student 2: He ran out of the house, but he got embarrassed when he realized he had forgotten his pants.

Student 3: etc., etc.

Activity 3

Have **you** ever had a really bad day? A day when everything went wrong, through no fault of your own? Describe the day, using *get*-passive where possible.

Activity 4

The purpose of this activity is to analyze native speakers' use of *get*-passives. Arrange to have a conversation with a native-speaker of English. Ask him or her to tell you about a really frightening experience s/he once had. Find out how it happened. Tape your conversation, and afterward listen to your recording to see if the *get*-passive was used and in what ways. Share your findings with the rest of the class.

UNIT

24

Modals of Probability and Possibility

Could, May, Might, Must

Task

One evening toward the end of March, a New York taxi driver found that someone had left a briefcase on the back seat of his cab. When he opened it, he found that the briefcase was empty, except for the things you can see on pages 257 and 258. Examine these carefully. Can you find any clues about the identity of the owner of the briefcase? Use the chart below to write down your ideas and to show how certain you are about them.

GUESSES	HOW CERTAIN ARE YOU?		
	Less Than 50% Certain (it's possible)	90% Certain (it's probable)	100% Certain (it's certain)
Name			
Sex			
Age			
Marital Status			
Occupation			
Likes and Interests			
Family and Friends			
Habits			
Recent Activities			
Future Plans			
Anything else?			

SUNDAY	MONDAY	TUESDAY	WEDNESDAY	THURSDAY	FRIDAY	SATURDAY
1	2 *Board meeting 10:30* Send papers to Washington	3 *meeting 8* lunch: Sally 1. leave for NYC: 7:00	4 Ash Wednesday *NYC EXECUTIVE*	5 *MEETING*	6 *Return from NYC meeting: 10:30 drinks: Bob Theater 8:30*	7 *wedding anniversary* *dinner - 8*
8 *golf 9:30*	9 *Report on NYC meeting due*	10 *Sally's birthday meeting with vice president 2 p.m. movie 8*	11 *PARIS* *arrive: 14.50*	12 *MEETING*	13	14 *Call Sally*
15 Purim	16 *Accountant: 9 lunch: Robert Hayward Call Paris office*	17 St. Patrick's Day *Opera 7:30*	18 *Visitors from Tokyo office dinner: Japanese restaurant - 7 p.m.*	19	20 *Export meeting*	21 Spring Begins *tennis 2 p.m. Mike* *kids home from school*
22 *golf 9:30*	23 *Japanese class*	24 *doctor: 8 Sales meeting 10:30*	25 *9:00 accountant tennis: Mike*	26 *lunch: Sally*	27 *doctor: 9 10:00 sales meeting Japanese class*	28 *check passport*
29 *TOKYO?*	30	31				

USE

Expressing Possibility and Probability

USE

- There are several ways of expressing possibility or probability. The form you choose depends on how certain you feel about the topic:

	Possible (less than 50% certain)	Probable (about 90% certain)	Certain (100% certain)
More Certain ↑ ↓ **Less Certain**	**(a)** He *may* smoke. **(b)** He *might* smoke. **(c)** He *could* smoke.	**(g)** He *must* smoke.	**(i)** He *smokes.*
More Certain ↑ ↓ **Less Certain**	**(d)** She *may* be a doctor. **(e)** She *might* be a doctor. **(f)** She *could* be a doctor.	**(h)** She *must* be a doctor.	**(j)** She *is* a doctor.

- For information on some other ways of using *could, might, may* and *must*, see Units 7, 8, and 15.

Focus 2

Modals of Probability and Possibility

FORM

- *Could, might, may* and *must* are modal auxiliaries, and like most other modal auxiliaries, they are followed by the infinitive without *to*:
    - **(a)** That woman looks familiar: She **could be** a movie star.
    - **(b)** Lila always gets excellent grades: She **must study** a lot.
- They do not change to agree with the subject:
    - **(c)** You **must know a lot** of interesting people.
      Carol **must know a lot** of interesting people.
    - **(d)** They **might be janitors**, but I doubt it.
      He **might be a janitor**, but I doubt it.
    - **(e)** I **may have the information** you need.
      Shirley **may have the information** you need.
- Negatives are formed without *do*:
    - **(f)** She **must not** like cats.
      They **might not** know about the party.

Exercise 1

Turn back to the Task.

Make statements about the owner of the briefcase. Use *could, might, may,* or *must* to show how certain you feel. Share your opinions with your classmates and be ready to justify them as necessary.

EXAMPLE: NAME: *In my opinion, the owner of the briefcase might be called C. Murray because this name is on the boarding pass. However, this boarding pass could belong to somebody else.*

1. SEX: In my opinion, the owner of the briefcase _____

   because _____

   _____ .

2. OCCUPATION: I believe she or he _____ because _____

   _____ .

3. MARITAL STATUS: This person _____ . I think this because

   _____ .

4. LIKES AND INTERESTS: _____

_____ .

5. HABITS: _____

_____ .

6. AGE: _____

_____ .

Focus 3

FORM

Probability and Possibility in the Past

FORM

- To express possibility and probability in the past:
  - Modal auxiliary + *have* + past participle
    - **(a)** I'm not sure how Liz went home; she **could have taken** a cab.
    - **(b)** There's nobody here; they **must have gone** out.

Exercise 2

Turn back to the Task. Make statements showing how certain you are about the person's **past** activities. Use *could, might, may,* or *must* as appropriate. Be ready to share and justify your opinions.

Exercise 3

In trying to solve crimes, detectives generally examine evidence carefully and then draw conclusions based on what they observe. Sometimes their conclusions are stronger (or more certain) than others, depending on on the evidence they have examined. Creative detectives (like Sherlock Holmes) are famous for examining *all* possibilities in a case. What might Sherlock Holmes conclude about the following people?

> **EXAMPLE:** 1. A woman with a yellow forefinger: *She must be a heavy smoker.*
> *She might be a painter, and she might have lost her paintbrush.*

Can you think of any other possibilities? Be ready to share your ideas with your classmates.

2. A very short man with bow legs: _____

_____

_____

3. A man with a very red nose: _____

_____

_____

4. A woman with rough, hard hands: _____

_____

_____

5. A woman with a fur coat, diamonds, and chauffeur-driven limousine: _____

_____

_____

6. A man with soft, white hands: _____

_____

_____

7. A man with a lot of tattoos: _____

_____

_____

Exercise 4

The police are investigating a murder. What might Sherlock Holmes conclude about the following pieces of evidence? Get together with your classmates to share your conclusions and decide who has the most interesting theory. How probable do you think this theory is?

> The victim was found in her bedroom on the second floor of her house. The front door and her bedroom door were locked from inside. There were two wine glasses on the table in her room; one was empty, the other was full. There was an ashtray with several cigarette butts in it. The victim had a small white button in her hand and several long, blond hairs. Her watch was found on the floor; it had stopped at 11:30. The drawers of the victim's desk were open, and there were papers all over the floor. Nothing appeared to be missing.

Exercise 5

You are a reporter for your local newspaper. The editor has asked you to report on the murder described in Exercise 4, describing what you think happened and why you believe this to be so. Make a headline for your report. Display your headline and your report so that your classmates can compare the different theories about the murder.

Focus 4

FORM ● MEANING

Future Probability and Possibility

FORM
MEANING

- *Could, might,* and *may* all express possibility in the future:

  (a) There are a few clouds in the sky; it $\begin{Bmatrix} \textbf{could} \\ \textbf{might} \\ \textbf{may} \end{Bmatrix}$ rain later.

  May shows that the speaker is a little more certain.

- *Must* is not used to express probability in the future. Instead, *will* and *be going to + probably* usually express this idea:

  (b) A: Where's Anna?
  B: She'll probably get here soon.

  (c) A: What's Jim going to do after he graduates?
  B: He's probably going to travel round the world on a motorcycle.

- We use *will* and *be going to* to express certainty about the future. For more information on how to use *be going to* and *will,* see Unit 3.

Exercise 6

Turn back to the Task. From the evidence given, what can you say about the person's **future** plans? Use *could, might, may, be going to,* or *will* + *probably* as necessary. Be prepared to share and justify your answers.

Exercise 7

Choose the *best* form from the choices given below.

1. **A:** Where's Rose?
   B: I'm not sure. She _____ in the library.
   is   might be   must be

2. **A:** My daughter just got a scholarship to Stanford!
   B: You _____ be very proud of her.
   could   must   might

3. **A:** How does Sheila get to school?
   B: I don't really know. She _____ the bus.
   might take   takes   must take

4. **A:** It's really cold in here today.
   B: Yes. Somebody _____ the window open.
   must leave   might leave   must have left

5. **A:** I wonder why Zelda always wears gloves.
   B: I don't know. She _____ some kind of allergy.
   may have had   has   may have

6. **A:** Have you heard the weather forecast?
   B: No, but look at all those dark clouds in the sky. I think it _____ rain.
   could   must   is probably going to

7. **A:** Did my mother call while I was out?
   B: I'm not sure. She _____ .
   might have   might   did

8. **A:** Ellen gave a violin recital in front of 500 people yesterday. It was her first public performance.
   B: Really? She _____ very nervous.
   could have been   must be   must have been

9. **A:** Are you coming to Jeff's party?
   B: I'm not sure. I _____ go to the coast instead.
   must   will   might

10. **A:** Can I speak to Professor Carroll?
    B: She's not in her office, and she doesn't have any more classes today, so she _____ home.
    might go   must have gone   will probably go

Exercise 8

Look back at the Task. Who is this person? What do you think happened to him or her? Complete the following newspaper article with your ideas about what might have happened to him or her.

MISSING MYSTERY PERSON

It has been a week since New York taxi driver Ricardo Oliveiro found a briefcase on the back seat of his cab. It has been a week of guessing and speculation: Who is the owner of this briefcase and where is he or she now? Several different theories have been proposed, but so far the most interesting is the one which follows....

Activities

Activity 1

Can you guess what these drawings represent? Get together with a partner and see how many *different* possible interpretations you can come up with for each drawing. Classify your interpretations as "Possible," "Probable," and "Certain." Compare your answers with the rest of the class. (You can find the "official" answers on page 267.)

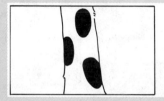 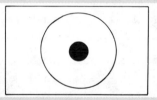 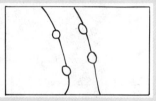

The purpose of this activity is to confuse your classmates. Form teams and create five different drawings of familiar things seen from an unusual point of view. Exchange papers. Each team receives drawings from another team. As a team, see how many different interpretations you can make for each drawing. Write them beside the drawing, showing how probable you think your interpretation is.

EXAMPLE:

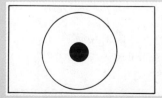

It could be a donut.
It might be a hat from above.
It could be an eyeball.

When you have made your guesses, exchange papers with another team until everyone has had a chance to "interpret" all the drawings. Which team got the most "correct" interpretations? Which team had the most creative interpretations?

Activity 2

Get together with a partner and examine the photographs below. What's going on? Who are the people? Create a story showing what you think might have happened and what might happen next. You can use the photographs in any order that you like. Compare your story with those of your classmates. In what ways do their interpretations differ from yours?

Activity 3

Show the photographs from Activity 2 to a native speaker. Ask him or her to tell you what she or he thinks might have happened and what might happen next. If possible, tape the answers. Listen to the tape and take special note of the different ways the native speaker expresses possibility and probability. Share your findings with the rest of the class.

Activity 4

In the Task, you looked at the contents of somebody's briefcase and made guesses about his or her identity. The purpose of this activity is to create your own "mystery person." Form groups and collect a number of items that somebody might carry in his/her pockets (tickets, bills, photographs, business cards, etc.). Choose between eight to ten items, put them in a bag, and bring them to class. Exchange bags with another group. With your group, examine the contents of your bag and try to decide on the possible identity of the owner, using the same categories as the Task. When everyone is ready, share your conclusions with the rest of the class, showing how certain you are. Remember, your classmates might ask you to justify your conclusions, so be ready to justify each one.

Activity 5

Write a profile of the mystery person your group presented to the class in Activity 4. Make sure you have an introduction and that you provide evidence to support your conclusions. When you finish writing, read your profile to see how much of the language discussed in this unit you were able to use.

"Official" Answers to Activity 1

1. A giraffe passing a window.
2. A pencil seen from the end.
3. A cat climbing a tree.

25

Noun Complements
That Clauses

Task

A. React to each of the following statements, using the following scale:

1	2	3	4	5
strongly agree	agree	neutral/ no opinion	disagree	strongly disagree

In the next ten years...

1. we will find a cure for AIDS.	1	2	3	4	5
2. the rain forests will disappear.	1	2	3	4	5
3. marijuana will be legalized in western countries.	1	2	3	4	5
4. people will become less dependent on automobiles.	1	2	3	4	5
5. crime will decrease.	1	2	3	4	5
6. we will stop killing animals for their fur.	1	2	3	4	5
7. homelessness will decrease.	1	2	3	4	5
8. communism as a political system will disappear entirely.	1	2	3	4	5
9. women will have the same economic rights as men.	1	2	3	4	5
10. there will be less racial discrimination.	1	2	3	4	5
11. there will be another world war.	1	2	3	4	5
12. drinking, like smoking, will become socially less acceptable.	1	2	3	4	5

B. Now find out what other students have said and tell them your opinions, using:

"I agree/strongly agree with the statement that in ten years..."
OR "I disagree/strongly disagree with the statement that in ten years..."
OR "I am neutral or have no opinion about the statement that in ten years..."

C. Report your class's opinions by using "think that," "believe that," "feel that," etc. For example, "Five people believe that . . . ," "Three people don't think that . . ."

Focus 1

FORM ● MEANING

Using *That* Clauses in Sentences

FORM
MEANING

- We often use *that* clauses (the word *that* + a sentence) with verbs that express beliefs, ideas, opinions, or facts.

  I know that. . . .
  I believe that. . . .
  I think that. . . .
  I doubt that. . . .

- A *that* clause is a noun phrase. It can be used as an object to complete a sentence.

Subject	Verb	Direct Object
The police	think	that they know who robbed the bank.

Exercise 1

What do you think about some of the statements in the Task? Complete the following to make statements that are true for you.

1. I know that
2. I am not certain that
3. I am convinced that
4. I doubt that

5. It is my opinion that
6. It is unlikely that
7. It is possible that
8. It is doubtful that

Focus 2

Making *That* Clauses Negative

FORM
MEANING

- To make a sentence with a *that* clause negative, the word *not* usually comes in the first part of the sentence—in the main clause, not in the *that* clause.

Main Clause	*That* Clause
(a) I **don't** think	that we will stop killing animals for fur.
NOT: I think	that we will **not** stop killing animals for fur.

- You can also make a *that* clause negative by using words which already include a "negative" meaning, such as *doubt, unlikely, uncertain.*

  (b) I **doubt** that we will stop killing animals for fur.

  (c) It is **unlikely** that we will stop killing animals for fur.

Exercise 2

Did you disagree with some of the opinions expressed in the Task? Tell some of your "negative" reactions, using *not* in your statement, and say why your opinion differs.

> **EXAMPLE:** *I don't believe that there will be another World War in the next ten years because....*

Focus 3

USE

When to Omit the Word *That*

USE

- With verbs like *know, believe,* and *think,* we can omit the word *that,* especially in speech, when it's not necessary to be formal.

  (a) Informal: I know the Taj Mahal's in India.

  (b) More formal: I know that the Taj Mahal is in India.

Exercise 3

Combine the two short statements in the conversation below into one longer statement using a *that* clause in your answer. If Person (b) starts his or her short statement with *It* or *That*, use *It* as the subject in your longer statement. (See Example 1.) If Person (b) starts his or her short statement with *I*, use that person's name as the subject in your longer statement. (See Example 2.)

EXAMPLES: 1. (a) Betty: We can buy a car.
          (b) Bob: It's possible.
          It's possible that Betty and Bob can buy a car.
      2. (a) Betty: It's raining.
          (b) Bob: I know.
          Bob knows that it's raining.

3. (a) Betty: My umbrella's broken.
   (b) Bob: That's unfortunate.

4. (a) Betty: We'll buy a car this week!
   (b) Bob: It's unlikely.

5. (a) Betty: I don't like my job.
   (b) Bob: That's too bad.

6. (a) Bob: I like my job.
   (b) Betty: I know.

7. (a) Bob: You should quit your job.
   (b) Betty: That's your opinion.

8. (a) Betty: We need the money.
   (b) Bob: I agree.

9. (a) Betty: The cost of living is rising.
   (b) Bob: It's true.

10. (a) Betty: I'm pregnant.
    (b) Bob: That's a surprise!

11. (a) Betty: We love each other.
    (b) Bob: We're lucky.

Exercise 4

Rewrite the following statements into one sentence, using a *that* clause. You do not need to use every word in the original statements as long as your statement makes sense and has all the important information.

EXAMPLE: 1. Learning another language is important for everyone. This is what our English instructor thinks.

    Our English instructor thinks (that) learning another language is important for everyone.

2. An open-minded attitude is helpful in learning a language. This is what our English instructor believes.

3. Many Americans have never studied a foreign language. It is shocking.

4. Since English is an important world language used in business, it is not necessary to learn another language. This is what many Americans feel.

5. Learning another language is one way of showing respect to people from other countries. I believe this.

6. Some of us speak three or four languages. This amazes our English instructor.

Activities

Activity 1

Use the rating scale and the statements in the Task to interview native speakers of English for their opinions. Summarize the results of your survey for the rest of the class.

Activity 2

In teams, imagine that you are members of a group of "world citizens" who have been asked by a panel of international policy-makers to think about ways to solve one of the world's problems.

First, you will need to choose a world problem and discuss some of the steps that must be taken in order to begin solving this problem. Then you will need to make formal suggestions to the panel. Use the following sentence beginnings to guide you in making your report:

We recommend that . . .
We suggest that . . .
We propose that . . .

Activity 3

In order to support your choices in Activity 2, you will need to make predictions about what might happen if your plan is **not** implemented/listened to. Use adjectives from the following list to make predictions about what could happen. (It is *certain* that . . . = strong prediction; It is *unlikely* that . . . = weak prediction.)

likely	unlikely
possible	certain
probable	doubtful

Activity 4

Before you present a final report to the international policymakers, you want to check to see if there is public support for your opinion. Make a short survey of people outside of your class to see if they agree with your opinions. You can model your survey after the Task, or you can design your own questionnaire, with a few specific questions about the issue you have chosen.

Activity 5

To follow up your work in the previous activities, write a short report that summarizes what you learned about one of the world's problems. In this report: 1) describe the problem; 2) report the results of the survey; 3) give your group's recommendations, and 4) predict the outcome if these recommendations are not followed.

UNIT 26

Phrasal Verbs

Task

What is happening in the cartoons below? First, work with a partner to describe the action in each sequence. Then, explain how the four sequences fit together to make a story.

Share your story with other classmates. When you have heard other people's stories, vote on whose story explains the four sequences the best. Whose story makes the most sense and is the most interesting?

Focus 1

Phrasal Verbs

FORM
MEANING

- Many common verbs are in two parts: verb + particle. We often call these **phrasal verbs.** It is usually difficult to guess the meaning of phrasal verbs, even if you know the meaning of the parts alone. A good dictionary will help you. For example,

  (a) The waiter did not **wait on** us for a long time. (People who **wait on** tables do very little "waiting"; nor do they do anything "on" tables or "on" people. To **wait on** means to serve people food.)

Exercise 1

Work with your original partner and look back at the cartoons in the Task. For each "frame" (each box) in the sequence, use at least one phrasal verb to describe what is happening, and write it in the list below. Be sure that your description fits in with the story you made up in the Task.

When everyone is finished, share your list with other students. If other students came up with different phrasal verbs to describe the action in the story, add these to your list.

SEQUENCE 1

1. _____

2. _____

3. _____

4. _____

SEQUENCE 2

1. _____

2. _____

3. _____

4. _____

SEQUENCE 3

1. _____

2. _____

3. _____

4. _____

SEQUENCE 4

1. _____

2. _____

3. _____

4. _____

Exercise 2

Add the missing particles to the common phrasal verbs in the following sentences. Use the list below. (Some of these are from your list in Exercise 1.)

break down	call up	find out	put off
take back	take up	throw away	get by
run out	look for	call on	throw out
take off	put on	wear out	

New Clothes, Old Clothes, Shopping for Clothes

Kent: Why are you taking (1) _____ your shoes? I thought you were going to go

for a walk.

Mieko: I am going to put (2) _____ my boots. It's raining outside.

Kent: I thought those boots were too small. You said you wanted to take them (3)_____

to the store. Did you find (4) _____ if they have a bigger size?

Mieko: I called (5) _____ the store. And the salesperson said they ran

(6) _____ of the old style. But they can look (7) _____

them in their warehouse if I want to wait. See these boots, though?—I've put

(8) _____ the decision too long!

Kent: Yes, your boots don't look new anymore. They're beginning to wear (9) _____

already.

Mieko: Yeah, but fortunately they feel like they're the right size now. They're comfortable.

So I can get (10) _____ with these, no problem. I hope they last a long

time, like my old ones. I finally threw those old ones (11) _____ four

years after I bought them!

Exercise 3

Replace the underlined verbs, along with other words in some sentences, with an appropriate phrasal verb from the list below. (Some of these are from your list in Exercise 1.)

pass away	run into	get on
call up	put off	go over
cheer up	drop in on	find out

Keeping in Touch with Friends, Talking about Troubles

1. Sally tried to <u>phone</u> Marie yesterday, but Marie's line was busy.
2. So she decide to <u>visit</u> her <u>unexpectedly</u>.
3. Earlier that day, Sally <u>saw</u> their friend Ron as he was leaving the apartment building.
4. He was ready to <u>enter</u> the bus to go to his sister's house.
5. He told Sally that his grandfather had <u>died</u>.
6. Of course, Sally was sorry to <u>hear</u> that.
7. She suggested to Marie that the three friends <u>postpone</u> the dinner party they had been planning.
8. Marie agreed, and she also thought they should do something to <u>make</u> Ron <u>feel better</u>.
9. They decided to <u>go</u> to Ron's sister's, in another part of the city, and give their family a bouquet of flowers and a casserole for dinner.

Focus 2

Separable and Inseparable Phrasal Verbs

FORM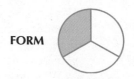

- We can separate some phrasal verbs. This means that the particle does not need to directly follow the verb. But if the word that separates the verb from the particle is a **pronoun**, the particle must move to a position after the pronoun.

  - **Separable phrasal verb:** turn on

    (a) She **turned on** the light. OR

    (b) She **turned** the light **on**.

    (c) She **turned** it **on**.
       NOT: She **turned on** it.

  - **Separable phrasal verb:** clean up

    (d) He **cleaned up** his room. OR

    (e) He **cleaned** his room **up**.

    (f) He **cleaned** it **up**.
       NOT: He **cleaned up** it.

- It is difficult to guess whether phrasal verbs are separable or inseparable; this is something that you will need to learn gradually. Even if a pronoun is used with an inseparable phrasal verb, the verb and the particle stay together.

  - **Inseparable phrasal verb:** run into

    (g) Yesterday I **ran into** my friend Sal. OR

    (h) Yesterday I **ran into** her.
       NOT: Yesterday I **ran** my friend Sal **into**.
       NOT: Yesterday I **ran** her **into**.

Exercise 4

Work with a classmate to come up with a list of all the phrasal verbs that you can remember from this unit so far. You have only five minutes to complete this list, so work quickly! If you have extra time, try to think of other phrasal verbs and add these to the list. In order to add these to the list, you must make sure you know the meaning of these phrasal verbs and can use them in a sentence.

When five minutes are up, your teacher will stop you and check to see whose list is the longest. If you added "new" phrasal verbs that aren't in this unit, your teacher will check to see if you can use these correctly in a sentence.

Your next task is to see if you can guess whether the phrasal verbs you have listed are separable or inseparable. Mark these with *S* for *Separable* or *I* for *Inseparable*. Look back at the way the phrasal verbs are used in sentences to help you decide.

Then check to see how your list compares with the list below.

Separable		Inseparable	
call up	put off	drop in	look for
calm down	take back	find out	pass away
cheer up	take off	get by	pay for
clean up	throw out	get in	run into
find out	turn off	get on	wait on
help out	turn on	get out	work out
look up	wake up	go over	
pick up	wear out		
put on			

Exercise 5

Are the <u>underlined</u> phrasal verbs correct in the following sentences? If you're not sure, use the list in Exercise 4 and the information in Focus 2. If a phrasal verb is used incorrectly, say what's wrong with it and correct it.

1. Cherie always shows up for work on time. She has to <u>get on</u> the bus at 7:00 A.M., but yesterday she overslept and didn't <u>get</u> it <u>on</u> until 8:00. She was late for work!

2. Last week Sharifah went through her closet and <u>threw</u> all the clothes that were several years old <u>out</u>. Later she <u>found out</u> that her sister had wanted her to keep some of these clothes.

3. When Nina <u>ran</u> Tim <u>into</u>, he pointed out that they had not seen each other for over a year. They promised to <u>drop in</u> on each other more often.

4. After Sandra called, Al gave Graham the message to <u>call</u> Sandra <u>up</u>. Graham tried to <u>call up</u> her, but he couldn't get through because her line was busy.

5. Eli's mother <u>passed</u> last year <u>away</u>. Since she died, he's <u>put</u> the decision about what to do with her house <u>off</u>.

6. When Sally and the other children arrived at camp, the camp counselor went over the rules: The girls had to <u>clean up</u> after breakfast, and the boys had to <u>clean up</u> after lunch.

Focus 3

When Not to Separate Phrasal Verbs

- If the noun or noun phrase that separates a phrasal verb is longer than three or four words, it sounds better if the phrasal verb is **not** separated.
  - **Separable phrasal verb:** throw out
    - **(a)** AWKWARD: Last week Sharifah went through her closet and **threw** all the clothes that were several years old **out**.
    - **(b)** CORRECT: Last week Sharifah went through her closet and **threw out** all the clothes that were several years old.
    - **(c)** CORRECT: She **threw** her old clothes **out**.
    - **(d)** CORRECT: She **threw out** her old clothes.

Exercise 6

Sentence 2 in Exercise 5 should not be separated, because the noun phrase is too long (see Example in Focus 3, above). Check the other answers in Exercise 5. Are any noun phrases too long to separate the phrasal verbs? Rewrite the sentence so that it does not sound awkward (if you didn't already do this in Exercise 5).

Activities

Activity 1

Take three separate pieces of paper, and on each one write down a different phrasal verb. Try to choose a phrasal verb that you can "mime"—that is, you can imitate the action—act it out silently—so that others can guess the word(s). For example, *look for* something you lost, *put on* or *take off* clothes, etc.

Your teacher will collect all the phrasal verbs you have written down. Your task is to take three sheets of paper and then mime them in sequence.

Activity 2

See if you can fill in the missing words in the following word puzzle and use each phrasal verb in a sentence. Sometimes the word is a missing particle that all the attached verbs use in phrasal verb combinations; other times the word is a missing verb that all the attached particles use in phrasal verb combinations.

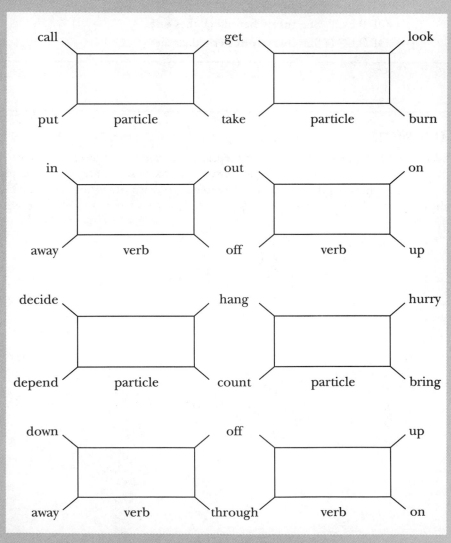

Activity 3

Phrasal verbs are very common in English. The following phrases or sentences are lines from popular songs of the late sixties and seventies. Interview native English speakers (who were born in the late forties through the early sixties) to see if they can recognize these songs. If so, can they remember the lyrics that follow these lines? Who sang the songs?

1. Don't let me down....
2. I'd love to turn you on....
3. Got up, got out of bed, dragged a comb across my head....
4. Each day when I wake up, before I put on my makeup....
5. You just keep me hanging on....
6. Wake up, little Suzie....
7. Hey, you, get off of my cloud....
8. Hang on, Sloopy....

Activity 4

In two teams, you will create a "chain story." You can assign your teacher or one student to write the sentences for the story on the board. The rules are

1. Each team will add only one sentence at a time to the story.
2. Each sentence must make sense as part of the story. In other words, each sentence must be logically "linked" to the previous sentence. (Your teacher will be the judge of this.)
3. Each sentence must contain a phrasal verb, and the phrasal verb must be used correctly.

Every time each team follows these rules correctly, they get one point. The team with the most points wins.

If you want this game to be especially challenging, there is one more rule: The phrasal verb in every new sentence must contain either the same particle as the phrasal verb in the previous sentence, or the same verb as the phrasal verb in the previous sentence.

27

Participles as Adjectives

THE 77 MOODS OF AKBAR & JEFF

LIFE IN HELL ©1988 BY MATT GROENING

HAPPY	SAD	DISMAYED	HUFFY	YEARNING	JUBILANT	DISTRAUGHT	SEDUCTIVE	PETULANT	BLISSFUL	FRUSTRATED
RAVING	SULLEN	ELATED	DEMURE	FRETFUL	DELIRIOUS	NAUGHTY	WHIMSICAL	SASSY	HYPERCRITICAL	SERENE
BLASÉ	HAUGHTY	SPUNKY	ASHAMED	BROODING	INTOXICATED	TINGLY	SEETHING	GOOFY	SULKY	CONTENTED
FROLICSOME	SARCASTIC	ABASHED	WOEFUL	GIDDY	CONTRARY	GRUMPISH	OVERJOYED	MOPY	PRISSY	BITTER
PRICKLY	FLIPPANT	SMUG	AMIABLE	INFURIATED	MOROSE	PERKY	TESTY	LACKADAISICAL	TOUCHY	CRANKY
ITCHY	LOVELORN	FRISKY	PERTURBED	LISTLESS	RESENTFUL	LONESOME	GLUM	DISTURBED	PLEASED	PEEVISH
COCKY	UNHINGED	MIRTHLESS	JADED	ENRAPTURED	DOLEFUL	INSCRUTABLE	LUSTFUL	JOLLY	DISGRUNTLED	SURPRISED

From Matt Groening, *The Big Book of Hell*, Random House, a Division of Panceon Books, New York (1990).

Task

A. Look through the adjectives above, which describe the many moods of the cartoon characters Akbar and Jeff. You have one minute to find as many *-ing* and *-ed* adjectives as possible, but you can only count the ones for which you know the meaning. Work in pairs or small groups so that you can ask other people about the meanings of words you don't know, or you can divide up the task of looking up the words in a dictionary.

_____-ing   _____-ed

_____   _____

_____   _____

_____   _____

_____   _____

_____   _____

_____   _____

B. Now match the drawings below with these adjectives.

elated   surprised   contented   seething
perturbed   yearning   frustrated   overjoyed

C. Some of these words are very similar in meaning. Underline those drawings and adjectives under B that show someone feels good. Circle those drawings and adjectives that show someone feels bad.

Focus 1

What *-ing* Words and *-ed* Words Describe

- Adjectives that end with *-ing* usually describe the **source**—the thing or person that makes us feel a certain way.
- Adjectives that end with *-ed* usually describe the **emotion**—how we feel about something.

SOURCE/BORING   EMOTION/BORED

Exercise 1

1. Draw arrows that start at the source (the reason for the feeling) and that point to the emotion (the way the person feels).
2. Use the word (on the right) to label the pictures with *-ing* adjectives (which describe the source) and *-ed* adjectives (which describe the emotion). The first one has been done for you.

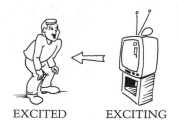

EXCITED   EXCITING

excite

disgust

shock

stimulate

amuse

embarrass

surprise

confuse

285

interest

inspire

Exercise 2

Make sentences that describe each of the illustrations in Exercise 1. Use both an *-ing* and an *-ed* adjective.

> **EXAMPLE:** 1. *The TV show was exciting. The person* (or "the TV viewer") *was excited.*

Exercise 3

Choose the correct adjective for each of the following sentences.

1. Melanie likes the family in the apartment above her, but sometimes she feels that their teenage boy is annoying/annoyed, especially when he plays his stereo too loudly.
2. However, she usually finds their presence upstairs very comforting/comforted.
3. Once she heard a frightening/frightened noise outside. She thought it was a prowler, so she called up her neighbors.
4. They invited her to their apartment for a relaxing/relaxed cup of tea and a soothing/soothed conversation.
5. This helped her to calm down, until she was no longer frightening/frightened.
6. Melanie especially likes Jane, the mother. Jane tells Melanie amusing/amused stories about her and her family members' daily life.
7. Jane's husband Bob is a shoe salesperson. Even though this may sound like a boring/bored job, it's not.
8. Lots of surprising/surprised things happen to shoe salespeople. Just last week, for example, a real prince came into the store with his bodyguards and bought 20 pairs of Italian leather shoes.

9. The prince thought Bob was such a polite and amusing/amused young man that he gave him a $50 tip.

10. Of course, Bob thought that this was very exciting/excited, and he took Jane and the family out to dinner that night.

11. Jane works part-time in a pet store as a dog groomer. She says that some of the customers never give their dogs baths. These dogs are sometimes so dirty and uncomfortable that it is shocking/shocked.

12. Jane's stories are so entertaining/entertained that Melanie usually doesn't mind the noise that Jane's teenage son makes.

13. In fact, Melanie was very disappointing/disappointed when she heard that Jane and her family might move.

Exercise 4

Circle all the *-ed* and *-ing* words in the following passage. Then decide whether the correct form of the adjective has been used. In other words, are there cases where the *-ing* adjective is used when the *-ed* adjective should be used (or vice versa)?

SHELLEY'S ANCESTORS

Shelley had an interested day yesterday. Three of her favorite cousins dropped in for an unexpected visit, and they had a very stimulating conversation. They told each other surprised stories about some of their relatives. Shelley was shocked by some of these stories. For example, when their great aunt—their grandmother's sister—was quite young, she traveled around the world, fell in love with a Dutch sailor, and had a baby but did not get married. Her embarrassing parents disowned her, but many years later they helped her raise the child. Another distant member of the family was a heroin addict in New York in the thirties, and according to Shelley's cousins' mother, he was quite a rude and disgusting fellow. This man's brother was a horse of a different color, though. Apparently he was an inspired and talented poet, who also created amused illustrations for children's books. After hearing all of these stories, Shelley realized that her family history was certainly not bored!

Activities

Activity 1

Can You Top That?

Choose an adjective below that describes an experience you have had (for example, an embarrassing moment, a boring day, an exciting date). Can you think of another experience that is even *more* embarrassing, *more* boring, or *more* exciting than the first one you thought of?

Circulate for 15 minutes and talk to your classmates to see if they have had an experience that "tops" yours—that is, an experience that is even more embarrassing, more boring, or more exciting than yours. After you have spoken to several classmates, report their experience to the class. Take a vote on who has had the most embarrassing, boring, exciting (etc.), experiences.

embarrassing	frightening
boring	horrifying
exciting	entertaining
disappointing	relaxing
shocking	disgusting
surprising	rewarding

Activity 2

Think of someone you know who is quite a character, or in other words, who stands out in some way or is easy to remember because of strong personality characteristics. Describe this person, and be sure to use some *-ed* and *-ing* adjectives in your description.

Activity 3

First think of as many *-ing* adjectives as possible. Your teacher will write each of these on a separate sheet of paper. As the game goes on, your group may add more to the list as needed.

Then you will use these words to play Password in teams or in pairs. In this game, one person (or team), the Clue-Giver, looks at the word on the piece of paper without letting the other person (or the other team) see it. Then they give a one-word clue that describes this word to the other person (or the other team), the Clue-Guesser.

The goal is to have the Clue-Guesser guess the word as soon as possible with as few clues as necessary. But the Clue-Giver can continue to give as many clues as needed in order for the word to be guessed.

Activity 4

Follow the directions for the first part of the activity above, this time using only *-ed* adjectives. Then mime these words, which are written on separate sheets of paper. When you "mime," you "act out" the word or phrase silently by using gestures and facial expressions, or by inventing some silent story that describes the word. The goal of this activity is like the last one: to have the other person (or the other team) guess what the word is as quickly as possible.

Conditionals
Future and Hypothetical

28

Task

What will happen if he doesn't stop drinking, smoking, and gambling? What do you think will happen if he stops drinking, smoking, and gambling?

You are probably sitting in a classroom right now. Or perhaps you are at home or in a library. Probably you are not in either of the following situations:

Which situation would you prefer to be in? Why? What would you do in this situation?

Focus 1

Future Conditionals

- We use future conditionals to make predictions about what will happen in the future. **Future conditionals** are formed by:

If Clause + (present tense)	Main Clause *(will/be going to* + base form of the verb)
(a) If he doesn't stop drinking	his wife will leave him.
(b) If I study hard,	I'll get a good grade.
(c) If it rains tomorrow,	I'm going to bring my umbrella.

Focus 2

Word Order in Conditionals

- In conditionals, the main clause can come first and the *if* clause can come second, with no difference in meaning:
    - **(a)** His wife will leave him if he doesn't stop drinking.
      If he doesn't stop drinking, his wife will leave him.
    - **(b)** I'll get a good grade if I study hard.
      If I study hard, I'll get a good grade.
    - **(c)** I'm going to bring my umbrella if it rains tomorrow.
      If it rains tomorrow, I'm going to bring my umbrella.
- When the main clause comes first, a comma is not needed.

Exercise 1

Make future conditional sentences that are true for you, using the following *if* clauses. If you prefer, you can switch the order of the clauses so that your main clause comes first.

1. If I get an *A* in this class,....
2. If you don't give me ten dollars right now,....
3. If my pants rip,....
4. If I lose this book,....
5. If you shout at me,....
6. If there is a fire alarm,....
7. If I don't see you tomorrow,....

Focus 3

FORM ● USE

Hypothetical Conditionals

FORM
USE

- We can also use conditionals to talk in the present tense about hypothetical situations—situations that will probably not happen. These **imaginary present conditionals**, or hypothetical conditionals, are formed by:

| *If* Clause   + | Main Clause |
(past tense)	(*would* + base verb)
(a) If Sherry came to class late,	she would be embarrassed.

(The hypothetical conditional is used in this sentence because Sherry **never** comes to class late.)

- For hypothetical conditionals, when *be* is the main verb in the *if* clause, we use *were,* the **subjunctive** form of the verb *be. Were* is used for all subjects (I, we, you, he, she, it, they).

| *If* Clause   + | Main Clause |
(*were*)	(*would*+ base verb)
(b) If I were on a desert island,	I would....
(c) If she were a man,	she would....

291

Exercise 2

The following passage tells a story about Sandira's fantasies. In each sentence, there is a situation that is not real or not likely. In other words, they are sentences that use hypothetical conditionals.

First, tell us what is **not** true about each sentence and the reason it is not true. Then, fill in the blanks in each sentence, and be sure to use the appropriate verb tense.

EXAMPLE: 1. Sandira _____ go to the movies every week if he _____ (have) enough money.

first step—what is not true about this sentence: Sandira does not go the movies every week because he doesn't have enough money.

second step—fill in the blanks: Sandira _would_ go to the movies every week if he _had_ (have) enough money.

2. If he _____ (be) rich, he _____ never cook at home, and he

_____ always go out to eat.

3. He _____ buy anything he wanted if he _____ (be) rich.

4. If he _____ (have) a girlfriend, he _____ also buy her whatever she

wanted.

5. If he _____ (buy) his girlfriend whatever she wanted, she _____

want to buy more and more.

6. If she _____ (buy) more and more, she _____ eventually run out of

things to buy.

7. She _____ fall out of love with Sandira if she _____ (run out) of

things to buy.

8. If she _____ (fall) out of love with him, he _____ be miserable.

9. If he _____ (be) miserable, he _____ go to the movies every week

to forget about his troubles.

Focus 4

Likelihood in Conditionals

MEANING

- The difference between future and hypothetical conditionals is not a difference of time. Both can talk about the future, even though hypothetical conditionals use verbs that look like the past tense form.
- The difference between real and hypothetical conditionals is a difference of likelihood: **future** conditionals talk about what really might happen; **hypothetical** conditionals talk about situations that will probably not happen.
  - **Hypothetical conditional:**
    - **(a)** If Harry became President of the United States, he would. . . . (The hypothetical conditional is used because Harry will probably never become President).
  - **Future conditional:**
    - **(b)** If Al becomes President of the United States, he will. . . . (The future conditional is used because Al might actually become President.)

Exercise 3

Tell whether the situations in the *if* clauses below are future (likely) or hypothetical (unlikely). What do the verb forms tell you about whether or not the situation is likely to happen? Respond to each underlined *if* clause with: "It really might happen" (likely), or "It probably won't happen" (unlikely).

1. If it rains, I will not have to water the garden.
2. If it rained, I would be very happy.
3. Marcy would quit her job if she got pregnant.
4. If I won the lottery, I would travel around the world.
5. Aunt Shira will give us a wedding shower if we decide on a wedding date.
6. If Laurel gets hurt again, her father will make her quit the girl's soccer team.
7. If the baby slept through the night without waking up, his parents would finally get a good night's sleep.
8. Jasmine would buy a big house if she were rich.

Focus 5

Hypothetical Conditionals in the Past

FORM
MEANING

- Another kind of hypothetical conditional talks about situations in the present or past in which the *if* clause could not be true.

If Clause + (past perfect)	Main Clause (*would/might* + *have* + **present perfect**)
(a) If he had not robbed a bank, (hypothetical: can't be true because he **did** rob a bank.)	he wouldn't have gone to jail.
(b) If Bill had proposed, (hypothetical: can't be true because Bill did **not** propose.)	she might have married him.

Exercise 4

Complete the following, using the given verb in your answers.

To complete the sentences, think about whether the sentence talks about: a) what really might happen (these sentences use future conditionals); or b) situations in the past in which the *if* clause could not be true (these sentences will use hypothetical conditionals).

EXAMPLE: 1. Gao became a doctor, but if he _____ (be) a truck driver, he _____ (learn) very different skills.

The *if* clause cannot be true, because Gao is not a truck driver; he's a doctor. The hypothetical conditional must be used.

Answer: Gao is a doctor, but if he _had been_ (be) a truck driver, he _would have learned_ (learn) very different skills.

2. Gao's wife is a doctor, too, but she is thinking of changing careers. If she _____

(change) careers, she _____ (be) _____.

3. Toni has lived in the United States and in New Zealand, so she speaks English, but if she

_____ (live) only in Brazil, she _____ (speak) _____.

4. But Toni _____ (speak) _____ if she _____ (move) to

France next year.

5. Mary's car is old. If it _____ (break down), she _____ (need)

   _____.

6. Because Mary has a car, she has driven to school every day this term. But if she

   _____ (not + have) car, she _____ (have to) _____.

7. Marcia has applied to graduate school. She _____ (start) school in the fall if she

   _____ (get) accepted to graduate school.

8. When Marcia was 21 years old, she quit school for several years to get married and raise

   a family. If she _____ (continue) her studies instead of raising a family, she

   _____ (begin) graduate school a long time ago.

Exercise 5

Complete the following hypothetical conditionals, using the given verb in your answers.

   To complete the sentences, think about whether the sentence talks about: a) a hypothetical situation that will probably **not** happen or b) situations in the present or past in which the *if* clause could not be true.

   EXAMPLE: 1. Eloise's husband has always been a thin man in good physical condition. If he suddenly _____ (become) fat, Eloise _____ (be) shocked. This is a hypothetical situations which will probably **not** happen because Eloise's husband has always been a thin man.

   Answer: Eloise's husband has always been a thin man in good physical condition. If he suddenly _became_ (become) fat, Eloise _would be_ (be) shocked.

2. Eloise started seeing a doctor about her cholesterol problem three years ago. If she

   _____ (knew) about her problem earlier, she _____ (change)

   her diet years earlier.

3. George's doctor says that one of the reasons George has high blood pressure is that he never

   expresses his anger. His doctor says that it is not healthy to "bottle it up." He says that if George

   _____ (get) angry once in a while, his blood pressure _____ (not +

   be) so high.

4. George never gets angry with his family. His children _____ (run away) from him

   if he ever _____ (yell) at them.

5. Dan, who doesn't earn very high wages, has owned Mazda trucks for years. If he _____ (have) a lot of money to buy a new truck, he _____ (buy) another Mazda.

6. When Dan graduated from college, his father gave him a used Mazda truck. Together they worked on the truck until it was in excellent condition. If Dan _____ (not + learn) how to repair Mazdas, he _____ (be) more enthusiastic about other models.

7. People who live in this area have forgotten how to conserve water. If it _____ (not + rain) so much last year, people _____ (remember) water conservation practices.

8. People _____ (be able) to water their lawns every day if it _____ (rain) more this summer. However, the forecast is that this area is going to experience a drought this summer.

Exercise 6

On one sheet of paper, write the following words and complete the hypothetical *if* clause.

If I were _____ . . .

Now, on another sheet of paper complete the main clause.

I would _____ .

a. Your teacher will collect and scramble your *if* clauses and your main clauses, and then you will take one of each. Read your sentence aloud to the rest of the class. Does it make sense?

b. After hearing everyone read their sentences, find the person who has the main clause that matches the *if* clause you have now.

c. Now find the person who has the *if* clause that matches your main clause.

Activities

Activity 1

1. Work in groups of four.
2. First, answer the following questions for yourself. Then do the same thing for each person in your group. Write down what you think each person would be. Don't show the members of your group your paper.
   a. If you were an animal, what would you be?
   b. If you were a color, what would you be?
   c. If you were food, what would you be?

   EXAMPLE: *If I were an animal, I would be a cat. If Terri were an animal, she would be a deer. I also think that Rachel would be a mouse, and Peter would be a flamingo.*

3. When you have all finished, share your ideas and compare what **you** think your group members would be with what **they** think they would be.

	You	Name	Name	Name
(a)				
(b)				
(c)				

Activity 2

In a paragraph or two, describe the most interesting results about **yourself** from the last activity. First tell why you described yourself the way you did. Then tell why you think your group members described you the way they did.

For example, if you said "If I were a color, I would be purple," but everyone else said you would be yellow, give us the possible reasons for these opinions.

Activity 3

Write an imaginary situation or a predicament on a piece of paper. For example, *What would happen if...* everyone in the world were 10 feet taller? *What would you do if...* you found somebody's purse with $200 in it and no identification? *What would happen if...* there were suddenly a huge earthquake?

After you write down one predicament, work with a team to do some "creative brainstorming" to solve the problem or describe the results. Then your team will tell some of your solutions to the other teams. They will try to guess the situation and tell what the *if* clause is. The team that guesses the situation most often wins.

Activity 4

You have all heard of the Beatles. Find people who are familiar with the words to their songs and complete the following lyrics:

(a) If I fell in love with you, would you promise to be true....

(b) What would you do if I sang out of tune, would you....

Peter, Paul, and Mary were a popular folk-singing group in the sixties. Find people who are familiar with Peter, Paul, and Mary lyrics, and see if they can help you finish this sentence:

(c) If I had a hammer...

What are the other *if* clauses in this song?

"Carousel" is a famous Rodgers and Hammerstein musical. Find people who can help you complete the *if* clause in the following song:

(d) If I loved you...

Question Review

From Matt Groening, *The Big Book of Hell*, Random House, a division of Panceon Books, New York (1990).

Task

What questions would you like to ask **your** teacher? Work alone or with other students to fill in the blanks on the following page.

Exercise 1

What are some of the different ways to ask questions? List as many question words or "openers" (*Do* . . . , *Can* . . . , *What* . . .) as you can think of. The Task gives you some ways, but there are more.

Focus 1

FORM ● MEANING
Yes/No Questions

- There are several different types of questions. One kind is the **yes/no** question. **Yes/no** questions are called that because they usually require a *yes* or *no* answer, and they are used to seek general agreement/acceptance (yes) or lack of agreement/refusal (no). They usually start with some form of *be* or *do*, or any first auxiliary verb (such as *have*), or with a modal such as *could* or *would*. *Yes/no* questions end with rising intonation.

- **Examples of *yes/no* questions:**
  - **(a)** Are you going to bed early tonight?
  - **(b)** Did you remember to lock the door?
  - **(c)** Have you been sleeping long?
  - **(d)** Could you close that window, please?

  Note: This last question requires an action rather than a *yes* or *no* verbal response.

Focus 2

FORM ● MEANING
Statement Form Questions

- **Statement form questions** are also a type of *yes/no* question. They appear to be the same as normal statements in form except that they use rising instead of falling intonation. Their function is different, however, because they ask for information that requires a yes or no answer.

- **Examples of statement form questions:**
  - **(a)** He's a student?
  - **(b)** They've already seen this video?
  - **(c)** You can take the bus to work today?
  - **(d)** She can't find her keys?

- These kinds of questions are fairly common in conversation, but they shouldn't be used too often. They are very informal and sometimes misunderstood because they sound like statements except for the rising intonation.

Focus 3

FORM ● MEANING
Negative *Yes/No* Questions

- We can also state *yes/no* questions in the **negative**. Sometimes if a speaker uses *not* in the question, he or she assumes that the answer is also negative.
  - **Examples of negative *yes/no* questions:**
    - **(a)** Aren't you going to study tonight?
      (Speaker assumes the answer is **no**—The listener is **not** going to study tonight.)
    - **(b)** Won't he teach her how to drive?
      (Speaker assumes the answer is **no**—He **won't** teach her how to drive.)
- Sometimes we use negative questions with *be* and *do* for emphasis, especially with descriptions. These kinds of questions are **exclamatory questions**. With these, the speaker expects agreement instead of a negative answer.
    - **(c)** Wasn't that a lovely play?
      (Speaker expects the listener to **agree**—Yes, it was a lovely play.)
    - **(d)** Doesn't the bride look beautiful?
      (Speaker expects the listener to **agree**—Yes, the bride looks beautiful.)

Exercise 2

Ask another person *yes/no* questions using the following:

1. Can you? . . .
2. Don't you ever? . . .
3. You're going to? . . .
4. Could you? . . .

5. Would you? . . .
6. You know how to? . . .
7. Won't you? . . .

Focus 4

FORM ● MEANING

Wh-questions

- **Wh-questions** are another common kind of question. They are also called Information questions because the answer to the question requires more than just a yes-or-no answer. Most *Wh*-questions begin with words that start with the letters *wh*, and they usually end with falling intonation.

  - **Examples of *Wh*-questions**
    - (a) **Where** is your next class?
    - (b) **Who** would like to borrow my book?
    - (c) **What** happened at the party after I left?
    - (d) **Why** are you smiling?
    - (e) **When** did they eat dinner?
    - (f) **How** old are you?
    - (g) **How many** times have you traveled overseas?
    - (h) **How much** does a new computer cost?

Exercise 3

Fill in the blanks below with an appropriate *Wh*-question word.

1. _____ do you live?

2. _____ is your address?

3. _____ time do you come to school every day?

4. _____ do you get here so early/late?

5. _____ often do you ride the bus every week?

6. _____ way do you come?

7. _____ do you come with?

8. _____ many times have you skipped class this term?

Exercise 4

For each sentence below, ask a question that goes with the answer. When you're finished, compare your questions with other students' questions.

1. Q: _____ ?

    A: The closet door is closed because the paint's dry, and so I put everything back in there.

2. Q: _____ ?

    A: The broom is in the closet, along with the mop, and some cleaning supplies.

3. Q: _____ ?

    A: The vacuum cleaner is probably still in the basement where you left it.

4. Q: _____ ?

    A: We need to clean the house because we're having some people over for dinner tonight.

5. Q: _____ ?

    A: Martha, Sam, and their kids are coming, and of course our neighbors, the Smiths.

6. Q: _____ ?

    A: They met them in the Smith's garden.

7. Q: _____ ?

    A: They met them there yesterday morning when we were gone.

8. Q: _____ ?

    A: The Smiths were planting flowers.

9. Q: _____ ?

    A: Martha and Sam are getting here by car.

10. Q: _____ ?

    A: They're taking Sam's car because Martha's is in the shop.

11. Q: _____ ?

    A: It's going to cost at least $200.

Focus 5

Tag Questions

- **Tag questions** are another kind of question that we commonly use in conversation. Like *yes/no* questions, they have to be answered with yes or no. They are used when the speaker predicts either a yes-or-no answer or when the speaker seeks agreement or confirmation.

  - Tag questions start with a statement and end with a "tag," or shortened question. If the verb in the statement is affirmative (positive), the tag is negative. If the verb in the statement is negative, the tag is affirmative.

  - The speaker expects the answer to agree with the **statement**, not with the tag. If the verb in the statement is affirmative, the speaker expects the answer to be affirmative. If the verb in the statement is negative, the speaker expects the answer to be negative.

    (a) You're going to bed early tonight, aren't you? (The verb in the statement is affirmative, so the speaker expects the answer to probably be yes.)

    (b) You can't go shopping with me today, can you? (The verb in the statement is negative, so the speaker expects the answer to probably be no—I can't go shopping with you today.)

- To agree with a speaker who asks a tag question and to confirm her opinion, use the same as the statement—negative or affirmative, **not** the same as the tag.

  - **Negative statement, affirmative tag**

    (c) Question: You're not cold, are you?
    Answer: No, I'm not. (if you agree with the statement, "You are not cold.")
    NOT: Yes, I'm not.

  - **Affirmative statement, negative tag**

    (d) Question: You're cold, aren't you?
    Answer: Yes, I am. (if you agree with the statement, "You are cold.")
    NOT: No, I am.

Focus 6

FORM ● USE

Tag Question Intonation

FORM
USE

- The **intonation** we use in a tag question is very important. If falling intonation is used, the speaker expects the listener to agree with the statement or verify that the statement is true.

  (a) His name is Tom, isn't it?

  (Because falling intonation is used, the speaker expects the listener to agree with the statement—Yes, his name is Tom.)

  (b) It's not going to rain today, is it?

  (Because falling intonation is used along with a negative statement, the speaker expects the listener to agree with the statement—No, it's not going to rain today.)

  (c) His name is Tom, isn't it?

  (d) It's not going to rain today, is it?

  (Because rising intonation is used, the speaker really wants an answer to the question. The speaker doesn't know whether the answer will be yes or no.)

Exercise 5

Your teacher will ask some tag questions. Circle **Y** if you think the expected answer is Yes and **N** if you think the expected answer is No.

1. Y	N	4. Y	N	7. Y	N
2. Y	N	5. Y	N	8. Y	N
3. Y	N	6. Y	N	9. Y	N

Exercise 6

Read each tag question aloud, using the intonation as marked. For each question, tell whether the speaker expects a certain answer or not, and if so, what the speaker expects the answer to be, yes or no. Answer the question the way you think the speaker expects it to be answered.

	(a) Is the speaker sure what the answer will be?	(b) If **yes** to (a), answer the question.
1. It's going to rain today, isn't it?		
2. You don't know where my umbrella is, do you?		
3. You're driving today, aren't you?		
4. It's not my turn to drive, is it?		
5. You made lunch for me, didn't you?		
6. I didn't forget to thank you, did I?		
7. I'm pretty forgetful, aren't I?		

Exercise 7

Look at the picture and then fill in the question or answer in each part below. All questions and answers are about this picture. (Note: For some of these, you will need to guess. There is more than one possible response.)

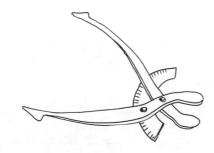

1. **Q:** _____ ?

    A: Builders, scientists, craftspeople, and others used to use it.

2. **Q:** _____ ?

    A: No, now there are more modern ones.

3. **Q:** When did people use it?

    A: _____ .

4. **Q:** _____ ?

    A: People often used this if they needed it in their jobs.

5. **Q:** _____ ?

    A: You hold it in your hand, and then you pull the legs apart.

6. **Q:** Those aren't real legs on it, are they?

    A: _____ .

7. **Q:** _____ ?

    A: It's made of two kinds of metal.

8. **Q:** _____ ?

    A: Because it's used in heavy and difficult kinds of jobs.

9. **Q:** Who made this thing?

    A: _____ .

10. **Q:** _____ ?

    A: An old farmhouse.

11. **Q:** _____ ?

    A: No, it's old.

12. **Q:** How old is it?

    A: _____ .

13. **Q:** _____ ?

    A: For decoration.

See the answer at the end of this unit.

(Idea from Ilyse Rathet Post)

Activities

Activity 1

Your English teacher has just quit her job and is now sunning on a beach in Tahiti. Your class is desperately searching for a new teacher. You have decided to take matters into your own hands and interview teachers yourselves. One of your classmates is an applicant for the position. Ask him or her some questions about her or his experience, interests, and future goals.

Activity 2

At school, you have recently lost a very unusual and very valuable piece of jewelry, perhaps a ring or necklace. Now you are sitting in class, and you notice that the person sitting beside you is wearing a ring/necklace just like the one you lost. Of course, you would like to ask the person some questions about it to find out if it might be yours.

You might want to role-play this in teams. One team can serve as coaches for the person who has lost the piece of jewelry. The other team can serve as coaches for the person who is wearing the piece of jewelry.

(Idea from Brenda Farmer)

Activity 3

Bring some unusual object to class (or a picture or drawing of the object, as in Exercise 7, above) that your other class members might not recognize, such as a kitchen gadget or an article of traditional clothing. Students can ask the person who brought the gadget any question except "What is it?" and "What is it used for?" The person who guesses correctly is the next one to show his or her object to the rest of the class.

Activity 4

With your classmates, brainstorm a list of questions that are useful for people learning English, in or outside the classroom setting. Vote on the question that is **most** useful and the question that is **least** useful.

To get you started, here are some examples of questions that students have found useful:

What does _____ mean?
Can you repeat that please?

Activity 5

What questions do North Americans ask you the most often? What questions do they **not** ask, which would be common where you come from? Work with your classmates to come up with a list of the most frequently asked questions and the questions that would be asked where you come from but that are not asked in North America.

Activity 6

Bring in a photograph and give it to your instructor. Each student will look at one photograph for 30 seconds and then give it back to the teacher. Other students will then ask the student any questions about the picture they studied and try to guess the situation. Try to use all types of questions: yes/no, Wh-, Statement form, and Tag. The person who brought in the picture can then tell the class whether their guesses were correct or not.

Activity 7

Write a list of questions about a topic that you want to know more about from native English speakers. For example, party behavior/party customs in this country or what are the best topics for "small talk."

Share your list of questions with other students to come up with a questionnaire. Then use this questionnaire to survey native speakers of English. Share the results of your survey with the rest of the class.

Activity 8

What's My Line?

Write down the name of an occupation on a piece of paper and give it to your teacher. Then each of you will take one slip of paper. That is **your** occupation, and you must answer other students' questions about this occupation. Other students will try to guess what your occupation is. They can ask any question except "What do you do?" or "What is your occupation?" Some examples of questions you might ask and be asked are, "Do you work with people?" "Where do you usually work?" "Did you need a college degree to do the work that you do?"

(Idea from Guy Modica)

Answer To Exercise 7:

It's an old-fashioned caliper, used to measure the diameter of tubes, etc.

UNIT

30

Emphatic Structures
Wh-clefts, Emphatic *Do*,
No versus *Not*

Task

Presidential elections in the United States are held every four years. A friend of yours is involved in a campaign to elect Barbara Tomas as President. She has been asked to make an important speech to persuade people to vote for Barbara Tomas; this speech has to draw attention to the candidate and emphasize her strong points. She has been working on the speech for a while and has nearly finished; however, she can't decide on the most effective way to present some of her ideas. She has written the same thing in several different ways and wants you to help her decide which sounds the most emphatic so that people will remember her message. Look at the notes she has written, and in each group of ideas underline the statement you think will sound best in the speech.

- Support B.T. today!
  ? { – There's no time to lose.
 – There isn't any time to lose. } ?

- We need a new voice in the White House.
  ? { – B.T. can bring peace, justice and compassion.
 – What B.T. can bring is peace, justice and compassion. }

- Look at what the current president has done.
  ? { – That isn't the way to run a country.
 – That's no way to run a country. } ?

- { – Your vote makes a difference.
 ? { – Your vote really does make a difference.
 – Your vote really makes a difference. } ?

° We don't want the same old stuff!

? { What we want is a woman in the White House.

We want a woman in the White House. }

° Other people say they care, but...

? { B.T. cares.

B.T. really cares.

B.T. really does care. } ?

Focus 1

MEANING

Overview of Some Emphatic Structures

MEANING

- There are many ways of emphasizing information in English. The following structures are common:
  - *Wh-cleft:*
    (a) Nonemphatic form: The world needs peace and justice. (neutral)
    (b) Emphatic form: **What the world needs** is peace and justice.
    Both (a) and (b) have the same meaning. In (b), the main focus of the sentence is "peace and justice."
  - **Emphatic *do:***
    (c) Nonemphatic form: I understand. (neutral)
    (d) Emphatic form: I **do** understand.
    (c) and (d) have the same meaning, but (d) places much more emphasis on the statement. Both *Wh*-clefts and emphatic *do* are more common in spoken English than in written English.
  - *No:*
    (e) Nonemphatic form: She doesn't have any money. (neutral)
    (f) Emphatic form: She has **no** money.
    We often use *no* to make a negative idea more emphatic.

Exercise 1

Turn back to the Task. Check (√) all the emphatic structures you can find. Which statements do you think your friend probably used in her speech? Why do you think this is so?

Focus 2

FORM

Wh-Clefts

FORM

- *Wh*-cleft sentences are divided into two parts:

Assumption		**Focus**
(what we already know or understand)		(new information: the emphasized part of the sentence)
(a) What the world needs	is	peace and justice.
(b) What we want	is	a woman in the White House.
(c) Where he goes at night	is	a mystery to me.
(d) What she is	is	an interfering busybody.

The assumption (something we already understand or believe) is introduced by a *Wh*-word and comes at the beginning of the sentence. The focus adds new knowledge or information to the sentence. An appropriate form of the verb *be* links the two parts of the sentence:

(e) What Barbara Tomas brings	is	compassion, peace, and justice for all.
(f) Where he went	was	none of your business.

- When there are two forms of *be* in a sentence, the **second** verb is the verb that links the two parts:

(g) What she is **is** a brilliant politician.

Exercise 2

Match the phrases in Part A with an appropriate word or phrase from Part B. Connect them with an appropriate form of *be* and write the complete sentences in the space below. The first one has been done for you.

A

1. What England is
2. What Florida produces
3. What Alexander Graham Bell invented
4. What Martin Luther King believed in
5. Where the United States President lives
6. What the capital of South Korea is
7. What "mph" means
8. Where the Pyramids are located
9. What Brazilians speak
10. What Americans eat at Thanksgiving
11. What Jimmy Carter was

B

turkey.
Seoul.

Portuguese.
a very small country.
in Egypt.
the 39th U.S. President.
racial equality.
in the White House.
citrus fruit.
the telephone.
miles per hour.

1. *What England is is a very small country* .

2. _____ .

3. _____ .

4. _____ .

5. _____ .

6. _____ .

7. _____ .

8. _____ .

9. _____ .

10. _____ .

11. _____ .

Focus 3

USE

How to Use *Wh*-Clefts for Emphasis

USE

- *Wh*-clefts are more common in spoken English than in written English. The *Wh*-phrase refers to a previously expressed (or understood) statement or idea:

  (a) A: How much money does the director earn?

  　　B: What she earns ⌐ is none of your business!

- We often use *Wh*-clefts to emphasize the difference between two ideas or opinions:

  (b) A: Mozart wrote plays.

  　　B: No. What Mozart wrote was **music** (not plays).

Exercise 3

Rewrite the underlined words using a *Wh*-cleft. The first one has been done for you.

1. Matt: Henry drives a Porsche.
   David: Don't be ridiculous. <u>He drives a Ford</u>. *What he drives is a Ford.*
   Matt: Really? He told me it was a Porsche.

2. Frank: Margo tells me you're a painter.
   Duane: That's right.
   Frank: Do you sell many of your paintings?
   Duane: Well, actually, <u>I paint houses.</u>

3. Nick: I'm tired. I'm going to take a nap.
   Lisa: No. <u>You need some exercise.</u>

4. Teacher: Do you have any suggestions about how we can improve this class?
   Fusako: <u>We'd like less homework.</u>
   Ricardo: And <u>we'd prefer a test every week.</u>
   Soraya: <u>I need more grammar to pass the TOEFL.</u>
   Bernadine: <u>And I'd like a different textbook.</u> This one is too boring.

5. Oscar: The city council is going to build a new shopping mall.
   Yoichiro: Not another shopping mall! <u>This town needs a good movie theater.</u>
   Oscar: I agree. There's nothing to do here.

6. Howard: Do you know Barry? He writes novels.
   Tessa: No he doesn't. <u>He writes instruction manuals.</u>
   Howard: Well, at least he's a writer.

7.   Lee: What are you getting Kim and Hiro for their wedding?

        Stella: <u>They'd really like a microwave,</u> but I can't afford that much, so I'm getting them a toaster.

8.   Greg: Mom, can you give me some money? I need a new skateboard.

        Mom: <u>You should get a job.</u> Then you can buy as many skateboards as you like.

        Greg: But all the other kids in my class have new skateboards!

        Mom: I'm sorry, but I'm not giving you any more money.

        Greg: Jimmy's mother always gives him money.

        Mom: Well, I'm not Jimmy's mother.

        Greg: Then maybe <u>I need a new mother!</u>

Focus 4

FORM

Emphatic *Do*

FORM

- We can also add emphasis to a sentence by stressing the auxiliary or the *be* verb:

  (a) I **will** do it.

  (b) He **is** French.

  (c) We **have** finished it.

- In sentences where there is no auxiliary or *be* verb, we can use *do* to add emphasis:

  (d) I like her work.   I **do** like her work.

  (e) They saw us.   They **did** see us.

- We often add extra emphasis with an emphatic adverb like *really* or *certainly*:

  (f) I **really do** like her work.

  (g) They **certainly did** see us.

- In spoken English, emphatic *do* is strongly stressed.

Focus 5

Some Ways to Use Emphatic *Do*

USE

- Emphatic *do* can add emphasis to a whole sentence:

  (a) A: I love you.
  B: Really?
  A: Yes, I really **do** love you.

This shows how strongly you feel about something or someone. Use it only when you need to add extra emphasis.

- Emphatic *do* can add emphasis to an imperative:

  (b) Do come in!

  (c) Do give him my best regards!

- Emphatic *do* can contradict a negative statement:

  (d) A: You didn't lock the back door.
  B: You're wrong. I **did** lock it.

This use of emphatic *do* is very common in arguments. In such situations, the *do* verb generally refers back to a previous statement:

  (e) A: Bob doesn't like this kind of music.
  B: That's not true. He **does** like it.

Exercise 4

Bruce and Gary are brothers, but they often have arguments. Read the following argument and underline all the places where you think it is possible to use emphatic *do*. Rewrite those sentences with an appropriate form of the *do* verb. The first one has been done for you.

Bruce: Did you take my flashlight? I can't find it anywhere.

Gary: Well, I haven't got it. I always return the stuff I borrow.

Bruce: No, you don't.

I do return the things I borrow!

Gary: That's not true! I return the things I borrow! It's probably on your desk. I bet you didn't

look for it there.

Bruce: No, I looked on my desk, and it's not there.

Gary: Well, don't blame me. You can't find it because you never clean your room.

Bruce: I clean my room!

Gary: Oh, no you don't!

Bruce: I certainly clean it up! I cleaned it up last night as a matter of fact.

Gary: You didn't.

Bruce: I really cleaned it up last night. Hey, there's my flashlight under your bed.

Gary: Well, I didn't put it there.

Bruce: I bet you put it there. Anyhow, that proves it: You take my stuff and you don't return it.

Gary: I told you before: I return everything I borrow. You just don't look after your things properly.

Bruce: I look after my things. Anyway, from now on, I'm going to lock my door and keep you out.

Gary: You can't. That door doesn't have a key.

Bruce: That's where you're wrong. It has a key and I'm going to lock you out!

Gary: Oh, shut up!

Bruce: Do you know something? You make me sick. You really make me sick.

Gary: Good!

Get together with another student and take the parts of Gary and Bruce. Read the dialogue, paying particular attention to the stress patterns of emphatic *do*. If possible, record yourselves and listen to how emphatic you sound.

Focus 6

FORM

Not versus *No*

- To emphasize a negative statement, we can use *no* + noun in place of *not/n't* + verb:
  - **(a)** They do not have any friends.   They have **no** friends.
  - **(b)** Tourists did not come to Birdlip this year.   **No** tourists came to Birdlip this year.
- We use *no* with non-count nouns:
  - **(c)** I have **no money**.
  - **(d)** I have **no time**.
  - **(e)** There's **no coffee** in the pot.
- We use *no* with plural count nouns:
  - **(f)** He has **no chairs** in his apartment.
- We use a plural noun here because we are referring to chairs in general, not to one specific chair. Notice the same principle in the following:
  - **(g)** She has **no pets**.
  - **(h)** There are **no teachers** here on Sunday.
- We use *no* with singular count nouns:
  - **(i)** He is taking the bus because he has **no car** today.

  We use a singular noun here because we are referring to a specific car, not to cars in general. We also use a singular noun when we refer to something that is **usually** singular:
  - **(j)** He has **no father** or mother.
    NOT: He has no fathers or mothers.
- *No* is a determiner and we cannot use it with other determiners:
  - **(k)** **No students** came to my office yesterday.
    NOT: No the students came to my office yesterday.
- We can combine *no* with other words to make compounds:

no + one	=	**no one**	I saw no one.
no + body	=	**nobody**	I saw nobody.
no + thing	=	**nothing**	I ate nothing.*
no + where	=	**nowhere**	I went nowhere.

  * The first syllable in *nothing* is pronounced differently from the other *no* + compounds.
- In standard English, there is only one negative word in each sentence:
  - **(l)** She **doesn't have any** money. OR She **has no** money.
    NOT: She doesn't have no money.

Exercise 5

Part One. Match the first part of the sentence, (A), with something from (B) that makes sense and is grammatical. The first one has been done for you.

Lily went to a party last night.

A

1. She had hoped to make some new friends, but she didn't meet

2. She had to drive home, so she didn't drink

3. She was very hungry, but when she arrived there wasn't

4. She talked to a few people, but she didn't have

5. Some people were dancing, but Lily didn't have

6. She wanted to sit down, but there weren't

7. Finally, she said to herself: "This party isn't

8. So she went home early and decided not to go to

B

any food left.

anyone to dance with.

any more parties.

anyone interesting.

any fun!"

any alcohol.

anything to say to them.

any chairs.

Part Two. Rewrite each sentence of Part One using *no* or an appropriate *no* + compound. Change the verbs as necessary. The first one has been done for you.

1. *She had hoped to make some new friends, but she met nobody interesting* .

2. _____ .

3. _____ .

4. _____ .

5. _____ .

6. _____ .

7. _____ .

8. _____ .

320

USE

When to Use *No*

USE

- Statements using *no* as the negative word instead of *not* emphasize what is missing or lacking. In speaking, we often stress the word *no* for extra emphasis:

  (a) I didn't have any friends when I was a child.

  I had **no** friends when I was a child.

  The *no* sentence emphasizes the lack of friends. The *n't (not)* sentence sounds more like a statement of fact. It sounds less emotional than the sentence with *no*.

- *No* + compound also emphasizes what is missing or lacking:

  (b) I didn't meet anybody interesting at the party.

  I met **nobody** interesting at the party.

  The first sentence sounds neutral, a statement of fact. The second sentence sounds more emotional, emphasizing the lack of interesting people.

  (c) I didn't learn anything new at the conference.

  I learned **nothing** new at the conference.

Exercise 6

Lily is describing the party to her best friend and is telling her what a miserable time she had. Imagine you are Lily and try describing the party from her point of view, emphasizing all the negative aspects of the evening. If possible, record yourself and listen to see how emphatic you sound.

Exercise 7

Emphatic language is very common in political speeches. Read the extracts from speeches below and notice the different ways each speaker uses language to emphasize his message. Underline any examples of the emphatic language discussed in this unit that you can find. Do you notice any other techniques the speakers use to get their points across?

1. Jesse Jackson: Speech to the Democratic National Convention, July 20, 1988

   When I was born late one afternoon, October 8, in Greenville, South Carolina, no writers asked my mother her name. Nobody chose to write down our address. My mama was not supposed to make it. You see, I was born to a teenage mother who was born to a teenage mother. I understand. I know abandonment and people being mean to you, and saying you're nothing and nobody, and can never be anything. I understand. . . . I understand when nobody knows your name. I understand when you have no name . . . I really do understand.

2. Robert F. Kennedy: Speech on the death of Martin Luther King Jr., April 4, 1968

   What we need in the United States is not division; what we need in the United States is not hatred; what we need in the United States is not violence or lawlessness, but love and wisdom, and compassion toward one another, and a feeling of justice toward those who still suffer within our country, whether they be white or they be black.

Activities

Activity 1

Organize a political campaign in class. Divide into groups. Each group represents a new political party. With your group, create a name for your party and draw up a list of all the things you stand for and all the things you will do if you are elected. Make a poster representing your beliefs and prepare a short speech to persuade people to vote for you. Each member of your group should be prepared to speak on a different aspect of your party's policy. Give your speeches to the rest of the class and decide who has the most persuasive approach. If possible, record your speech and afterward, listen to what you said, taking note of any emphatic structures you used and how you said them.

Activity 2

Get together with another student. Think of a relationship or a situation in which people often have disagreements (for example, parent/child; brother/sister; boyfriend/girlfriend; husband/wife; roommate/roommate, and so on). Choose one such relationship and brainstorm all the possible issues these people might argue about. Choose **one** issue and take the role of one of the people in the situation (your partner takes the role of the other). Create the argument these two people might have on this issue. Write your dialogue and prepare to perform it in front of the class. Before you perform, check to see how emphatically you state your point of view. If possible, record your dialogue, and afterward listen to see whether you used any emphatic structures and how you said them.

Activity 3

Get together with another student and look at the poem below.

LESSONS FROM LIFE

I have learned many lessons from life.

I have learned from many different people.

And in many different ways.

What I have learned from my family is _____

What I have learned from my friends _____

What I have learned from _____

And what _____

These are the lessons I have learned

From my life.

Can you think of a way to complete the missing parts? Share your finished poem with the rest of the class.

Activity 4

Get together with another student or form small groups and look at the poem below.

They are old.

They have been here for a long time.

They are _____ .

They have no _____ and no _____ .

Nobody _____ .

What they really want is _____ .

They are old.

They have been here for a long time.

Brainstorm all the things that *they* could refer to in this poem. Choose **one** and complete the poem with this as your topic. Give the poem a title. Display your poem so everyone can enjoy it.

Activity 5

Look at the poems you and your classmates wrote in Activity 4. Decide which ones are pessimistic and which ones are optimistic about the topic. Choose one of the poems (it can be the one you wrote or it can be one written by other students). Using this poem, try to rewrite it from another point of view. For example, if the original poem was pessimistic, can you rewrite it so that it is optimistic? If it was optimistic, can you rewrite it so that it is pessimistic? Share your results with the rest of the class.

Index